*Dedicated to Rev. Msgr. Francis J. Schneider, J.C.D., Rector,
and to all the faculty, staff, and students, past and present,
on the Seventy-fifth Anniversary of the
Seminary of the Immaculate Conception,
Huntington, Long Island, New York*

Foreword

By His Eminence William Cardinal Baum

Pope John Paul II is perhaps best remembered by the nations of the world for his affirmation of the *dignity of the human person*. This affirmation was rooted in his conviction that Jesus Christ is the answer to every human question. In the ministry of the Word, the mystery of man comes alive. In Jesus Christ, the Word Incarnate, the Living God himself discloses to each one of us the fullness of our own humanity. Throughout the ministry of Pope John Paul II, in his encyclicals, his catecheses, and his discourses, and especially in his speeches before the United Nations, this was his constant exhortation to the world: that every human person has great dignity and value. This universal dimension of the unique revelation in Christ was the message he bore to all, Christians and non-Christians alike.

Karol Wojtyla's vision of the dignity of every person was grounded in his personal experience and carefully developed by his formidable intellectual and spiritual powers. One of his primary insights into human dignity came through his experience of human suffering.

His mother died when he was a child, his only brother several years later. He was barely nineteen when Nazi Germany invaded Poland. When his father died a few years after that, he was on his own in hostile circumstances. During these years and the decades of Communist oppression that followed, he saw many people suffer simply because of their moral integrity and adherence to the faith.

It was during the Second Vatican Council (1962–65) that the Church at large became aware of Cardinal Wojtyla's insights into the dignity of every man and woman, particularly because of his major contribution to the Pastoral Constitution *Gaudium et Spes.* He laid out the intellectual and philosophical roots in his foundational book *The Acting Person.*

Pope John Paul II quickly showed that this would be a theme of his pontificate in his early encyclicals. *Redemptor Hominis, Dives in Misericordia,* and *Dominum et Vivificantem* are devoted to the Persons of the Blessed Trinity in relationship to one another and to the life of the world. This thorough reflection on the one God's self-revelation as three divine Persons made it possible for him to address the question of the nature of man, who is made in the image of that Triune God. These relationships reveal the awesome dignity of each human life.

In *Dominum et Vivificantem,* he pronounced that the spirit of the Father and of the Son is given to the Church for the sake of the fulfillment of every human person. He developed the teaching of the Second Vatican Council that each and every person is called to holiness and everlasting life.

In his personal vision of holiness he was strongly influenced by St. Louis de Montfort. He came to see himself, with Mary, as being bound up in the mystery of Christ and of the pilgrim Church. He wanted this awareness to be available to everyone. In his rich Marian devotion, he entrusted his life and his papacy to the protection of the Blessed Mother.

His personal prayer nourished his understanding of human dignity. One had only to observe him at prayer to be aware that he was taking with him into the presence of God the personal lives and sufferings of all those entrusted to his pastoral care.

My own experiences and memories provide a cherished familiarity with the Servant of God John Paul II. He was motivated in his every action by the fundamental truths of Christian belief, that is: the triune nature of God; the incarnation of the divine Word; redemption in and by Jesus Christ; and the role of the Blessed Virgin Mary in the economy of salvation. With every minute of his life, he unfailingly proclaimed the truth of essential human dignity, and in so doing, changed the world. He was the greatest man of his time.

May he rest in eternal peace, and may his memory be everlasting. Praised be Jesus Christ, now and forever.

William Cardinal Baum, S.T.D.
Penitenziere Maggiore Emerito
Vatican City State
Feast of the Ascension, May 5, 2005

Preface

The task of assembling this material was begun before the death of Pope John Paul II on April 2, 2005. Often I would bring my thoughts about these selections from the late pontiff's writings to my meditation in the chapel of the seminary crypt as I would prepare for Mass. I wondered how I would order the selections and indeed which selections would I make. I was helped in this matter by the very presence of a mosaic of Jesus as the *Christos Pantocrator* (Christ the Ruler). In that image the vestiges of the Church rest at his feet: fanciful Gothic stonework is in ruins; a bishop's miter and a bishop's crosier lie amid both the rubble and the bones of those bishops who might have worn them. Now that Pope John Paul has passed away, this image serves as a stark reminder that even the Bishop of Rome, like the bishops of Brooklyn and Rockville Centre whose bodies rest here, bows in death before the majesty of the Son of God.

As I received the news of the death of the man formally known as Karol Wojtyla, I found myself asking what the legacy of both his teaching and action would be. Having served in several capacities in Rome during his pontificate, I am compelled to say that his was a unique legacy of humility and grace. He was a gifted teacher and a dramatic articulator of the gospel. I, therefore, have made these selections in an attempt to show his universal personality and the quiet yet urgent character of his personal depth. I am struck by three core elements of his ministry as Bishop of Rome. They are ecumenism, phenomenological philosophy, and his use of the word "solidarity."

Ecumenism: I remember being present on the steps of St. Peter's Basilica on the day Pope John Paul II inaugurated his pontificate. I was, at that time, a staff member of the Secretariat for Promoting Christian Unity. How surprised we all were, when more representatives of other religious traditions and families appeared than for deaths of either Pope John XXIII or Pope Paul VI, themselves both ecumenical pontiffs. Personally, the new pope expressed his wonder at what he should do before so many diverse expressions of the Christian faith. To the White Father Pierre Duprey, at that time Undersecretary of the Secretariat for Promoting Christian Unity, he said, "You must help me because I've had no previous experience of anything at all like this in Krakow."

The Orthodox, Anglican, and Protestant leaders sat near the new pope during the Mass of inauguration. At the end of the ceremonies, he came directly before them waving his crosier, which like that of Pope Paul VI was styled as a crucifix. He lifted the shepherd's staff, emphasizing the body of the Savior, as if to say, "In Christ, we are already all one."

It was a sign of what was to come. One year later, a curial address for the Feast of Sts. Peter and Paul, a kind of "state of the union" message to the cardinals, colleagues, and collaborators, was devoted entirely to the theme of ecumenism. The fact that this theme characterized all his administrative and pastoral activity so early on in his pontificate came as something of a shock to all those in attendance. Nonetheless, he was firm in his expression of those seminal truths of the Pauline message: there is indeed one Lord, one faith, one baptism. As the chief steward of the household of God, John Paul understood that his task was global—not out of a sense of politics or culture, but out of a sense of communion of spirituality.

Whence did he derive such an understanding of this aspect of his ministry? I believe that he carried the tools with him in the two suitcases he brought to take up residence in the Apostolic Palace: one was his spirituality, and the other was his philosophy.

Phenomenological philosophy: Pope John Paul's philosophy is so bound up with his mode of spirituality that it is impossible to separate them. His was a spirituality in which he, like St. Thérèse of Lisieux, was always aware of the presence of grace. Every time I came near him, I was always aware that the man was living in the presence of God. You just had to be close to him when he prayed to be convicted of that truth, because the focus of his attention was definitely somewhere other than where his body was. Everyone who had the privilege of kneeling with him, as he prepared to celebrate Mass or while he made his thanksgiving after Mass, would actually feel his spirit of holiness. He was unworldly. He rejected the profane. He was both sensitive and attentive. He seemed constantly to be in adoration before the majesty of God, even when surrounded by the crowds who were attracted to him as iron to a magnet.

John Paul II was a graced individual who was called to lead the Church in extraordinary times. He did so by enunciating the faith. The Spirit of God acted not because of him, but in and through him. His pontificate literally reconfigured the map of Europe and lifted what one thought would be the perpetual shadow of unease inherent in the very concept of Cold War. What was said by the Roman poet and playwright Terence can be said of John Paul II: "Nothing human is foreign to me." The difference is that the late pontiff saw everything human through the splendor of grace. The words of George Bernanos, author of *The Diary of a Country Priest,* were both enunciated and demonstrated by Pope John Paul: "All is grace." The late Holy Father's belief in this was the source of his abundant optimism, his humor, and his joy. He was also like Bernanos, however, in the shrewd realism he brought to his understanding of the dual threat of secularism and materialism to the human quest for unity in the transition from the twentieth to the twenty-first century: "Faith is not something which one *loses,* we merely cease to shape our lives by it." That line, too, is from *The Diary of a Country Priest.* How profound the sentiment of that understated sentence.

Everything interested him. His attitude was rooted in his capacity to understand what is human. To catch a glimpse of his sense of "the human," one has to open and unpack the second suitcase, which he carried with him when he crossed the threshold of the Apostolic Palace, whereby we find that very definitely he was a perennial philosophical student of *phenomenology.* Through his professor, Roman Ingarden, he had a direct link to the monumental thoughts of philosophers Edmund Husserl and Edith Stein, the latter of whom he was later to canonize as St. Teresa Benedicta of the Cross, the name she chose when she left the classroom for the Carmelite Order in Cologne.

It is from the thinking of these three persons as well as that of Max Scheler, whom he always admired, that he made his own personal philosophical synthesis. This is found in his treatise *The Acting Person.* Through his unique concept of "participation," which he defined as the fundamental dynamic of the adult human being, he achieved remarkable insight into the "dignity of man and woman." That "dignity" was represented by his unique term for humans in relationship as "neighbors." Whether as professor, bishop, or cardinal, he enunciated the belief that each individual is on a track of continual formation through life events to become what God intended. His words for wisdom as the apex of maturity are "a sense of responsibility through human interaction."

"Neighboring" was the subtext of his entire pontificate. As pope, he was to envision his task as helping all human beings "see into the other" and find there also an individual not unlike themselves. He envisioned the cluster of multiple human communities as destined to interact with each other. Whether as individuals or a community in the public domain, people were designed to "covenant" or "share their uniqueness." He expressed this best in a book about marriage and human sexuality entitled *Love and Responsibility.* "Neighboring" is not, then, merely a pleasant desideratum by which one may freely choose to be in or not be in a relationship with another. *Rather, it is a necessary sharing of humanness.* The concept of "participation" implies that each one of us is in the process of searching out the fulfillment of our destinies. This is equally true of all forms of human community, whether political, social, economic, fraternal, or religious. *Papa* Wojtyla on every occasion expressed the fundamental personalistic value of human activity as being "together with others." People come together in "solidarity." For John Paul II, solidarity meant standing together with others.

Solidarity: From the inception of his pontificate, I was always impressed by the late Holy Father's insistent and emphatic reference to the concept of "solidarity." At first, I saw it through its political references, especially to Poland, where the solidarity movement ultimately brought Poland its freedom. Later, another personal assignment in Rome led me to track the pontiff's pilgrimages and journeys. Even a scanning of all his speeches, encyclicals, and other texts made me aware of a profound and emphatic use of that word, even far from the borders of Poland.

After a while, I became conscious of the truth that his doctrine of "participation" extended beyond being together "with" others to being together also "for" others. The image of marriage, which he continually held up, became more than a reference point. It became an icon, because in his continued examination of the purity and blessedness of the marital union, it really came down to one truth: two people in one life.

In the ecumenical and global dimension, however, truth involves certainly more than two people. A life in Christ—that is the destiny for us all. It is our task to share, to enter into communion, to covenant with one another. Certainly, in light of the events of the last decade, and especially after September 11, 2001, it became clear that this has to go even beyond the relationship among Christians.

As pope, John Paul II reached out to beg pardon of historical Judaism for the tragic displays of Christian anti-Semitism in the past. He is definitely the first pope to call Muslims "brothers." As the journalist Luigi Accattoli observed, *"Brother* is definitely a title that the Christian tradition reserves for *brothers in the faith."* It is with this profoundly philosophical understanding of brotherhood within the entire human family that one becomes aware also of Karol Wojtyla's sense of morality. It is one of humility. This is the premise of "neighboring."

In 1994, the late Holy Father addressed by letter the College of Cardinals, reminding them that the great Jubilee Year 2000 was beginning to cast its shadow. As with an audible sigh, he spoke of the division that still exists within the greater Christian family—a division that provides a poor witness for a world waiting to be healed of the tragedies of the twentieth century. These are tragedies he personally experienced. One needs to allude to them directly here because the mere fact of their drama underscores the authenticity of his words. He was witness to the invasion of his country by a foreign and terrifying power. He saw the execution of his friends. He lived in fear for his own life. While not even a full adult, he was bereft of all of his immediate family and he lived a unique kind of painful solitude. Only his faith provided him comfort. Years later, someone tried to murder him and, as a result, he had to continue his pontificate as a man physically and, as he himself admitted, personally wounded. If anyone had cause to understand that forgiveness is not hypocrisy but rather a very necessary value for survival of the human community, it was he. Therefore, he stated in his memorandum to the cardinals the following: "With an attitude of full receptivity to the action of the Holy Spirit, the Church and Christians fulfill this task with renewed diligence in approaching the year 2000. The imminence of the end of the second millennium invites all to an examination of conscience and to suitable ecumenical initiatives so that in the face of the Great Jubilee they may find themselves, if not fully reconciled, at least in less opposition and division than they were during the course of the second millennium." This pope spoke logically about the scandal caused to the world by deeds of pernicious and deliberate intent, enacted in the name of Christ, that openly contradict the will of Christ.

Thus I come back to the crypt chapel of the Seminary of the Immaculate Conception in Huntington, New York. In looking at the image of the broken crosier, I have come to realize that several themes motivated, both personally and ecclesiologically, the pontificate of Pope John Paul II. They include grace, participation, neighboring, contemplation, and prayer. To summarize: all truth leads to this one truth of the human heart—we all were made for relationships with other human beings.

We were made for authentic love. Thus one also sees with understanding Karol Wojtyla's life-long enthusiasm for the biography and writings of St. John of the Cross, who wrote as a synthesis of his own doctrine: "In the evening of life, we shall be judged on love." Thus no one can beseech Christ's forgiveness when he sits in majesty and judgment over the death of prelates or the ruins of various periods of Church history "if we have not beseeched the forgiveness of the brother or the sister with whom we are called to stand in solidarity."

To date, no synthesis of the pope's thinking or spirituality has been achieved, so rich and diverse is his body of writing! What has been attempted so far, by others, provides facets of the depth of the pope's sentiment and reason. With the theme of solidarity perpetually in mind, I have sought to provide a variety of meditations for every day of the year. I am grateful to all those who have helped me in the process.

Here I wish to express my gratitude to the following for all their kindness to me. In particular, I thank my colleagues at the seminary, Fathers Peter Vaccari, Charles Caccavale, and James Massa, of the Diocese of Brooklyn, and Richard Henning, of the Diocese of Rockville Centre. I thank the seminary librarian, Elyse Hayes, and her assistants, Frances Brophy and Carol Breckner, for their patience and their multiple deeds of kindness. I acknowledge gratefully the support of Mrs. Bernadette Grodman, the seminary business manager. To work with such a staff is a joy for any editor or author.

I also thank Brother Owen Sadlier, O.S.F., also of the seminary faculty, for his rich insight and his guidance. I wish to express gratitude to Father Xavier Hayes, C.P., and Margaret Hoenig, of the Society of Our Lady of the Way, for all of their hard work in seeing that this task was completed on time. They are both ever faithful, ever hard working. Special thanks go to four students of the seminary who worked with me at a rapid pace and under pressure, Thomas Tassone, Allan Arneaud, Matthew Nannery, and Janusz Mocarski, whose advice on Polish culture and theater has been invaluable. I also thank close friends Gretchen Schumacher and Daniel Levans, who likewise helped me accomplish a great deal in a short time. I cannot overlook the kindness and generosity of my monastery rector, the Very Reverend Jack Douglas, C.P., the vicar of the monastery, Fr. Stanislaus Wasek, a very good friend, and all of the Passionist Community at Immaculate Conception Monastery, Jamaica, New York. Last and with profound gratitude, reverence, and affection, I acknowledge the generous support of the entire community of the Seminary of the Immaculate Conception. My thanks, most especially to Monsignor Francis J. Schneider, seminary rector, are sincere and abundant. On the occasion of the seminary's seventy-fifth anniversary, I can only say, *Ad Multos Gloriosque Annos!*

Jerome-Michael Vereb, C.P., S.T.D.
Seminary of the Immaculate Conception
Huntington, New York
Feast of the Visitation of Mary, May 31, 2005

INTRODUCTION

The name of the venerable Servant of God John Paul II will be one of the most significant names of the last century and, I am convinced, of this century hardly begun. The impact of his thought and personality is profound. It will take more than a generation of scholars to unpack the richness of his teaching. It will take more than a generation of historians of the Church and society to evaluate his place in the pantheon of thinkers and leaders who shaped our world and set forth trajectories for the future development of human and Christian history.

My own esteem and admiration for Pope John Paul II has been nurtured by the experience of working in the Roman Curia during the first eight years of his pontificate. Like most others standing in St. Peter's Square on October 18, 1978, I had heard the name of Karol Wojtyla only when Cardinal Felici came to the Loggia to proclaim *"Habemus Papam ... Karolum ... Wojtyla di Polonia."* An Italian woman near me in the square queried *"Bologna?"* to which I replied *"No, Signora, Polonia."* Her concern that he might not speak Italian was alleviated when the new Holy Father greeted us in perfect Italian and showed us his warm and engaging personality and shy wit when he said, "Please correct me when I am speaking your—no, I mean our—language."

There was not much to correct then, or at all, in this incredible pontificate of twenty-six years. Nor was there any aspect of human life that would not be studied, prayed over, and given deeper significance as a result of this man's pontificate of mediating God's plan of salvation. Father Jerome Vereb, C.P., in this book offers contemporary readers a fascinating and helpful primer on one of the most basic foundation stones of John Paul II's intellectual and spiritual project: the human person, whose value and dignity inhere in his or her humanity. The roots of this project can be found in the late pontiff's early life struggles and their context, twentieth-century Poland. As Cardinal Baum presciently notes in his Foreword, one can find this theme emerging with conviction and clarity in the Holy Father's philosophical writings long before he was elected pope.

Shortly after the pope was elected, my own work on the staff as Undersecretary of the Pontifical Commission for Justice and Peace did bring me into personal contact with the pope, but not on a regular basis. Mine was modest work, but one that depended very much on an attentive and accurate understanding of, and formation in, the thought and the vision of the new pontiff regarding issues of justice and peace.

Early on, the Secretary of the Pontifical Council, Father Roger Heckel, S.J. (later coadjutor bishop of Strasbourg, France), suggested that one of the ways our office could contribute to the work of the new Holy Father would be to publish an annual booklet that would contain the principle messages of the new pope in the field of social justice, along with commentary by Father Heckel and me. Within a few months we came to joke about the suggestion, as it became obvious that no "booklet" would ever be able to summarize or even adequately list the voluminous number of discourses, homilies, messages, and letters that this pope was producing in the field of Catholic social doctrine. Each of us chose certain themes in his writings and offered those to the public with our commentary. They were a good forum to make known the thoughts of the pope in the area of Catholic social teaching. They are still helpful today in recording and interpreting the first five years of his pontificate.

As Father Jerome makes evident in this book, the human person lies at the heart of the pope's teaching. However, it is not just any conception of the human person. It is not a reductionist sense of human existence, nor is it a deification of humanity. His clear and unambiguous vision of humanity and of the concrete person is shaped by his faith. Here shines a depth and richness to be had only from encounter with Jesus Christ, who "reveals man to man." Although Pope John Paul II constantly calls everyone to reflect on what he says, regardless of whether or not they share the faith, he does not hesitate to insist that the understanding of "man" is properly theological and Christological. It is theological because God, and God alone, is the author of life and the shaper of human destiny. It is Christological because, following the first part of the Vatican II document *Gaudium et Spes* (22, 45), the Holy Father shows how *the* Incarnation of the Son of God radically changes the meaning of human existence. Christ the Redeemer reveals the depths of dignity and value of human beings, thus offering everyone the option to live a humanity that would otherwise be impossible.

In so doing, the venerable Servant of God lays claim to one of the important presuppositions of Catholic social doctrine: "Faith and social justice are not to be separated one from the other." In the aftermath of the council, there was a resurgence in the many works of social justice. An example of this was the flourishing in the 1970s of national justice and peace commissions around the world. Although much was gained and a new kind of Catholic witness soon became evident, in many places a danger was not avoided and a certain mistake took hold. The danger was the control of Catholic social justice by "ideology"; the mistake was to subject the Catholic vision of the person to philosophical and ideological limitations of inadequate interpretations of the human person. Among these were some forms of liberation theology in Latin America, but this tendency was present in projects of North American and European justice and peace movements also. When faith ceases to nourish commitment to social justice, then the actions of even the most dedicated and well meaning can become compromised by the forces of "ideology and politics."

Knowing this, the pope was convinced from his formidable intellectual analysis and experience of the primacy of faith. The result was his insistence on the project of "man before God" as the way to discover the claims of social justice and as a guide for responding to the concrete issues that constantly challenge society. In western Canada, John Paul II cried out that the poor nations of the world will rise up to condemn the rich; his appeal was not a Marxist critique. It was the distress of a pastor who sees the suffering of his people and who calls those with power and resources to their responsibility. When in the *favelas* of Rio de Janeiro he encountered the poor in the midst of the most primitive of economic and social conditions, his reaction was not the despair of the revolutionary; instead it was the clear-sighted conviction of the pastor who wished to see human dignity restored and human living flourish for all.

The genius of the Catholic theological tradition flourishes in the relationship between faith and reason. The venerable Servant of God John Paul II was both philosopher and theologian. Both those roles became subsumed into his universal pastoral mission.

Although he begins and ends with faith, the Holy Father's proposals about the person in society and the commonweal within the creation, destined by God, for the good of all, were also open to be grasped, understood, and affirmed by every man and woman of goodwill. This was demonstrated when he traveled to the United Nations in New York or spoke to international agencies and other global entities. He invited those who heard him to reflect on the validity of what he had to say by testing it against their own experience and understanding and against the experiences and examples that human history constantly offers. He wedded in his own homilies and discourses natural moral reasoning with the revelation that is the deposit of faith of the Church. In so doing, he opened up new vistas for understanding the human person in society.

I recall his 1981 encyclical *Laborem Exercens*, on the meaning of human labor. The Holy Father's "social encyclicals," *Laborem Exercens, Solicitudo Rei Socialis,* and *Centesimus Annus,* should not be read separately from the whole ensemble of his work, in which the social questions are placed within his theological vision, especially as presented in his first four encyclicals, *Redemptor Hominis, Dives in Misericordia, Dominum et Vivificantem,* and *Redemptoris Mater.* He had a rare capacity to analyze and throw new light on some of the most challenging social questions of the day. All of his thinking is based upon his vision of the Blessed Trinity at work in contemporary human society.

Laborem Exercens was planned to be promulgated in May of 1981, ninety years after Pope Leo XIII's pronouncement on labor, *Rerum Novarum.* On May 13, the pope was shot. He spent the next months in the Gemelli Hospital in Rome. This postponed the publication of *Laborem Exercens.* It gave the pope a rare opportunity to reread his own work. His convalescence gave him time to ponder exactly what he wished to say free from other distractions. The result is a "social encyclical" that classically stands with *Rerum Novarum* and *Quadragesimo Anno,* its predecessors.

It has become commonplace—and correct—to cite how influential John Paul II was in bringing about the demise of Marxist Communism in Europe. As Vaclev Havel noted when he greeted the pope in Prague after the fall of the Soviet Union and its satellites: "When everyone else lied to us, you alone always spoke the truth." Speaking the truth remains the major reason why Pope John Paul II made such an impact on his own times and will *continue* to have an influence. Three moments come immediately to my mind. The first was the Polish pope's second visit to his native country after General Wojciech Jaruszelski had instituted martial law. He spoke clearly and forcefully to the "president" of Poland in words that were direct, leaving the general visibly shaking before the television cameras. The second was his encounter with President Fernando Marcos and his wife, Imelda, at the Philippine presidential palace in Manila. There the Holy Father gave a discourse on human rights that effectively shattered the artificial and false attempts by the Marcoses to hide their abysmal record on human rights. The third was in Havana when John Paul II celebrated Sunday Mass in the *Plaza de la Revolución*. There he set forth in a calm but studied way the principles of Catholic social doctrine about the human person, the priority of personal freedom, and religious freedom as President Fidel Castro sat in the front row directly below the Holy Father's gaze.

Perhaps no area of human living is more challenging and more difficult to guide with ethical principles than economics. The macroeconomics presented by the G–7, the World Bank, and the International Monetary Fund came under close scrutiny during the pontificate of John Paul II. The negative effects of globalized economies did not escape his attention.

Conscious as he was of the importance of the creation of capital as illustrated by his recognition of the positive aspects of the free-market system in *Centesimus Annus,* he never lost sight of the stark reality of poverty. In my encounters with him after specialized meetings at the Commission for Justice and Peace, he would stress his concern through his questions about development in the context of global poverty. He encouraged the work being done on issues such as international debt; he addressed the challenge of globalization with a sensitivity to those who were adversely affected, without falling prey to the easy and cheap analyses of condemnation. For Pope John Paul II, economics had a human face and the many faces of the world's poor served to call the responsible parties and "actors" to a greater effort to use capital for human advancement and to end the exploitation of the poor by blind economic forces. The Holy Father's references to the "social mortgage" stem from the Catholic social principle of the universal destination of all created goods. His emphasis on subsidiary and solidarity lifted up a vision of human creative achievement within the context of a solidarity that left no one outside the sphere of its influence. In a very practical way, the Holy Father pressed this vision forward when he founded the John Paul II Foundation for the *Sahel* (the geographic area of Africa currently experiencing severe drought conditions) and entrusted 30 million *deutschemarks* to projects that would advance the development of the African nations that stretched from Mauritania to Somalia.

In these and in so many other moments too numerous to mention, John Paul II echoed the words of the Lord: "The truth will set you free." Truth, freedom, human dignity, social justice that is more than *quid pro quo*, peace that is built not on might or convenience but on the inherent dignity of the human person, and the principles that ensure the common good in a just society—these are the themes that continually recur in his thoughts and his actions.

All these *never* became slogans or catchwords. Rather, they were part of a whole that found its inspiration and its point of reference in the Lord, who "loved his own to the end" (John 13:1). Ultimately social justice can never be complete in and of itself. It will always be to some extent deficient, because it can never satisfy the deepest desires of the human heart. Only a person can do that! And only the Second Person of the Blessed Trinity, the eternal Son of God, offers the ultimate answer that alone can satisfy the human heart. As the ultimate expression of love, Jesus Christ offered his own life "for the salvation of the world."

The venerable Servant of God John Paul II came to us as the Servant of the Servants of God and taught the Church and the world truths about God, about ourselves, and about the society in which we live. In the closing years of his pastoral ministry, when he was physically limited, he showed us the depth of his love by his suffering with dignity and returning to the Father in a death that touched the hearts of the whole world. Ultimately, his gift to us was the gift of priestly love, coupled with his life journey, his rich but sometimes harsh experiences, and his spirit-driven wisdom, poured out for the edification and the sake of the Church, "that the world might believe" (John 17:21). We all give thanks to God for this good and holy man, this venerable Servant of God, this venerable Servant of the Servants of God, John Paul II.

Most Reverend William Murphy, S.T.D, L.H.D.
Bishop of Rockville Centre
Feast of St. Philip Neri, May 26, 2005

January

———— ⚬⚬⚬ ————

The Legacy of Pope John Paul II

I express the most profound trust that, in spite of all my weakness, the Lord will grant me every grace necessary to face, in accordance with his will, any task, test, or suffering that he sees fit to ask of his servant during his life. I am also confident that he will never let me fail through some attitude I may have, words, deeds, or omissions in my obligations to this holy Petrine See.

The Testament of Pope John Paul II, Undated Page

⎯⎯∞⎯⎯

You Are a Power

All together you are an enormous power: the power of intelligences and consciences! Show yourselves to be more powerful than the most powerful in our modern world! Make up your mind to give proof of the most noble solidarity with humankind: the solidarity founded on the dignity of the human person. Construct peace, beginning with the foundation: respect for all the rights of man, those connected with his material and economic dimension as well as those connected with the spiritual and interior dimension of his existence in this world. May wisdom inspire you! May love guide you, that love which will suffocate the growing threat of hatred and destruction! Men of science, commit all your moral authority to save humankind from nuclear destruction.

Message to UNESCO, June 2, 1980

January 3

Bonds of Peace

In his address to the United Nations on October 4, 1965, Pope Paul VI stated a profound truth when he said: "Peace, as you know, is not built up only by means of politics or the balance of forces and interests. It is constructed with the mind, with ideas, with works of peace." The products of the mind—ideas—the products of culture, and the creative forces of peoples are meant to be shared. Strategies of peace that remain on the scientific and technical level and merely measure out balances and verify controls will never be sufficient for real peace, unless bonds that link peoples to one another are forged and strengthened. Build up the links that unite people together. Build up the means that will enable peoples and nations to share their culture and values with one another. Put aside all the narrow interests that leave one nation at the mercy of another economically, socially, or politically.

Letter to the General Assembly of the United Nations, June 11, 1982

Called to Dialogue

You are thus called, as Christians and experts in the social disciplines, to play a role of mediation and dialogue *between concrete ideals and realities.* It is a role that sometimes requires you to be "pioneers," for you have to point out new paths and new solutions to deal more justly with the burning problems of the contemporary world. Reflection on the democratic system today cannot be limited merely to considering political orders or institutions, but must broaden our personal horizons to the problems posed by the development of science and technology, to those introduced into the economy of finance by the spread of globalization, to the new rules to regulate international organizations, to the questions that have arisen from the growing and rapid development of the world of communications in order to work out a model of democracy that is authentic and complete.

Letter to Cardinal Camillo Ruini for Italian Catholic Social Week,
October 4, 2004

January 5

A Missionary Concern

The mission of Christ the Redeemer, which is entrusted to the Church, is still very far from completion. As the second millennium after Christ's coming draws to an end, an overall view of the human race shows that this mission is only beginning and that we must commit ourselves wholeheartedly to its service. It is the Spirit who impels us to proclaim the great works of God: "For if I preach the gospel, that gives me no ground for boasting. For necessity is laid upon me. Woe to me if I do not preach the gospel!" (1 Cor. 9:16). In the name of the whole Church, I sense an urgent duty to repeat this cry of St. Paul. From the beginning of my pontificate I have chosen to travel to the ends of the earth in order to show this missionary concern. My direct contact with peoples who do not know Christ has convinced me of the *urgency of missionary activity,* a subject to which I am devoting the present encyclical. The Second Vatican Council sought to renew the Church's life and activity in the light of the needs of the contemporary world. The council emphasized the Church's "missionary nature," basing it in a dynamic way on the trinitarian mission itself. The missionary thrust therefore, belongs to the very nature of the Christian life, and is also the inspiration behind ecumenism: "That they may all be one ... so that the world may believe that you have sent me" (John 17:21).

Encyclical Redemptoris Missio, *December 7, 1990*

The Message of the Star

The *theme of light* dominates the Solemnities of Christmas and Epiphany, which in the first centuries were—and still today are in the East—celebrated together in a single great "Feast of Lights." The light appears in the warm intimacy of the holy night of Christmas Eve; Christ, the Light of Humanity, is born. He is the "Sun that shall dawn upon us from on high" (Luke 1:78). He is the son that came into the world to dispel the darkness of evil and flood it with the splendor of divine love. John the Evangelist writes: *"The true light that enlightens every man came into the world"* (John 1:9). On today's Solemnity of the "Epiphany," a word for "manifestation," we are struck by the theme of the light. The Messiah who showed himself in Bethlehem to the lowly shepherds of the region continues to reveal himself as the light of every people of every time and place. To the Magi, coming from the East to adore him, the light of the one "who has been born King of the Jews" (Matt. 2:2) appears in the form of a heavenly body, so bright as to attract their attention and guide them to Jerusalem. Thus he sets them on the trail of the ancient messianic prophecies: *"A star shall come forth from Jacob, and a scepter shall rise from Israel"* (Num. 24:17). How striking is the symbol of the star that recurs in all the images of Christmas and Epiphany!... The star we contemplate over the crib *also speaks to the heart and the mind of the man of the third millennium.* It speaks to *secularized* man, awakening in him the nostalgia of his condition as pilgrim in search of the truth with a *deep desire for the absolute.*

Homily, St. Peter's Basilica, January 6, 2002

———∞∞———

The Duty of the Church

Open the doors to Christ! His gospel in no way detracts from the human person's freedom, from the respect that is owed to every culture and to whatever is good in each religion. By accepting Christ, you open yourselves to the definitive Word of God, to the One in whom God has made himself fully known and has shown us the path to himself. The number of those who do not know Christ and do not belong to the Church is constantly on the increase. Indeed, since the end of the Second Vatican Council it has almost doubled. When we consider this immense portion of humanity, which is loved by the Father, and for whom he sent his Son, the urgency of the Church's mission is obvious. Our own times offer the Church new opportunities in this field: we have witnessed the collapse of oppressive ideologies and political systems; the opening of frontiers and the formation of a more united world due to an increase in communications; the affirmation among peoples of the gospel values, which Jesus made incarnate in his own life (peace, justice, brotherhood, concern for the needy); and the kind of soulless economic and technical development that only stimulates the search for the truth about God, about man, and about the meaning of life itself. God is opening before the Church the horizons of a humanity more fully prepared for the sowing of the gospel. The moment has come to commit all of the Church's energies to a new evangelization. No believer in Christ, no institution of the Church can avoid this supreme duty, to proclaim Christ to all peoples.

Encyclical Redemptoris Missio, *December 7, 1990*

———∞∞∞———

The Power of the Creed

In my first encyclical, in which I set forth the program of my pontificate, I said that "the Church's fundamental function in every age, and particularly in ours, is to direct man's gaze, to point the awareness and experience of the whole of humanity toward the mystery of Christ." The Church's universal mission is born of faith in Jesus Christ, as is stated in our trinitarian profession of faith: "I believe in one Lord, Jesus Christ, the only Son of God, eternally begotten of the Father.... For us men and for our salvation he came down from heaven: by the power of the Holy Spirit he became incarnate from the Virgin Mary, and was made man." The redemption event brings salvation to all, "for each one is included in the mystery of the Redemption and with each one Christ has united himself forever through this mystery." It is only in faith that the Church's mission can be understood and only in faith that it finds its basis.

Encyclical Redemptoris Missio, *December 7, 1990*

January 9

---⚬⚭⚬---

Impelled by Love

Those who love God, the Father of all, cannot fail to love their fellow human beings, whom they recognize as brothers and sisters. Precisely for this reason, they cannot remain indifferent to the fact that many men and women do not know the full manifestation of God's love in Christ. The result, in obedience to Christ's commandment, is the missionary drive *ad gentes* (to all the peoples), which every committed Christian shares with the Church, which is missionary by nature. This drive is felt above all by the members of institutes, whether of the contemplative or of the active life. Consecrated persons, in fact, have the task of making present even among non-Christians Christ, who is chaste, poor, obedient, prayerful and missionary. While remaining ever faithful to their charism, they must know that they have a special share in the Church's missionary activity, in virtue of their interior consecration made to God. The desire so often expressed by Thérèse of Lisieux, "to love You and make You loved," the ardent longing of St. Francis Xavier that many, "meditating on what the Lord God will expect from them and from the talents he has given them, would be converted, using the right means and the Spiritual Exercises to know and feel within themselves the divine will, and so, adapting themselves more to that will than to their own inclinations, they would say: 'Lord, here I am, what do you want me to do? Lead me wherever you will,'" and other similar testimonies of countless holy men and women manifest the irrepressible drive that distinguishes and ennobles the consecrated life.

Apostolic Exhortation Vita Consecrata, *March 25, 1996*

---∞---

The Meaning of the Twentieth Century

The century just ended has seen remarkable advances in science, which have considerably improved people's life and health. These advances have also contributed to our dominion over nature and made easier people's access to culture. Information technology has made the world smaller and brought us closer to one another. Never before have we been so quickly informed about the daily events affecting the lives of our brothers and sisters in the human family. But *one question can be asked: Was this century also the century of "brotherhood"?* Certainly an unqualified answer cannot be given. As the balance is made, the memory of bloody wars that have decimated millions of people and provoked massive exoduses, shameful genocides that haunt our memories, as well as the arms race, which fostered mistrust and fear, terrorism and ethnic conflicts that annihilated peoples who had lived together in the same territory, all force us to be modest—in many cases to have a penitent spirit. The life sciences and biotechnology continue to find new fields of application, yet they also raise the problem of the limits imposed by the need to safeguard people's dignity, responsibility, and safety. Globalization, which has profoundly transformed economic systems by creating unexpected possibilities for growth, has also resulted in many people being relegated to the side of the road. Unemployment in the more developed countries and extreme poverty in too many countries of the Southern Hemisphere continue to hold millions of women and men back from progress and prosperity.

Address to the Diplomatic Corps, Vatican City, January 10, 2000

A Sense of Responsibility

We know one thing today more than in the past: we will never be happy and at peace without one another, much less if some are against others. The humanitarian efforts deployed during recent conflicts and natural catastrophes inspire praiseworthy initiatives of volunteerism, which reveal a greater sense of altruism, especially among the younger generation. The phenomenon of globalization has somewhat changed the role of states: citizens have become more and more involved, and the principle of subsidiarity has undoubtedly contributed to greater balance between the forces present within civil society.... This means that the *men and women of the twenty-first century will be called to a more developed sense of responsibility.* First, their personal responsibility, in fostering a sense of duty and honest labor; corruption, organized crime, and passivity can never lead to a true and healthy democracy. But there must also be an equal sense of responsibility toward others: an attitude of concern for the poor, participation in structures of mutual assistance in the workplace and in the social sphere, respect for nature and the environment....We must renounce idols such as prosperity at any price, material wealth as the only value, science as the sole explanation of reality. The rule of law must be applied and respected by everyone and in all places, so that individual liberties can be effectively guaranteed and equal opportunity become a reality for all people. And God must have his rightful place in people's lives: the first place.

Address to the Diplomatic Corps, Vatican City, January 10, 2000

---- ∞ ----

The Mission of the Disciple of Christ

The disciple of Christ is constantly challenged by a spreading "practical atheism"—an indifference to God's loving plan, which obscures the religious and moral sense of the human heart. Many either think and act as if God did not exist or tend to "privatize" religious belief and practice, so that there exists a bias toward indifferentism and the elimination of any real reference to binding truths and moral values. When the basic principles that inspire and direct human behavior are fragmentary and even at times contradictory, society increasingly struggles to maintain harmony and a sense of its own destiny. In a desire to find some common ground on which to build its programs and policies it tends to restrict the contribution of those whose moral conscience is formed by their religious beliefs.

Address to the Bishops of New Jersey and Pennsylvania, November 11, 1993

⁓

More About Sin

Another point is that sin constitutes conflict with God. People worry about this matter a great deal, wondering where this conflict with God springs from and whether it is found in every sin.... We choose God when we choose ourselves, and we are constantly choosing or refusing God. In each action, when we choose ourselves, we are choosing (or refusing) God—this is how closely we are linked to God! So why does sin always give rise to conflict with God? I would say that it is because sin is against the "ideology" of God. God's ideology is that of creation, and it lies in creating and in developing the good, particularly in the moral order. Sin, on the other hand, destroys. In the first place it destroys the fundamental good with which we are all imbued. Sin destroys the good, which is the person, the good that is myself. I did not give myself existence, and I do not own myself. In the final analysis, not even my parents gave me existence. God has a fundamental right over us, since he created us. As his creatures we are in a certain manner pervaded by the ideology of God, who creates and through whom all growth takes place. And if I wreak ruin and destruction around and within myself, this is ideological conflict with God: I am professing some ideology other than his.

The Way to Christ

———∞———

The Gift of Old Age

The teaching and language of the Bible present old age as a "favorable time" for bringing life to its fulfillment and, in God's plan for each person, as a time when everything comes together and enables us better to grasp life's meaning and to attain "wisdom of heart." "An honorable old age comes not with the passing of time," observes the book of Wisdom, "nor can it be measured in terms of years; rather, understanding is the hoary crown for men and an unsullied life, the attainment of an old age" (Wisd. of Sol. 4:8–9). Old age is the final stage of human maturity and a sign of God's blessing. In the past, great respect was shown to the elderly. "Great was once the reverence given to the hoary head," says Ovid, a Latin poet. Centuries earlier, the Greek poet Phocylides had admonished: "Respect gray hair: give to the elderly sage the same signs of respect that you give your own father." And what of today? If we stop to consider the current situation, we see that among some peoples old age is esteemed and valued, while among others this is much less the case, due to a mentality that gives priority to immediate human usefulness and productivity. Such an attitude frequently leads to contempt for the later years of life, while older people themselves are led to wonder whether their lives are still worthwhile.

Letter to the Elderly, October 1, 1999

—∞∞∞—

The Grandeur of the Disabled

Disabled persons are fully human subjects with inalienable rights. The starting point for every reflection on disability is rooted in the fundamental convictions of Christian anthropology: even when disabled persons are mentally impaired or when their sensory or intellectual capacity is damaged they are fully human beings and possess the sacred and inalienable rights that belong to every human creature. Indeed, human beings, independently of the conditions in which they live or of what they are able to express, have a unique dignity and a special value from the very beginning of their life until the moment of natural death. The disabled person, with all the limitations and sufferings that scar him or her, forces us to question ourselves with respect and wisdom on the mystery of man. In fact, the more we move about in the dark and unknown areas of human reality, the better we understand that it is in the more difficult and disturbing situations that the dignity and grandeur of the human being emerges. The wounded humanity of the disabled challenges us to recognize, accept, and promote in each one of these brothers and sisters of ours the incomparable value of the human being created by God to be a son or a daughter in the Son.

Discourse at the Vatican for the International Symposium on the Dignity and Rights of the Mentally Disabled Person, January 5, 2004

---◯◯◯◯---

Monasticism: A Natural Platform for Mutual Understanding

God continues his work in you and with you in his own way, as Jesus foretold when speaking to his disciples: *"In the world you have tribulation, but be of good cheer, I have overcome the world"* (John 16:33). *Be faithful to your history.* Our secularized world is indebted to you for the witness of your communities that put God in the center place. Through the liturgy, study, and work may you be an example of Christian life that is fully oriented to God, respectful of humankind and creation. I am aware of your contacts with *monks and nuns of other religions:* these are important relationships that can prove fruitful. I urge you to deepen *ecumenical relations with our brothers and sisters of eastern Europe.* Monasticism is a natural platform for mutual understanding. This is extremely important at this moment in history in order to preserve the Christian roots of Europe. I am pleased that as the great *Benedictine family,* you are increasing by rediscovering your common heritage. Dear brothers and sisters, continue on your way following the footsteps of St. Benedict and St. Scholastica: "Prefer nothing whatsoever to Christ!" (*Rule of Benedict* 72:11). Faithful to this rule of life you will experience a future full of God's gifts. May the Blessed Virgin Mary obtain them for you. I entrust you to her as I wholeheartedly bless you and all your communities.

Message to Benedictine Abbots and Abbesses, General Assembly at the Vatican, September 23, 2004

Listening to God's Word

The liturgy once again proposes for our meditation the Gospel episode of Jesus's visit to the house of *Martha and Mary* (Luke 10:38–42). While Martha is totally taken up with household tasks, Mary is seated at the Master's feet listening to his word. Christ affirms that Mary *"has chosen the good portion, which shall not be taken away from her." Listening to the word of God* is the most important thing in our lives. Christ is always in our midst and desires to speak to our hearts. We can listen to him by meditating with faith on Sacred Scripture, by recollection in private and communal prayer, by silent meditation before the Tabernacle, from which he speaks to us of his love. Christians, especially on *Sundays,* are called to meet and listen to the Lord. This happens most completely through participation in the Holy Mass, and during sacred services, during which Christ prepares the Banquet of the Word and the Bread of Life for the faithful, but other moments of prayer and reflection, of rest and brotherhood can also be profitably combined to make the *Lord's Day* holy. When through the action of the Holy Spirit God takes up his dwelling in the heart of believers, it becomes easier for them to serve the brethren. This is what happened in a unique and a perfect way to Mary, the most holy Mother of God.

Discourse at the Vatican, July 18, 2004

Ecumenism: A Search for Unity

This year, the theme of the Week of Prayer for Christian Unity was suggested by an ecumenical group in the city of Aleppo, Syria, which reminds me of the pilgrimage I had the joy of making to Damascus. I recall with special gratitude the warm welcome I received from the two Orthodox patriarchs and the Greek Catholic patriarch. Ecumenism is not genuine unless there is *"interior conversion. For it is from newness of attitudes of mind, from self-denial and unstinted love that desires of unity take their rise and develop in a mature way"* (*Unitatis Redintegratio*). For me, a profound spirituality of peace and pacification is more keenly felt not only by those who are directly involved in ecumenical work, but by all Christians. Indeed, the cause of unity concerns every believer, called to belong to the one people of those redeemed by the blood of Christ on the cross. The search for unity among Christians is constantly spreading, thanks to timely initiatives involving the various contexts of ecumenical commitment. Among these signs of hope I would like to list the growth of fraternal love and the progress reported in the theological dialogues with the various churches and ecclesial communities. It has been possible in these to reach an important convergence, to a varying degree and with different specificity, on topics that were deeply controversial in the past. Taking these positive signs into account, we must not be discouraged by the old and new difficulties we encounter, but face them with patience and understanding, relying always on divine help.

Discourse at the Vatican, January 21, 2004

The Gift of Dialogue

What has been said about ecumenical dialogue since the end of the Second Vatican Council inspires us to give thanks to the Spirit of Truth promised by Christ the Lord to the apostles and the Church (John 14:26). It is the first time in history that efforts on behalf of Christian unity have taken on such great proportions and have become so extensive. This is truly an immense gift of God, one that deserves all our gratitude. From the fullness of Christ we receive "grace upon grace" (John 1:16). An appreciation of how much God has already given is the condition that disposes us to receive those gifts still indispensable for bringing to completion the ecumenical work of unity. An overall view of the last thirty years enables us better to appreciate many of the fruits of this common conversion to the gospel that the Spirit of God has brought about by means of the ecumenical movement.

Encyclical Ut Unum Sint, *May 25, 1995*

A Year of Anguish

My sentiments of joy in the New Year are overshadowed, unfortunately, by the enormous catastrophe that on December 26, 2004, struck different countries of Southeast Asia and as far as the coasts of East Africa. It made for a painful ending of the year just past: a year troubled by other natural calamities such as the devastating cyclones in the Indian Ocean and the Antilles and the plague of locusts that desolated vast regions of northwest Africa. Other tragedies also cast a shadow on 2004, like the acts of barbaric terrorism that caused bloodshed in Iraq and other countries of the world, the savage attack in Madrid, the terrorist massacre in Beslan, the inhuman acts of violence inflicted on the people of Darfur, and the atrocities perpetrated in the Great Lakes region of Africa. These events have caused great anguish and distress, and we would feel a tragic concern for the future of humanity were it not for the fact that from the cradle of Bethlehem there comes to us a message, both divine and human. In Jesus Christ, who comes into the world as the brother of every man and woman, it is God Himself who asks us not to yield to discouragement, but to overcome every difficulty, however great it may be, by strengthening the common bonds of our humanity and by making them prevail over all other considerations.

Message to Ambassadors Accredited to the Vatican, January 10, 2005

The Content of the Fact of Sin

The content of the Gospels is deeply human, since it is the truth about man's life, and this is precisely why it also contains the negative aspect. The picture presented in the Gospels is real and true.... Each period of history is full of negative aspects of sin, and our contemporary world has its full share. We must face up to the fact that there are many of these in us and around us. Let us imagine some ordinary human situation we could meet with any day in our office, home, or laboratory. One or more of these places may be dominated by an unpleasant atmosphere, an atmosphere of animosity, or at least insensitivity, an atmosphere that contaminates and in some way affects everything and everyone; and this atmosphere may exclude or marginalize some people. Today we often hear talk about broken or marginalized people. Where does this atmosphere come from? It comes from us, from somebody who gives it form—maybe one or two of us, or maybe all of us. We probably all contribute to it, some of us actively and others passively, some of us through commission and others through omission. It is a very common situation. At home doors are slammed, and the different members of the family do not speak to one another; they live their lives closed off from one another, as if they were total strangers and there were a wall between them. This too is a common situation. We must admit that in these situations it is often more a case of general human suffering and dissatisfaction and of hidden tears than of some consciously and freely willed evil.

The Way to Christ

---∞∞∞---

Preparing to Be Witnesses

By increasing your knowledge, broadening your culture, deepening your faith, and affirming your convictions, you prepare yourselves to be those vigorous witnesses to truth and to love that our age calls for, our age in which man, isolated in the lonely crowd, no longer knows what it is to live, to love, to suffer, and to die. What is man? This question must be answered: the challenge of practical materialism, religious indifference, and caustic skepticism must be met. Yes, what is man, lacerated between the infinitude of his desires and the finiteness of his pleasures, between his persistent search for the truth and the bit-by-bit knowledge that comes to him? Today even those who have doubts about God, and from this arrive pretty quickly at having doubts about man, feel with a more or less vivid awareness the need to establish and to guarantee respect for man, respect for his life in all of its phases of development, respect for the love he has for others, respect for the liberty of his convictions and of his conscience. Must not the Catholic university contribute in responding to these fundamental questions regarding man with all the seriousness that their gravity demands?

Address at Louvain University, Louvain, Belgium, May 23, 1985

A Deep Question

One last question, and an even deeper one: Why is sin conflict with Christ? Nietzsche wrote a philosophical work entitled *Beyond Good and Evil*. Human beings do have a desire to place themselves beyond good and evil in an effort to achieve personal freedom beyond morality, liberating themselves from what is most human—in other words, morality. However, Christ rejected such an idea, placing himself in the center between good and evil and taking a personal part in the conflict between good and evil as it is found in every human being. By doing so he made it the duty of each of us to do the same. Therefore, any person who tries to place himself beyond good and evil, beyond morality, is not with Christ. We have already said that the Christian is a person whose place is beside Christ; this person therefore takes on the whole burden of morality—for morality *is* a burden as well as an instrument of elevation. The person who wants to be with Christ must take on his shoulders the whole burden of morality, which will be the instrument of his elevation. If we refuse this burden, we are in conflict with Christ. We try to thrust the Cross away from us, because morality is the Cross; and everything that has been written about the Cross in numerous studies, novels, and plays cannot be compared with the single concept of morality as Cross. Christian morality, and morality in general, means the Cross. We may even try to thrust the Cross away from us; but Christ did not thrust it from his shoulders; and therefore sin is conflict with Christ.

The Way to Christ

———∞∞∞———

Dignity and Education

Now Christ says: "You will know the truth, and the truth will make you free" (John 8:32). Of the words contained in the Gospel these are certainly among the most important, for they refer to man in his totality. They explain what *the dignity and greatness proper to man* are built upon from within, in the dimensions of the human spirit. A knowledge that frees man does not depend on education alone, even of university standard—an illiterate person can have it too, though education, the systematic knowledge of reality, should serve the dignity of the human person. It should therefore serve the truth. The service of truth is also carried out *in the work* that you will be called upon to perform when you have completed the program of your education. At school you have to acquire the program of your education. At school you have to acquire the intellectual, technical, and practical skills that will enable you to take your place usefully in the great world of human work. But although it is true that the school has to prepare you for work, including manual work, it is equally true that *work itself is a school in which great and important values are learned:* it has an eloquence of its own that makes a valid contribution to human culture.

Apostolic Letter to the Youth of the World, March 31, 1985

———— ∞ ————

God Calls Families to Holiness

In fact, through the family all human life is oriented toward the future. In the family man comes into the world, grows, and matures. In it he becomes an increasingly mature citizen of his country and an increasingly aware member of the Church. The family is also the first fundamental environment where every person identifies and fulfills his own human and Christian vocation. Lastly the family is a community that cannot be replaced by any other. This is what we can glimpse in today's liturgical readings.... In fact, the family is the particular and, at the same time, fundamental community of love and life on which all other communities and societies are based. Therefore, in invoking the blessings of the Most High upon families, let us pray together for all the great societies that we represent here. Let us pray for the future of the nations and states and for the future of the Church and the world.

Address to Families, Rio de Janeiro, Brazil, October 5, 1997

⊶⊷

Present at the Creation

The book of Genesis reveals first and foremost the cosmic dimension of creation. Man's appearance occurred within the immense horizon of the creation of the whole cosmos: it is not accidental that this takes place on the last day of the world's creation. Man entered the Creator's work at the moment when all the conditions necessary for human life were in place. Man is one of the visible creatures; at the same time, however, in Sacred Scripture it is said that he alone was made "in the image and likeness of God." The wonderful union of body and spirit was a decisive innovation in the process of creation. But in the human beginning, all the greatness of the visible creation gains a spiritual dimension. The intellect and will, knowledge and love—all this enters into the visible cosmos at the very moment of man's creation. It enters it showing, from the beginning, the copenetration of the life of the body with the life of the soul. Thus a man leaves his father and mother and is joined to his wife, to become one flesh; however, this conjugal union is rooted at the same time in the knowledge and love that is in the spiritual dimension.... The text of the Letter to the Hebrews recalls that the sanctification of marriage, like that of any other human reality, was accomplished by Christ at the price of his Passion and Cross. He reveals himself here as the new Adam. Just as in the natural order we all descend from Adam, so in the order of grace and sanctification we all originate in Christ. The sanctification of the family stems from the sacramental character of marriage.

Address to Families, Rio de Janeiro, Brazil, October 5, 1997

Letter to Prisoners

Today the pope turns to you with this letter, to bear witness to you of Christ's love and the ecclesial community's attention. Christ and the apostles experienced the reality of "prison," and St. Paul was jailed several times. Jesus says in the Gospel: "I was in prison and you came to me" (Matt. 25:36). He feels solidarity with your condition and encourages everyone who shares your problems. His death on the cross is also a supreme witness to love and acceptance. Crucified between two men condemned to the same punishment, he promises salvation to the good thief who repented: "Truly, I say to you, today you will be with me in paradise" (Luke 23:43). An act of extreme mercy, an extreme gift that can give confidence even to those who feel totally lost. With this act of forgiveness, the Lord speaks to humanity in every age. The plan of salvation is for everyone. *No one should feel excluded.* Christ knows every person intimately; with his justice he overcomes every human injustice; with his mercy, he conquers evil and sin. So let the Lord dwell in your hearts! Entrust your hardship to him! He will help you bear it.

Letter from the Vatican, September 30, 1997

———∞∞∞———

The Importance of Benedict

St. Benedict lived in the dark times that came with the collapse of the Roman Empire. For many, disorder brought despair and the escapism, which despair always breeds. But Benedict's response was different. Obeying impulses long known in the Christian East, he turned from all that was familiar and entered his cave, "searching for God." (*Rule*, 58:7). There Benedict grasped the very core of biblical revelation, which begins with the original chaos described in the book of Genesis and comes to its summit in the light and glory of the Paschal Mystery. He learned that even in darkness and in emptiness we can find the fullness of light and life. The mountain that Benedict climbed was Calvary, where he found the true light that enlightens all (John 1:9). How right it is then that the *sacro speco* (the Holy Shrine) at Subiaco contains the image of Benedict contemplating the Cross, since from the Cross alone comes the light, the order, and the fullness of God for which all men and women long. There alone does the human heart find rest.

Discourse from the Vatican to the Benedictine Abbesses and Prioresses,
September 16, 1998

———⊷———

Listen

The first word of his *Rule* reveals the core of Benedict's experience in the cave: *Ausculta,* "Listen!" This is the secret: Benedict listens, trusting that God is there and that God will speak. Then he hears a word in the silence; and thus he becomes the father of a civilization, the civilization born from contemplation, the civilization of love born from listening to the word that springs from the depths of the Trinity. Benedict *became* the word he heard, and slowly his voice "went forth through all the world" (Ps. 19:4). Disciples came, then monasteries appeared, then a civilization grew around them—not only salvaging what was precious in the classical world, but opening as well an unimagined path into a new world. It was the sons and daughters of St. Benedict who reclaimed the land, who organized society, who preached the gospel as missionaries, who wrote the books as scholars, nurturing all that makes for a truly human life. It is astonishing to consider how much came from so little: "This is the Lord's doing and a marvel in our eyes" (Ps. 118:23).

Discourse from the Vatican to the Benedictine Abbesses and Prioresses,
September 16, 1998

The Magnanimity of God

The *Rule* Benedict wrote is unforgettable not only for its burning passion for God and its wise concern for the discipline without which there is no discipleship, but also for its radiant *humanitas* (humanity). The *Rule* breathes a spirit of hospitality grounded upon the belief that the other is no enemy, but is Christ himself who comes as guest; and this is a spirit who is given only to those who have known the magnanimity of God. In the *Rule* of Benedict we find an order that is strict but never stern, a light that is clear but never cold, and fullness that is absolute but never overwhelming. In a word, the *Rule* is radical but always hospitable—which is why, when other monastic rules disappeared, the *Rule of Benedict* triumphed and continues to work its power even today in the lives of your communities. Our society knows darkness at the end of this century. In such a time, the luminous figure of Benedict stands in our midst, pointing as always to Christ. You have been called in a special way into that mystery of light—which is why the Church continues to look to your communities so expectantly. We look to you because you are those who are not afraid to enter the cave that is dark and empty, who listen in a truly contemplative silence, who hear the word of God and *become* that word; those who help shape a truly civilized world where anxiety and despair lose their power, and the peace of Easter is experienced in the *tranquillitas ordinis* (in the harmony of order).

Discourse from the Vatican to the Benedictine Abbesses and Prioresses,
September 16, 1998

Every House a Church

It is a great joy for me to visit as the first Roman parish precisely yours, to which I am linked by a special memory. In the years of the immediate postwar period, as a student in Rome, I used to go nearly every Sunday to Garbatella to help in the pastoral service. Some moments of that period are still alive in my memory, although it seems to me that, in the course of over thirty years, many things have changed enormously here. All Rome has changed.... Now buildings occupy all the green spaces surrounding the city. These buildings speak of the people who inhabit them. You, beloved parishioners, are these inhabitants. You make up the citizens of Rome and at the same time a definite community of the People of God. The parish is just such a community. It is so and becomes ever more so by means of the gospel, which is proclaimed here regularly, and also because the sacramental life is lived here. Coming to you today, in the name of Christ, I am thinking particularly of what Christ himself transmits to you by means of his priests, your pastors. I am thinking also of how much Christ operates by means of all of you.... I address all the families who live in this parish community and make up a part of the Church of Rome. To visit the parishes as part of the diocese called Church, it is necessary to reach all the "domestic churches," that is, all the families. This, in fact, was the name given to families by the Fathers of the Church. "Make your home a church," St. John Chrysostom urged.

Homily, St. Francis Xavier Parish, Garbatella, Rome, December 3, 1978

February

The Mission of the Church

Today an enormous amount of work is needed on the part of the Church. In particular, the lay apostolate is needed. It is absolutely essential to develop a strong sense of mission. The Church in Europe and on every continent has to recognize that it is always and everywhere a missionary church. Mission belongs so much to its nature that at no time and in no place, even in countries of long-established Christian tradition, can the Church be other than missionary. The sense of mission, renewed by the Second Vatican Council, was further promoted by Pope Paul VI. Hence the apostolic exhortation *Evangelii Nuntiandi*, in which Pope Paul spoke from the heart. I sought to continue along the same path, as my first document, *Redemptor Hominis*, can testify. In this mission, received from Christ, the Church must work tirelessly. She must be humble and courageous, like Christ himself and his apostles. If she encounters obstacles, if she is criticized in various ways—maybe accused of so-called proselytism or of trying to clericalize social life— she should not be discouraged. Most of all, she should not cease to proclaim the gospel. St. Paul was already aware of this when he wrote to his disciple: "Proclaim the message, be persistent whether the time is favorable or unfavorable, convince, rebuke and encourage with the utmost patience in teaching" (2 Tim. 4:2). St. Paul testifies to another urgent inner imperative when he says: "Woe to me if I do not proclaim the gospel!" (1 Cor. 9:16).

Memory and Identity

Christ Is Inseparable from the Church

"Christ yes, the Church no!" is the protest heard from some of our contemporaries. Despite the negative element, this stance appears to show openness toward Christ, which the Enlightenment excluded. Yet it is only an appearance of openness. Christ, if he is truly accepted, is inseparable from the Church, which is his mystical Body. There is no Christ without the Incarnation; there is no Christ without the Church. The Incarnation is prolonged, in accordance with his will, and is the community of human beings that he constituted, guaranteeing his constant presence among them: "And remember I am with you always, . . ." (Matt. 28:20). Admittedly, the Church, as a human institution, is continually in need of purification and renewal; the Second Vatican Council acknowledged this with courageous candor. Yet the Church, as the Body of Christ, is the normal locus for the presence and the action of Christ in the world. It could be said that these ideas express the thinking behind the initiatives adopted for the education of the second millennium after Christ's birth and the launching of the third. I spoke of this in the two apostolic letters I wrote at that time to the Church and to all people of goodwill. In both I stressed that the Great Jubilee concerned the entire human race to an unprecedented degree. Christ belongs to the history of all humanity and gives shape to that history. He brings it to life, as only he can, like the yeast in the Gospel. From all eternity God's plan has been accomplished in Christ . . . .

Memory and Identity

The World Perfected

The image of the Church presented by the Dogmatic Constitution *Lumen Gentium* needed in some way to be completed. John XXIII himself wisely sensed this, when, in the last weeks before his death, he decided that the Second Vatican Council would prepare a special document concerning the Church in the modern world. This task proved to be extremely fruitful. The Pastoral Constitution *Gaudium et Spes* expressed the Church's openness to the whole content of the concept of "world." In Sacred Scripture, of course, this world has a dual meaning. When, for example, the sacred authors speak of the "spirit of this world" (1 Cor. 2:12), they mean everything in the world that separates us from God; today we would express this under the heading of secularization. Yet this negative meaning of "world" in Scripture is balanced by the positive meaning: the world is God's creation, the world is the sum of the goods that the Creator has given to man, entrusting them to him as a task to be completed with initiative, insight, and responsibility. The world, which is like the theater of man's history, bears the marks of his travail, his triumphs, and his failures. Damaged by man's sin, it has been redeemed by Christ crucified and risen and now, with man's active cooperation, awaits its glorious fulfillment. Paraphrasing the words of St. Irenaeus, one might say: *Gloria Dei—mundus secundum amorem Dei ab homine excultus,* the glory of God is the world perfected by man according to God's love.

Memory and Identity

———∞∞∞———

The Human Dimension of the Mystery of the Redemption

Man cannot live without love. He remains a being that is incomprehensible for himself; his life is senseless, if love is not revealed to him, if he does not encounter love, if he does not experience it and make it his own, if he does not participate intimately in it. This is why Christ the Redeemer "fully reveals man to man himself" (*Gaudium et Spes,* 22). This is the human dimension of the mystery of the Redemption. Man finds again the greatness, dignity, and value that belong to his humanity. Man becomes newly "expressed" and is newly created. "There is neither Jew nor Greek, there is neither slave nor free, there is neither male nor female; for you are all one in Christ Jesus" (Gal. 3:28). The man who wishes to understand himself thoroughly—and not just in accordance with immediate, partial, often superficial, and even illusory standards and measures of his being—he must, with his unrest, uncertainty, and even his weakness and sinfulness, with his life and death draw near to Christ. He must enter into him with all his own self; he must appropriate and assimilate the whole of the reality of the Incarnation and Redemption in order to find himself. If this profound process takes place within him, he can then bear fruit not only of adoration of God, but also of deep wonder at himself. How precious man must be in the eyes of the Creator, if he "gained so great a Redeemer" and if God gave his only Son in order that man should not perish but have eternal life.

Encyclical Redemptor Hominis, *March 4, 1979*

—∞∞∞—

Technological Progress in Context

The essential meaning of this "kingship" and "dominion" of man over the visible world, which the Creator himself gave man for his task, consists in the priority of ethics over technology, in the primacy of the person over things, and in the superiority of spirit over matter. This is why all faces of present-day progress must be followed attentively. Each stage of that progress must, so to speak, be X-rayed from this point of view. What is in question is the advancement of persons, not just the multiplying of things that people can use. It is a matter—as a contemporary philosopher has said and as the Second Vatican Council has stated—not so much of "having more" as of "being more.".... We all know well that the areas of misery and hunger on our globe could have been made fertile in a short time, if the gigantic investments for armaments at the service of war and destruction had been changed into investments for food at the service of life.

Encyclical Redemptor Hominis, *March 4, 1979*

---∞∞∞---

Mystery of the Trinity

We are invited to meditate on the supreme reality of God to us by the Incarnate Word. Trusting in the divine word of Jesus, we believe in *God the Father*, who is absolute and eternal creative power; we believe in *God the Son*, the consubstantial Word of the Father, who by his incarnation in the womb of the Virgin Mary took on a soul and body like our own and died on the cross for the salvation of humanity; we believe in *God the Holy* Spirit, the uncreated Person who proceeds from the Father and the Son as their eternal love, the "Consoler" promised by Jesus to his pilgrim Church on earth. O Most Holy Trinity, we thank you for this supreme and ineffable revelation! The mystery, however, remains unfathomable in itself and inaccessible: a mystery of love, a mystery of light, but also a mystery of infinite transcendence, "Truly you are a hidden God!" (Isa. 45:15). And so meditation and gratitude should always be accompanied by adoration; the latter in turn must be translated into a witness of fraternal communion which makes believers "one." We all remember the prayer of Jesus: "As you, Father, are in me, and I in you; I pray that they may be one in us, that the world may believe that you sent me" (John 17:21).

Angelus Message, St. Peter's Basilica, May 17, 1991

The Incarnation and the Heritage of the Popes

God entered the history of humanity and, as a man, became an actor in that history, one of the millions of human beings, but at the same time unique! Through the Incarnation God gave human life the dimension he intended from the beginning. It was to Christ the Redeemer that my feelings and thoughts were directed when after the canonical election I was asked: "Do you accept?" I replied: "With obedience and faith to Christ, my Lord, and with trust in the Mother of Christ and of the Church, in spite of the great difficulties, I accept." Today I wish to make that reply known publicly, thus showing that there is a link between the first fundamental truth of the Incarnation and the ministry that, with my acceptance of my election as Bishop of Rome, has become my specific duty. I chose the same names chosen by my beloved predecessor. Indeed, as soon as he announced to the Sacred College on August 26, 1978, that he wished to be called John Paul—such a double name being unprecedented in the history of the papacy—I saw in it a clear presage of grace for the new pontificate. Since that pontificate lasted thirty-three days, it falls to me not only to continue it, but to take it up again at the same starting point. By following the example of my predecessor in choosing these two names, I wish to express my love for the unique inheritance left to the Church by Popes John XXIII and Paul VI and my readiness to develop that inheritance with God's help.

Encyclical Redemptor Hominis, *March 4, 1979*

Evangelization Through Love of Neighbor

"Now is the time for a new creativity in charity" (*Novo Millennio Ineunte*). How could I fail to mention in this context that great Missionary of Charity Mother Teresa of Calcutta? In the days following my election to the See of Peter, I met this great little missionary sister, who from then on would often visit me to tell me where and when she had succeeded in opening new houses to provide a home for the poorest.... I met Mother Teresa on many other occasions, and every time I was able to witness new signs of her passionate commitment to care for the poorest of the poor. Mother Teresa died in Calcutta, warmly remembered for her wonderful work, which her great multitude of spiritual daughters continue. During her lifetime many people regarded her as a saint, and when she died, her sanctity was universally recognized. I thank God that I was privileged to beatify her on October 19, 2003.... I said then, "The witness of Mother Teresa's life reminds us all that the Church's evangelizing mission is achieved through charity and is nourished through prayer and attentive listening to the Word of God. This missionary style is eloquently expressed by the image of Blessed Teresa clasping the hand of a child while fingering her rosary beads with her other hand. Contemplation and action, evangelization and respect for the human person: Mother Teresa proclaims the gospel through her life of total dedication to the poor and total dedication to prayer." This is the mystery of evangelization through love of neighbor springing from love of God.

Rise, Let Us Be on Our Way

———— ⸾⸾⸾ ————

The Source of Vocation

I set off in search of the source of my vocation. It is there ... in the Upper Room in Jerusalem. During the Great Jubilee of the Year 2000 I was able to pray in the Upper Room (Mark 14:15), where the Last Supper took place.... There Christ, *having loved his own to the end* (John 13:1), instituted the apostles as priests of the New Covenant. I see him bending before each of us, successors of the apostles, to wash our feet. I hear him as if he were speaking to us these words: *"Do you realize what I have done for you? ... If I, therefore, ... have washed your feet, you ought also to wash one another's feet. I have given you an example to follow, so that as I have done for you, you also should do"* (John 13:12–15). Together with Peter, Andrew, James, and John ... let us listen: *"As the Father has loved me, so I have loved you. Remain in my love! If you keep my commandments, you will remain in my love, just as I have kept my Father's commandments and remain in his love. I have told you this so that my joy might be in you and your joy might be complete. This is my commandment: love one another as I have loved you. No one has greater love than this, to lay down one's life for one's friends. You are my friends if you do what I command you"* (John 15:9–14). Is not the *mysterium caritatis* (mystery of charity) of our vocation contained in these sayings? These words of Christ ... are at the root of every vocation in the Church. From them flows the life-giving sap that nourishes every vocation; because the Son wishes to be a friend to everyone: because he gave his life for all.

Rise, Let Us Be on Our Way

February 10

---❦---

The World of Culture

It is well known that not all bishops are particularly interested in a dialogue with scholars. Many of them give greater priority to their pastoral responsibilities, understood in the broadest sense, than to their rapport with men of learning. In my view, however, members of the clergy, priests and bishops, do well to take the trouble to establish personal contacts with the academic world and its leading figures. A bishop, in particular, should be concerned not only with his own Catholic academic institutions, but should also maintain close links with the whole university world: reading, meeting others, discussing, informing himself about their activities. Obviously, he himself is not called to be a scholar, but a pastor. Yet as a pastor, he cannot fail to take an interest in this part of his flock, since it is his task to remind scholars of their duty to serve the truth and thus to promote the common good. In Krakow I also tried to maintain a good rapport with the philosophers.... My personal outlook moves, so to speak, between two poles: Aristotelian Thomism and phenomenology. I was particularly interested in Edith Stein, an extraordinary figure, for her life story as well as her philosophy.

Rise, Let Us Be on Our Way

February 11

The Bond Between Love and Truth

The responsibilities that weigh on a bishop's shoulders are many. I have discovered this, and I know how hard it is to find time for everything. Yet this experience has also taught me the great need for recollection and study. He has to have a profound theological formation, constantly updated, and a wide-ranging interest in thought and culture. These are treasures that all thinking people share. For this reason I would like to say something about the importance of reading in my life as a bishop. This has been a dilemma for me: What am I to read? I have always tried to choose what was most essential; so much has been published and not everything is valuable and useful. It is important to know how to choose and to consult others about what is worth reading. From my earliest childhood I loved books. My father introduced me to reading. He would sit beside me and read to me, for example, Sienkiewicz and other Polish writers. After my mother died, he continued to encourage me to explore good literature .... In my reading and in my studies I always tried to achieve a harmony between faith, reason, and the heart. These are not separate areas, but are profoundly interconnected, each giving life to the other. This coming together of faith, reason, and the heart is strongly influenced by our sense of wonder at the miracle of a human person—at man's likeness to the Triune God, at the immensely profound bond between love and truth, and the mystery of mutual self-giving and the life that it generates, and our reflections on the succession of human generations.

Rise, Let Us Be on Our Way

———∞∞∞———

We Have to Be Converted Anew

"Every perfect gift is from above, coming down from the Father of lights" (James 1:17). We for our part cannot weaken this faith and confidence with our human doubting and our timidity. In consequence, we must all be converted anew every day. This is a fundamental exigency of the gospel, addressed to everyone. If we have the duty of helping others to be converted, we have to do the same continuously in our own lives. Being converted means returning to the very grace of our vocation; it means meditating upon the infinite goodness and love of Christ, who has addressed each of us and, calling us by name, has said: "Follow me." Being converted means continually "giving an account" before the Lord of our hearts about our service, our zeal, and our fidelity, for we are "Christ's servants, stewards entrusted with the mysteries of God." Being converted also means "giving an account" of our negligences and sins, of our timidity, of our lack of faith and hope, of our thinking only "in a human way." Let us recall in this regard the warning that Christ gave to Peter himself. Being converted means seeking again the pardon and strength of God in the sacrament of reconciliation, and thus always beginning anew, and every day progressing, overcoming ourselves, making spiritual conquests, giving cheerfully, for "God loves a cheerful giver." Being converted means "to pray continually and never lose heart" (Luke 18:1). *In a certain way, prayer is the first and the last condition for conversion,* spiritual progress, and holiness.

Letter to All Priests, Holy Thursday, 1979

Sanctify Your Lives

Be a single thing among yourselves, the pillars and props of unity among Christ's flock and its shepherds, sent by Christ. Do not be concerned about prestige, about self, about pride, but be "a heart and a soul." Vigorously promote the unity of a divided Christianity! Be holy! Yes. Sanctify your lives and fill your minds only with what is holy. Only when your own life takes on the immutable attributes of the gospel will you succeed in making men marvel and drawing them in. And, in your testimony to the world, you serve the sanctification of the world. Be Catholic, universal, open, worldly. Do not shut yourselves up in your worries and in your problems. Your contribution is needed for all humanity, for the Third World, for Europe, for America, so that there can be a new beginning.

Address in Roman Catholic Cathedral, Munich, Germany,
November 18, 1980

─────◦◦◦◦─────

Communion with the Bishop

The desire to be the transparency of Christ for others places you in a position of great importance and dignity, as men and women consecrated in the Church for the good of all humanity. Your duties have a profound ecclesiastical and social impact, since you can offer something of your own, that is, the gifts of a rich spirituality and the vast capacity for disinterested love. From the perspective of your integration into the Church, I encourage you to rejoice in your special presence, in full and faithful communion with the hierarchy, since there cannot be a genuine integration into the Church outside of the center of communion, which is the bishop in his diocese. Thus you will be the true light, the light of Christ in his Church, light that radiates its own self-fulfillment.

Address to Religious, Asuncion, Paraguay, May 17, 1988

—∞∞∞—

Christ's Salvific Work

As a result of Christ's salvific work, man exists on earth *with the hope* of eternal life and holiness. And even though the victory over sin and death achieved by Christ in his Cross and Resurrection does not abolish temporal suffering from human life or free from suffering the whole historical dimension of human existence, it nevertheless *throws a new light* upon this dimension and upon every suffering: the light of salvation. This is the light of the gospel, that is, of the "good news." At the heart of this light is the truth expounded in the conversation with Nicodemus: "For God so loved the world that he gave his only Son" (John 3:16). This truth radically changes the picture of man's history and his earthly situation: in spite of the sin that took root in this history both as an original inheritance and as the "sin of the world," the sum of personal sins, God the Father has loved the only begotten Son; that is, he loves him in a lasting way. And then in time, precisely through this all-surpassing love, he "gives" this Son, that he may strike at the very roots of human evil and thus draw close in a salvific way to the whole world of suffering in which man shares.

Apostolic Letter Salvifici Doloris, *February 11, 1984*

———∞∞∞———

Christ's Mission of Suffering

Christ drew close above all to the world of human suffering through the fact of having *taken this suffering upon his very self.* During his public activity, he experienced fatigue, homelessness, and misunderstanding even on the part of those closest to him, but, more than anything, he became progressively more and more isolated and encircled by hostility, especially the hostility of putting him to death. Christ was aware of this, and often spoke to his disciples of the sufferings and death that awaited him: "Behold we are going up to Jerusalem; and the Son of Man *will be delivered* to the chief priests and the scribes, and they will condemn him to death and deliver him to the Gentiles; and they will mock him, and spit upon him, and scourge him, and kill him and after three days he will rise" (Mark 10:33–34). Christ goes toward his Passion and death with full awareness of the mission he has to fulfill precisely in this way. *Precisely* by means of this *suffering* he must bring it about "that man should not perish, but have eternal life" (John 3:16). Precisely by means of his Cross he must strike at the roots of evil planted in the history of man and in human souls. Precisely by means of his Cross he must accomplish *the work of salvation.* This work, in the plan of eternal love, has a redemptive character.

Apostolic Letter Salvifici Doloris, *February 11, 1984*

———∞———

Fostering Holiness

Today a renewed commitment to holiness by consecrated persons is more necessary than ever, as *a means of promoting and supporting every Christian's desire for perfection.* "It is therefore necessary to inspire in all the faithful a true longing for holiness, a deeper desire for conversion and personal renewal in a context of ever more intense prayer and of solidarity with one's neighbor, especially the most needy" (*Tertio Millennio Adveniente*). To the degree that they deepen their friendship with God, consecrated persons become better prepared to help their brothers and sisters through valuable spiritual activities such as schools of prayer, spiritual exercises and retreats, days of recollection, and spiritual dialogue and direction. In this way people are helped to grow in prayer and will then be better able to discern God's will in their lives and to commit themselves to the courageous and sometimes heroic demands that faith makes on them. Consecrated persons "at the deepest level of their being ... are caught up in the dynamism of the Church's life, which is thirsty for the Divine Absolute and called to holiness. It is to this holiness that they bear witness" (*Evangelii Nuntiandi*). The fact that all are called to become saints cannot fail to inspire more and more those who by their very choice of life have the mission of reminding others of that call.

Apostolic Exhortation Vita Consecrata, *March 25, 1996*

Truth with Gentleness

Another painful chapter of history to which the sons and daughters of the Church must return with a spirit of repentance is that of the acquiescence given, especially in certain centuries, *to intolerance and even the use of violence* in the service of truth. It is true that an accurate historical judgment cannot prescind from careful study of the cultural conditioning of the times, as a result of which many people may have held in good faith that an authentic witness to the truth could include suppressing the opinions of others or at least paying no attention to them. Many factors frequently converged to create assumptions that justified intolerance and fostered an emotional climate from which only great spirits, truly free and filled with God, were in some way able to break free. Yet the consideration of mitigating factors does not exonerate the Church from the obligation to express profound regret for the weaknesses of so many of her sons and daughters who sullied her face, preventing her from fully mirroring the image of her crucified Lord, the supreme witness of patient love and of humble meekness. From these painful moments of the past a lesson can be drawn for the future, leading all Christians to adhere fully to the sublime principle stated by the Second Vatican Council: "The truth cannot impose itself except by virtue of its own truth, as it wins over the mind with both gentleness and power" (*Dignitatis Humanae*).

Apostolic Letter Tertio Millennio Adveniente, *November 14, 1994*

---∞∞∞---

Prayer for Christian Unity

This, then, is one of our tasks as Christians as we make our way to the year 2000. The approaching end of the second millennium demands of everyone *examination of conscience* and the promotion of fitting ecumenical initiatives, so that we can celebrate the Great Jubilee, if not completely united, then *at least much closer to overcoming the divisions of the second millennium.* As everyone recognizes, an enormous effort is needed in this regard. It is essential not only to continue along the path of dialogue on doctrinal matters, but above all to be more committed to *prayer for Christian unity.* Such prayer has become much more intense after the Second Vatican Council, but it must increase still more, involving an ever greater number of Christians, in unison with the great petition of Christ before his Passion: "Father ... that they also may be one in us" (John 17:21).

Apostolic Letter Tertio Millennio Adveniente, *November 14, 1994*

The Role of Christians in the World

Christians, and especially the members of the laity, are called by God to become interested in the world in order to transform it according to the gospel. Your personal commitment to truth and honesty occupies an important position in the fulfillment of that task, because a sense of responsibility to truth constitutes one of the fundamental meeting points between Church and Society, between Church and each man and woman. The Christian faith does not provide ready-made solutions to the complex problems of our contemporary society, but it does provide a deep understanding of human nature and its needs, calling you to tell the truth in charity, to take up your responsibilities as good citizens, and to work along with your neighbor to construct a society in which genuine human values are fostered and intensified through a shared Christian vision of life.

Address in Nairobi, Kenya, May 7, 1980

The Church Finds Its Power in the Sacrifice of Christ

Every ecclesial action is objectively rooted in the work of salvation in the redemptive action of Christ, and attains its power from the sacrifice of the Lord, from his blood spilled on the cross. The sacrifice of Christ, always present in the work of the Church, constitutes her power and her hope, the most mysterious and greatest gift of grace. The Church is well aware that her history is a story of sacrifice and self-denial. As consecrated laypeople, you experience the truth of that every day in the area of activity and mission that each of you has led. You know what dedication that work requires in the struggle of oneself against the world and its lusts; but it is the only way to achieve true inner peace, the peace that only Christ can and knows how to give. This evangelical path, often traversed in solitude and suffering, is precisely the path that gives you hope, because in the Cross you are sure of being in communion with our Lord and Redeemer. Extending the gift of Redemption to all the works of man is the mission that the Spirit has given you. It is a sublime mission; it requires courage, but it is always a cause of happiness for you, if you live in the fellowship of charity with Christ and your brothers and sisters. The Church of 2000 therefore expects strong collaboration from you on the arduous path of sanctifying the world.

Message to the World Congress of Secular Institutes, Rome, Italy,
August 26, 1988

February 22

———— ∞ ————

The Art of Authentic Living

Not all are called to be artists in the specific sense. Yet, as Genesis has it, all men and women are entrusted with the task of *crafting their own life:* in a certain sense they are to make of it a work of art, a masterpiece. It is important to recognize the distinction, but also the connection, between these two aspects of human activity. The distinction is clear. It is one thing for human beings to be the authors of their own acts, with responsibility for their moral value; it is another to be an artist, able to respond to the demands of art and faithfully to accept art's specific dictates. That is what makes artists capable of producing *objects,* but it says nothing as yet of their moral character. We are speaking not of molding oneself, but simply of actualizing one's productive capacities, giving aesthetic form to ideas conceived in the mind. The distinction between the moral and the artistic aspects is fundamental, but no less important is the connection between them. Each conditions the other in a profound way. By producing a work, artists express themselves to the point where their work becomes a unique disclosure of their own being.... In shaping a masterpiece, artists ... in some way reveal their own personality by means of it. For them art offers both a new dimension and an exceptional mode of expression for spiritual growth. Works of art speak of their authors; they enable us to know their inner life, and they reveal the original contribution that artists offer to the history of culture.

Letter to Artists, April 4, 1999

---✾✾✾---

Friendship

You know as well as I that when people, young people like you or older people like me, take the time to meet one another and to show their friendship, simply and sincerely, to help one another as best they can, that is *happiness!* It is this fraternity among all the inhabitants of the earth that the Lord desires so strongly. You know that Jesus came and that he remains, mysteriously but truly, among us. He continues to seek this universal brotherhood with us; he brings us together to make us members of his Body. Of course, no one individual alone can realize this plan for friendship in the world and unity within each country and among all the peoples of the earth. But everyone has to make his or her contribution: a personal irreplaceable contribution. I know you understand me, for I can see it in your young faces.

Meeting with Elementary School Children in Montreal, Canada,
September 11, 1984

I Come as a Witness

One of you, a young girl from Quebec, wrote to me: "Give us your secret of responding to love and of having confidence in Jesus." I have not come to reveal a secret to you. I have come as a witness, as John the Baptist came, to witness to the light. I have come to invite you to open your eyes in the light of life to Christ Jesus. If we listen to his word, if we follow him, if we discover the greatness of his love for all men and women of every age, then we will know that life is worth living, and better still, that it is worth giving. However, there is darkness: when life disappoints us, when life owes us, when we do not find happiness, when the heart hardens, and when brothers and sisters are divided and fight one another. The world no longer recognizes the One who has called it to life, a life that should blossom in the universal fraternal union.... In the darkness, our blinded gaze can no longer perceive the Father, whose love remains faithful, in spite of the estrangement of his sons and daughters; in spite of all breaches in friendships, "in him there is no darkness" (1 John 1:5). "The light shines in the darkness, a darkness that did not overcome it." The word was "the true light which gives light to all." "The Word became flesh and made his dwelling among us" (John 1:5, 9, 14). In regard to the dark side of your questions I would like to say to you: "Stand erect and hold your heads high, for your deliverance is near at hand" (Luke 21:28). Jesus the Son of God, "True God from True God, Light from Light," lives among us.

Olympic Stadium Address to Youth, Montreal, Canada, September 11, 1984

Growing Old

The passing of the years brings its frailties. You may be forced to give up activities that you once enjoyed. Your limbs may not seem as pliable as they used to be. Your memory and your eyesight may refuse to give service. And so the world may cease to be familiar—the world of your family, the world around you, the world you once knew. Even the Church, which you have loved for so long, may seem strange to many of you as she goes forward in this period of renewal. Yet, despite changes and any weaknesses you may feel, you are of great value to all. Society needs you and so does the Church. You may not be able to do as much as before, but what counts above all is what you are. Old age is the crowning point of earthly life, a time to gather in the harvest you have sown. It is a time to give of yourselves to others as never before. Yes, you are needed, and never let anyone tell you that you are not. The Masses you have attended throughout your life, the devout Communions you have made, the prayers you have offered enable you to bestow rich gifts upon us. We need your experience and your insights. We need the faith that has sustained you and continues to be your light. We need your example of patient waiting and trust. We need to see in you the mature love that is yours, earned by the effort of your lives lived in both joy and sorrow. And yes, we need your wisdom, for you can offer assurance in times of uncertainty. You can be an incentive to live according to the higher values of the spirit. These values link us with people of all time, and they never grow old.

Address to the Elderly, Vancouver, British Columbia, September 18, 1984

A Vocation to Greatness

Christ is the servant of human Redemption! Thus: "Whoever would be great among you must be your servant" (Matt. 20:26). Down through the centuries people have come on pilgrimage (to Santiago de Compostela, Spain), to the apostle James, to whom Christ said, "You will drink my cup" (Matt. 20:23). Young people have come to the tomb of the apostle *to learn* that gospel truth: *"Whoever would be great among you must be your servant."* In these words we find *the essential criterion of human greatness.* The criterion is new. It was new in the time of Christ and continues to be so two thousand years later. It implies a transformation, *a renewal of the criteria by which the world is governed.* "You know that the rulers of the Gentiles lorded over them, and their great men exercised authority over them. It shall not be so with you" (Matt. 20:25–26). A criterion by which the world is governed is the criterion of *success.* To have power ... to have economic power, so as to make the dependence of others be seen. *To have cultural power in order to manipulate consciences.* To use ... and to abuse. Such is the "spirit of this world." Does this mean perhaps that power in itself is evil? Does this mean that the economy—economic initiative—is in itself bad? No! By no means. *Both of them can also be a way of serving.* This is the spirit of Christ, the truth of the gospel. This truth and this spirit are expressed through the apostle, who—according to his mother's wish—would be the first; however—following Christ—he became a servant.

Message for World Youth Day, Santiago de Compostela, Spain,
August 20, 1989

February 27

—∞∞∞—

Winners and Losers

In your eyes, there must be neither winners nor losers, but rather men and women who need to be helped to leave error behind, persons to be supported in their efforts to recover from the effects, including the psychological ones, of violence, abuse of power, and the violation of human rights. You need to remind the "losers" that it is not enough to adapt to changed social situations; instead, what is required is sincere conversion and, if necessary, expiation. And the "winners" need to hear continually the exhortation to *forgiveness,* so that there will come about the authentic peace that derives from following the gospel of mercy and of charity. Like the Good Shepherd, welcome and seek out every person. All people, but particularly the young, are looking for "spiritual fathers," enlightened guides, teachers of evangelical consistency. *Listen, encourage, support, and lead God's people* along the paths of truth and holiness: *this is your mission,* and it obviously requires of you a constant effort to be faithful and to love Christ, the Redeemer of Man. Set always before yourselves the example of Jesus: carry on a daily conversation with the divine Master, a conversation of openness through his word and a readiness to follow. In this way you will become *instruments of the Holy Spirit,* whom he has sent.

Pilgrimage Address at the Cathedral, Vilnius, Lithuania, September 4, 1993

---∽∞∾---

The Sermon on the Mount

There are eight Beatitudes, and the first one declares: "Blessed are the poor in spirit, for theirs is the Kingdom of Heaven" (Matt. 5:3). The mountain in Galilee on which Jesus uttered the Beatitudes is one only, but there are many places all over the earth where the same affirmations are proclaimed and listened to.... Among you there are many poor people. The Church in Brazil wishes to be the Church of the Poor. She wishes this first Beatitude of the Sermon on the Mount to be realized in this great country. The poor in spirit are those who are most open to God and to "the mighty works of God" (Acts 2:11). Poor, because they are ready to accept always the gift from above that comes from God himself. The poor in spirit are those who live in awareness that they have received everything from the hands of God as a gratuitous gift and to value every good received. Constantly grateful, they repeat incessantly: "Everything is grace. Let us thank the Lord our God." Jesus said to them at the same time that they are "pure in heart" and "meek"; it is they who "hunger and thirst for righteousness," they who frequently "mourn," they who are "peacemakers" and "persecuted for righteousness' sake." It is finally they who are "merciful" (Matt. 5:3–10). The poor, the poor in spirit, are the most merciful. Their hearts open to God are for that very reason most open to men also. They are ready to offer their help, ready to share what they have.... They always find an extra place in the midst of the straits in which they live.

Speech at Favela Vidigal, Rio de Janeiro, Brazil, July 2, 1980

March

———⁂———

March 1

The Needs of Young People

The mystery of the Church is the mystery of the life of Christ, the mystery of the living Christ. And this is the mystery we are living, together with our people. *All our pastoral efforts are aimed at assisting the faithful to share more intimately in the life of Christ....* This great treasure must be presented in an especially dynamic way to *the young people of the Church.* It is they who are assailed most by the problems of the modern world; it is they who need a particular grace from Christ to endure the Christian combat with temptation and sin. In Christ young people can find the answers to the deep questions that are the basis of all Christian choices. How greatly they need the pastoral support of their bishops, together with their priests, in order to develop and persevere in their Christian vocation. In speaking of young people and their needs, *we cannot ignore the formidable problems of narcotics* in the world today as well as the causes of this phenomenon and the means needed to face this crisis of humanity. The whole human community must be mobilized to confront this issue. But here the Church has a specific task of educating about human dignity, the respect of self, the values of the spirit, and the search for the true joy that abides in the heart and not in the passing exhilaration of the senses.

Address to Youth, Bangkok, Thailand, May 11, 1984

March 2

We Are Called to Peace

We are called to seek peace and justice and to promote them among men. "Peace": this is one of the names of the one God, whom we joyfully worship. It is a gift of his goodness and is manifest in man's life as benevolence, reconciliation, and forgiveness for his peers. Concrete solidarity must be shown with the victims of oppression, hatred, and atrocities. We must be near to those whose towns have been burned down and bombarded, those who have had to leave their homes and take refuge elsewhere, the women who have suffered violence, and those who have been unjustly arrested and imprisoned in concentration camps. As I have had the opportunity to say in Assisi on the occasion of the Prayer Meeting for Peace in the Balkans on January 9–11, 1993, "Both Christianity and Islam inculcate in us a commitment to persevere in the pursuit of justice and peace for them and all the victims of the conflict.... Since all human beings have been created by God and all are members of the one human family, we have a duty to come to the aid of all." Christians and Muslims, in defending the value of life together and in respect for every person, are called to show God's mercy and compassion and work to make the entire human race God's family on earth.

Draft of Address to Have Been Given in Sarajevo, September 8, 1994

───⊗⊗⊗───

The Basis of Trust

Why do the hearts of children trust their parents? This is certainly an expression of love, upon which is built the whole of civilization and culture, beginning with the fundamental interhuman bonds. However, this love still more depends on truth. Spouses have a mutual trust because they believe in each other, because they meet each other in truth. Children trust their parents because they expect from them truth, and the amount they trust depends on the extent to which they receive the truth from them. Truth, therefore, is the basis of trust. And truth is also the power of love. And, *vice-versa,* love is also the power of truth. In the power of love man is ready to accept even the most difficult, the most demanding truth.

Homily in Wroclaw, Poland, June 21, 1983

The Purpose of Pilgrimage

Making pilgrimages is a very traditional practice among us Christians. Particular places are regarded as especially sacred because of the holiness and virtue achieved by individuals who lived there; and their sacredness increases with the passage of time, through the prayers and sacrifices of the pilgrim multitudes who visit them. So virtue generates further virtue, grace attracts grace, and the goodness of one saintly man or woman, held in permanent remembrance by a whole people, continues to transmit itself down through the centuries, bringing refreshment, inspiration, and healing to the spirit of succeeding generations. And thus we are helped and encouraged in the difficult ascent to goodness of life.

Sermon in Krakow, Poland, June 10, 1979

The Dignity of the Human Person

Can it still be a surprise to anyone that the pope born and brought up in this land, the pope who came to the See of St. Peter from the diocese in whose territory is situated the camp of Auschwitz, should have begun his first encyclical with the words *Redemptor hominis* (Redeemer of humankind) and should have dedicated it as a whole to the cause of man, to the dignity of man, to the threats to him, and finally to his inalienable rights, which can so easily be trampled on and annihilated by his fellow men? Is it enough to put man in a different uniform, arm him with the apparatus of violence? Is it enough to impose on him an ideology in which human rights are subjected to the demands of the system, completely subjected to them, so as in practice not to exist at all? ... Auschwitz is *a testimony of war*. Or is it a disproportionate growth of hatred, destruction, and cruelty? It cannot be denied that it also manifests near capabilities of human courage, heroism, and patriotism, but the fact remains that it is the reckoning of the losses that prevails. That reckoning prevails more and more, since each day sees an increase in the destructive capacity of the weapons invented by modern technology. Not only those who directly bring about wars are responsible for them, but also those who fail to do all they can to prevent them.

Visit to Auschwitz, June 7, 1979

─⟨⟩⟨⟩⟨⟩─

My Own Old Age

In this spirit, dear elderly brothers and sisters, as I encourage each of you to live with serenity the years that the Lord has granted you, I feel a spontaneous desire to share fully with you my own feelings at this point of my life, after more than twenty years of ministry on the throne of Peter and as we await the arrival, now imminent, of the third millennium. Despite the limitations brought on by age, I continue to enjoy life. For this I thank the Lord. It is wonderful to be able to give oneself to the very end for the sake of the Kingdom of God! At the same time, I find great peace in thinking of the time when the Lord will call me from life to life! And so I often find myself saying, with no trace of melancholy, a prayer recited by priests in celebration of the Eucharist: *In hora mortis meae voca me, et tube me venire ad te,* "At the hour of my death, call me and bid me come to you." This is the prayer of Christian hope, which in no way detracts from the joy of the present, while entrusting the future to God's gracious and loving care.

Letter to the Elderly, October 1, 1999

The Experience of War

As I have already said, my priestly vocation took definitive shape at the *time of the Second World War, during the Nazi occupation.* Was this a mere coincidence, or was there a more profound connection between what was developing within me and external historical events? It is hard to answer such a question certainly. In God's plan, nothing happens by chance. All I can say is that the tragedy of the war had its effect on my gradual choice of a vocation. It helped me to understand, in a new way, *the value and importance of a vocation.* In the face of the spread of evil and the atrocities of the war the meaning of the priesthood and its mission in the world became much clearer to me. The outbreak of the war took me away from my studies and from the university. In that period I also lost my father, the last remaining member of my immediate family. All this brought with it, objectively, *progressive detachment* from my earlier plans; in a way it was like being uprooted from the soil in which up until that moment my humanity had grown. But the process was not merely negative. At the same time a light was beginning to shine ever more brightly in the back of my mind: *the Lord wants me* to become a *priest.* One day I saw this with great clarity; it was like an interior illumination, which brought with it the joy and certainty of a new vocation. And this awareness filled me with great inner peace.

Gift and Mystery

———∞∞∞———

Human Dignity

Man's intimate relationship with God in the Holy Spirit also enables him to understand himself, his own humanity, in a new way. Thus that image and likeness of God, which man is from his very beginning, is fully realized. This intimate truth of the human being has to be continually rediscovered in the light of Christ, who is the prototype of the relationship with God. There also has to be rediscovered in Christ the reason for "full self-discovery through a sincere gift of himself to others," as the Second Vatican Council writes: precisely by reason of this divine likeness, which "shows that on earth man ... is the only creation that God wishes for himself in his dignity as a person, but as one open to integration and social communication (*Gaudium et Spes,* 24). The effective knowledge and full implementation of the truth of his being come about *only by the power of the Holy Spirit.* Man learns this truth from Jesus Christ and puts it into practice in his own life by the power of the Spirit, whom Jesus himself has given to us.

Encyclical Dominum et Vivificantem, *May 30, 1986*

The Dignity of Woman

However, God's intention goes well beyond what is revealed in Genesis. In Mary, God created a feminine personality that greatly surpasses the ordinary condition of woman as it appears in the creation of Eve. Mary's perfection and her unique excellence in the world of grace are fruits of the particular divine benevolence that seeks to raise everyone, men and women, to the moral perfection and holiness proper to the adopted children of God. Mary is "blessed among women"; however, every woman shares in some way in her sublime dignity in the divine plan. The remarkable gift to the Mother of the Lord not only testifies to what we could call God's respect for woman, but also emphasizes the profound regard in God's plans for her irreproachable role in human history. Women need to discover this divine esteem in order to be ever more aware of their lofty dignity. The historical and social situations that cause the reaction of feminism were marked by a lack of appreciation of woman's worth; frequently she was relegated to a second-rate or even marginal role. This did not allow her to express fully the wealth of intelligence and wisdom contained in her femininity. Indeed, throughout history women have often suffered from scant esteem for their abilities and sometimes even scorn and unjust prejudice. Despite important changes, this state of affairs unfortunately continues even today in many nations and parts of the world. The figure of Mary shows that God has such esteem for woman that any form of discrimination lacks a theoretical basis.

Discourse at the Vatican, November 29, 1995

———— ∞ ————

Visit to the Chief Rabbis at Hechal Shlomo

It is with deep respect that I visit you here today and thank you for receiving me at Hechal Shlomo. Truly this is a uniquely significant meeting, which—I hope and pray—will lead to increasing contacts between Christians and Jews, aimed at achieving an ever deeper understanding of the historical and theological relationship between our respective religious heritages. Personally, I have always wanted to be counted among those who work, on both sides, to overcome old prejudices and to secure ever wider and fuller recognition of the spiritual patrimony shared by Jews and Christians. I repeat what I said on the occasion of my visit to the Jewish community in Rome, that we Christians recognize that the Jewish religious heritage is intrinsic to our own faith: "You are our elder brothers" (*Address at the Synagogue of Rome,* April 13, 1986). We hope that the Jewish people will acknowledge that the Church utterly condemns anti-Semitism and every form of racism as being altogether opposed to the principles of Christianity. We must work together to build a future in which there will be no more anti-Judaism among Christians or anti-Christian sentiment among Jews. There is much that we have in common. There is so much that we can do together for peace, for justice, for a more human and fraternal world. May the Lord of heaven and earth lead us to a new and fruitful era of mutual respect and cooperation, for the benefit of all!

Discourse, Israel, March 23, 2000

—∞∞∞—

My Lord and Savior

Without doubt, Christ is and presents himself especially as Savior. He does not regard it as his mission to condemn people according to merely human principles (John 8:15). He is, first of all, the one who teaches the way of salvation and not the accuser of the guilty. "Do not imagine that I will be your accuser before the Father; the one to accuse you is Moses ... for it was about me that he wrote" (John 5:45–46). In what then does judgment consist? Jesus replied, "The judgment of condemnation is this—the light came into the world, but men loved darkness rather than light, because their deeds were wicked" (John 3:19). It must therefore be said that in the presence of this light, which is God revealed in Christ, in the presence of this truth, each one is judged by one's own deeds. The will to save humanity on God's part is definitively manifested in Christ's word and work in the entire Gospel up to the Paschal Mystery of the Cross and Resurrection. It becomes at the same time the deepest foundation and the central criterion of all judgment of human works and consciences. This thought corrects the all too human way of viewing God's judgment as a cold act of justice or some kind of revenge. Christ is the last link in the chain of God's love for us all.

Discourse at the Vatican, September 30, 1987

---∞∞∞---

To the Catholic Scout Movement

You have desired to renew *your "promise"* before the pope, and I am delighted to be a witness to your resolution *to be faithful to God,* who calls you to live communion and friendship with him; *faithful to yourselves,* in the search for and realization of the project that the Father in his love has worked out for each one; *faithful to your neighbor,* who expects of you the gift of a fully human and Christian commitment. The Scout Law helps you in this commitment of fidelity. Through it, as your founder, Lord Baden-Powell, used to like to say, *you can make the impossible possible.* The pope looks to you with trust and hope and accompanies you with his prayers and sympathy in the great adventure of life. I ask you, *Brownies and Cubs,* to do "your best" every day to grow joyfully in your circle and in your pack, discovering the marvels of creation. I urge you, *Guides and Explorers,* to "always be ready" to do good, while with your troop you experience responsibility and learn to be active members of the ecclesial and civil community to which you belong. I ask you, *Rangers and Rovers,* to do your utmost to make the verb "to serve" the motto of your life, in the conviction that the gift of yourselves is the secret that can make human life beautiful and fruitful. Lastly, I am thinking of you who have the difficult but exalted role of chiefs in the association. You have been entrusted with the *responsibility of accompanying on their way through life a great many children and young people who expect you to help them grow harmoniously,* in order to contribute to building a world of friendship and solidarity.

Discourse at the Vatican, October 23, 2004

———∽∾∽———

The Conscience

Like all things human, the conscience can fail and encounter illusions and errors. It is a delicate voice that can be overpowered by a noisy, distracted way of life or almost suffocated by a long-lasting and serious habit of sin. Conscience needs to be nurtured and educated, and the preferred way to form it—at least for those who have the grace of faith—is to relate it to the biblical revelation of the moral law and authoritatively interpret it with the help of the Church and the Holy Spirit.

Go in Peace

Consider Forgiveness as a Preparation for Lent

Throughout his life, Jesus proclaimed God's forgiveness, but he also taught the need for mutual forgiveness as the condition for obtaining it. In the Lord's Prayer, he makes us pray: "Forgive us our trespasses, as we forgive those who trespass against us." With that *as* he places in our hands the measure with which we shall be judged by God. The parable of the unforgiving servant, punished for his hardness of heart toward his fellow servant, teaches us that those who are unwilling to forgive exclude themselves from divine forgiveness by this very fact: "So my heavenly Father will also do to every one of you, if you do not forgive your brother or sister from your heart" (Matt. 18:35). Our prayer itself cannot be pleasing to the Lord unless it is preceded, and in a certain sense "guaranteed" in its authenticity, by a sincere effort on our part to be reconciled with our brother and sister who may have "something against us"; only then will it be possible for us to present an offering pleasing to God.

Go in Peace

About Reconciliation

The difficulty of forgiving does not arise only from circumstances of the present. History carries with it a heavy burden of violence and conflict that cannot easily be shed. Abuses of power, oppression, and wars have brought suffering to countless human beings; and even if the causes of these sad events are lost in the distant past, their destructive effects live on, fueling fear, suspicion, hatred, and division among families, ethnic groups, and whole peoples. These are facts that sorely try the goodwill of those who are seeking to overcome their past conditioning. *The truth is that one cannot remain a prisoner of the past,* for individuals and peoples need a sort of "healing of memories," so that past evils will not come back again. This does not mean forgetting past events; it means reexamining them with a new attitude and learning precisely from the experience of suffering that only love can produce healing, whereas hatred produces only devastation and ruin.

Go in Peace

The Warmth of Human Relationships

Certainly, forgiveness does not come spontaneously or naturally to people. Forgiving from the heart can sometimes be heroic—the pain of losing a child, a brother or sister, one's parents, or one's whole family as a result of war, terrorism, or criminal acts can lead to the total closing off of oneself from others. People who have been left with nothing because they have been deprived of their land and home—refugees and those who have endured the humiliation of violence—cannot fail to feel the temptation of hatred and revenge. Only the warmth of human relationships marked by respect, understanding, and acceptance can help them to overcome such feelings. Thanks to the healing power of love, even the most wounded heart can experience the liberating encounter with forgiveness.

Go in Peace

March 17

Authentic Peace: A Free Act of Love

Real peace is not just a matter of structures and mechanisms. It rests, above all, on the adoption of a style of human coexistence marked by mutual acceptance and a capacity to forgive from the heart. We all need to be forgiven by others, so we must all be ready to forgive. Asking and granting forgiveness is something profoundly worthy of every one of us; sometimes it is the only way out of situations marked by age-old and violent hatred. Forgiveness, in its truest and highest form, is *a free act of love;* but precisely because it is an act of love, it has its own intrinsic demands, the first of which is respect for the truth.

Go in Peace

———∽∞∾———

Forgiveness Requires Truth

God alone is absolute truth, but he made the human heart open to the desire for truth, which he then fully revealed in his Incarnate Son. Hence, we are all called to live the truth. Forgiveness, far from precluding the search for truth, actually requires it. Evil that has been done must be acknowledged and, as far as possible, corrected.

Go in Peace

———⊗⊗⊗———

A Pope's Prayer

Lead in truth, O Christ, the fathers and mothers
of families in the Church,
urged on and strengthened by the sacramental grace of marriage,
and aware of being on earth the visible sign of
your unfailing love for the Church.
Lead in truth, O Christ, the young people of the Church.
Let them not be attracted by the new idols,
such as exaggerated consumerism, prosperity at all costs,
moral permissiveness, protest expressed with violence,
but rather let them live with the joy of your message,
which is the message of the Beatitudes.
Lead in truth, O Christ, all the faithful of the Church.
May we become before the world courageous
witnesses to your mission of salvation,
happy to be sons and daughters of God—
with You—and all humanity!
Lead us in truth, O Christ, always! Amen.

Go in Peace

Lent: A Time of Rediscovery

Lent is the way of truth. Man must rediscover himself in all his truth before God. He must also reread the truth of divine teachings, of divine commandments, of the divine will—he must compare his conscience with them. The way of salvation passes through here; it is the way of hope. And so the Church prays again:

Be mindful of your mercy, O Lord, and of your steadfast love,
for they have been from of old.
According to your steadfast love remember me,
for your goodness' sake, O Lord!

(Ps. 25:6–7)

Lent is the way of truth; it is the time for the reawakening of consciences. Above all it is the way of love and mercy. Only through love does truth reawaken man to life. Only love, which is mercy, enkindles hope. The Lenten fast is love's great cry. A penetrating cry. A definitive cry. It is the great time of mercy. If only everyone would recognize this way.

Discourse at the Church of Sant' Andrea delle Fratte, Rome, Italy,
February 28, 1982

Humility of Heart: A Necessary Component

And so the Church continues to pray in the liturgy:

Good and upright is the Lord:
   he shows sinners the right path;
he leads the humble in justice,
   and shows the lowly his way.
            (Ps. 25:8–9)

The Church prays for humility of the human heart. She prays that man, through humility, may be found in the truth, that he may be found in interior truth—that in this way he will be able to meet love, which is stronger than sin and death, stronger than any evil, and that he may be guided by the divine Word: "Not on bread alone does man live, but on every word that comes from the mouth of God" (Matt. 4:4).

Discourse at the Church of Sant' Andrea delle Fratte, Rome, Italy,
February 28, 1982

The Sense of Interior Joy

Then the main current of Lent must flow through the interior man, through hearts and consciences. The essential effort of repentance consists of this. In this effort the human determination to be converted to God is invested with the predisposing grace of conversion and, at the same time, of forgiveness and spiritual liberation. Penance is not just an effort, a weight, but it is also a *joy.* Sometimes it is a great joy of the human spirit, a delight that other sources cannot bring forth.

Discourse at the Vatican, February 28, 1979

March 23

The Nature of Joy

Contemporary man seems to have lost, to a certain extent, the flavor of this joy (the joy of penance). He has also lost the deep sense of that spiritual effort that makes it possible to find oneself again in the whole truth of one's interior being. Many causes and circumstances, which are difficult to analyze,... contribute in this connection. Our civilization—especially in the West—closely connected with the development of science and technology, catches a glimpse of the need of intellectual and physical effort, but it has lost to a considerable extent the sense of the effort of the spirit, the fruit of which is man seen in his interior dimensions. When all is said and done, man living in the currents of this civilization very often loses his own dimension; he loses the interior sense of his own humanity. The effort that leads to the fruit, just mentioned, becomes alien to this man as well as the joy that comes from it: the great joy of finding again and of meeting the joy of conversion (*metanoia*), the joy of penitence.

Discourse at the Vatican, February 28, 1979

The Path to Easter

The severe liturgy of Ash Wednesday and, subsequently, the whole period of Lent is—as preparation for Easter—a systematic call to this joy that fructifies from the effort of patiently finding oneself again: "By your endurance you will gain your lives" (Luke 21:19). Let no one be afraid to undertake this effort.

Discourse at the Vatican, February 28, 1979

March 25

Mentorella: The First Pilgrimage

We read in St. Luke's Gospel that after the Annunciation Our Lady went into the hill country to visit her kinswoman Elizabeth. It is there that she uttered the famous hymn the Magnificat. This (Mentorella, a Marian shrine run by the Polish Fathers high in the hills surrounding Rome) is a place in which man opens himself to God in a special way—a place where, far from everything yet close to nature, man can talk intimately with God and feel in his inmost self what God requires of him. Man is bound to glorify God, his Creator and Savior. He should be a mouthpiece of all created things, proclaiming the Magnificat in their name. He should declare the wonderful works of God, and at the same time show forth his own relationship with God. Whenever I have been in Rome (as a seminarian, student, priest, and bishop) this place has helped me to pray, and that is why I wish to come here this afternoon. Prayer, which in so many ways expresses our relationship to the living God, is the pope's first duty and his first message, *the first condition of his service to the Church and to the world.* The Mother of Christ went into the hill country to proclaim the Magnificat. May the Father, the Son, and the Holy Spirit accept the pope's prayer in this sanctuary and bestow the gifts of the Holy Spirit on all who pray here.

First Papal Pilgrimage to Mentorella, Italy, October 29, 1978

March 26

The Annunciation and the Season of Lent

At the end of the second century, St. Irenaeus, a disciple of St. Polycarp (himself a disciple of St. John), already pointed out Mary's contribution to the work of salvation. He understood the value of Mary's consent at the time of the Annunciation, recognizing in the Virgin of Nazareth's obedience to and faith in the angel's message the perfect antithesis of Eve's disobedience and disbelief, with a beneficial effect on humanity's destiny. Just as Eve caused death, so Mary, with her "yes," became "a cause of salvation" for herself and for all mankind. But this affirmation was not developed in a consistent and systematic way by the other Fathers of the Church. Instead, this doctrine was systematically worked out for the first time at the end of the tenth century in the *Life of Mary* by a Byzantine monk, John the Geometer. Here Mary is united to Christ in the whole work of Redemption according to God's plan, sharing in the cross and suffering for our salvation. She remained united to the Son "in every deed, attitude, and wish." Mary's association with Jesus's saving work came about through her Mother's love, a love inspired by grace, which conferred a higher power on it. *Love's creative passion proves to be the most compassionate.*

Discourse at the Vatican, October 25, 1995

March 27

—❈—

Look to the Cross

In the time of Lent we must all look to the Cross with special attention in order to understand afresh its eloquence. We cannot see in it only a memory of the events that happened about two thousand years ago. We must understand the teaching of the Cross as it speaks to our times, to modern men: "Jesus Christ is the same yesterday and today and forever" (Heb. 13:8). In the cross of Jesus Christ there is expressed an intense call to *metanoia,* to conversion: "Repent and believe in the gospel" (Mark 1:15). And we must accept this call as addressed to one and all of us especially on the occasion of Lent. To live Lent means conversion to God by means of Jesus Christ.

Letter on the Spirit of Lent, the Vatican, February 28, 1979

〜∞〜

The Means of Conversion

Christ himself indicates to us in the Gospel the rich program of conversion. Christ—and, after him the Church—also proposes to us, in the time of Lent, the means that serve for this conversion. It is a question in the first place of prayer; then of alms deeds and of fasting. We must accept these means and introduce them into our lives in proportion to the needs and possibilities of man and of the Christian of our times. Prayer always remains the first and fundamental condition of approach to God. During Lent we must pray, we must make an effort to pray more, to look for the time and the place to pray. *It is prayer in the first place that brings us out of indifference and makes us sensitive to the things of God and the soul.* Prayer also educates our consciences, and Lent is a particularly suitable time to reawaken and educate conscience. Just in this period the Church reminds us of the indispensable necessity of sacramental confession, in order that we may be able to live the resurrection of Christ *not only in the liturgy, but also in our own soul.*

Letter on the Spirit of Lent, the Vatican, February 28, 1979

March 29

Understanding the Eloquence of the Cross

Alms deeds and fasting as means of conversion and of Christian repentance are closely connected with each other. Fasting means self-mastery; it means being demanding with regard to ourselves; being ready to renounce things—and not just food—but also enjoyment and the various pleasures. And alms deeds—in the wider and essential application—means readiness to share joys and sadness with others, to give to one's neighbor, to the needy in particular; to share not only material goods, but also the goods of the spirit. And it is just for this reason that we must open to others, feel their different needs, sufferings, and misfortunes, and seek—not only in our resources, but above all in our hearts, in our way of behaving and acting—the means to prevent their needs or to bring relief to their sufferings or misfortunes. In this way, therefore, addressing God by means of prayer, *we at the same time address man.* Being demanding with ourselves and generous with others, we express our conversion in a way that is both concrete and social. Through fuller solidarity with men, with the suffering and especially with the needy, we unite with the suffering and crucified Christ.

Letter on the Spirit of Lent, the Vatican, February 28, 1979

Temperance

A temperate man is one who is master of himself. One in whom passions do not prevail over reason, will, and even the "heart." A man who can control himself! If this is so, we can easily realize what a fundamental and radical value the virtue of temperance has. It is even indispensable in order that man may fully be a man. It is enough to look at someone who, carried away by his passions, becomes a "victim" of them—renouncing of his own accord the use of reason (such as, for example, an alcoholic, a drug addict)—to see clearly that "to be a man" means respecting one's own dignity, and therefore, among other things, letting oneself be guided by the virtue of temperance.

Discourse at the Vatican, November 22, 1978

The Contemplative Life: The Value of Solitude

To attend to God is considered by the masters of the spiritual life to be the most noble and lofty form of activity of the human being, in that the latter concentrates the whole of himself in worshiping and listening to the Infinite Being, who desires the salvation of all mankind. It is understandable, then, how this prayer of praise is accompanied by prayer of propitiation and supplication in order that the divine will might be accomplished. And the more innocent and pure the soul that presents the prayer, the more acceptable it is to God.... Not only do I ask you to persevere in your generous resolutions, but I exhort you to advance more and more in friendship with God, to stir up continually the flame of love, as it were, *volcanoes covered with snow*. In the present time with all its difficulties, may your prayer, nourished by sacrifice in solitude and silence, draw God's merciful goodness upon the earth.

Discourse for the Enclosed Camaldolese Nuns at the Basilica of Santa Sabina, Rome, Italy, February 28, 1979

April

Discipleship Even unto the Cross

"Master, where do you live?" This evening, my dear young people, you have come to follow Christ as he advances on the way to his Passion. Lift your eyes to the face of the One who comes toward you and calls you. Whom do you seek in this Jesus, marked by sorrow, "his appearance was so marred, beyond human semblance" (Isa. 52:14)? He is the Servant of God, the Son of the Most High, who, carrying our pain, has made himself the servant of us all. Look upon him, listen to him in his pain and trial! It is in him, who experienced human weakness in everything except sin, that you will find healing for your hearts. *Through the weakness of a humiliated and despised man, God manifested his omnipotence.* Jesus, the Innocent One, by freely accepting to go to the extreme of obedience to his Father, who had sent him, became the witness of God's boundless love for all humanity. The mystery of our salvation is accomplished in the silence of Good Friday when a man, abandoned by all, bearing the weight of our sufferings, was delivered up to death on a cross, his arms wide open in the gesture of embracing every man and woman. Could greater love be shown? A mystery that is difficult to grasp, a mystery of infinite love! A mystery that inaugurates the new and transfigured world of the Kingdom. On this cross, death has been overcome; from the death of the Son of God made man, life has sprung. His fidelity to the Father's divine plan of love has not been in vain, it has led to the Resurrection.

Letter to Cardinal James Francis Stafford for World Youth Day,
August 22, 1997

—∞∞—

The Suffering Christ Today

The suffering Christ still dwells among the men and women of today. In order to reveal his power, God has come to share our deepest misery. In every person who is afflicted, beaten, mistreated, rejected, we can discover the Lord who travels the paths of humanity bearing his cross. Dear friends, the Crucified One is ever with you, by the side of those who toil, who suffer, who die. All of you who toil and labor under your burden, come to where Christ dwells, carry your cross with him, present him the offering of your lives, and he will give you rest (Matt. 11:28). At your side, the loving presence of Mary, Mother of Jesus and your mother, will guide you and give you courage and comfort. In a world in which evil appears to triumph, where hope sometimes seems extinguished, be close to one another as Christ has made himself close to you, in union with the martyrs of the faith, of brotherhood and of concern for others, with the witnesses to justice and freedom, with the victims of intolerance and discrimination, with all those who in so many nations torn apart by hatred or war have given their lives for their brothers and sisters. Do not look away; have the courage to reach out, to make a fraternal gesture, after the example of Simon of Cyrene, who helped Jesus on his way to Calvary. Be daring artisans of reconciliation and of peace. Live together in solidarity and brotherly love. Make the Cross of the Savior shine so as to announce to the world the victory of the Risen One, the victory of life over death!

Letter to Cardinal James Francis Stafford for World Youth Day,
August 22, 1997

———— ∽∞∞∽ ————

The Love That Transforms

Dear friends, contemplating the Cross of Christ, listening in silence to the word he addresses to you, discover this God who counts on man, who confides in you and never despairs of anyone. He offers you his strength in order to make fruitful the seeds of peace and reconciliation, which are in everyone's heart. The most humble acts of charity and fraternity witness to the presence of God. This evening, gathered together as members of the Church, Jesus again invites you to be open to his loving gaze upon you, to receive the forgiveness that will give you the courage to start out again on the road of life. He calls you to enter his light in order to begin a time of conversion and reconciliation. The sacrament of penance, which is being offered for you to receive, is the sacrament of a love accepted and shared in the joy of a reconciled heart and of rediscovered brotherhood. Dear friends, accept the love that transforms your lives and opens to you the horizons of truth and freedom.

Letter to Cardinal James Francis Stafford for World Youth Day,
August 22, 1997

———— ◇◇◇ ————

No Greater Love

"Jesus, looking upon him, loved him" (Mark 10:21). This is how the Gospel describes the meeting between Jesus and the rich young man. And this is how the Lord looks upon each of us. His eyes, full of affection, are fixed today on the young people of Cuba. And I, in his name, embrace you, for I see in you the living hope of the Church and of Cuba. Christ has told us, *"No one has greater love than this, to lay down one's life for one's friends. You are my friends if you do what I command you. . . . I have called you friends"* (John 15:13–15). Christ offers you his friendship. He gave his life so that those who wish to answer his call can indeed become his friends. His is a friendship that is deep, genuine, loyal, and total, as all true friendship must be. This is how young people ought to relate to one other, for *youth without friendship is impoverished and diminished.* Friendship is nourished by sacrifice for the sake of serving one's friends and truly loving them. And *without such sacrifice there can be no real friendship, no truly healthy youth, no future for one's country, no genuine religion.* Listen, then, to the voice of Christ! In your lives, Christ is drawing near and saying to you: "Follow me." Do not close yourselves off from his love. Do not turn away. Heed his message. Each of you has received a call from him. He knows each of you by name. Let yourselves be guided by Christ as you seek what can help you to achieve your full potential. *Open the doors of your heart and your life to Jesus.*

Discourse to the Young People of Cuba, Camagüey, January 23, 1998

April 5

The Practicality of the Passion

Virtue is that inner strength that leads to self-sacrifice for love of what is good and enables people not only to do good deeds, but also to give the very best of themselves. Virtuous young people are what makes a country great. Cuba's future depends on you, on how you build your character and on how you translate into action your commitment to transform the world. And so I say to you: with fortitude and temperance, with justice and prudence, face the great challenges of the present moment; *return to your Cuban and Christian roots,* and do all that you can *to build a future of ever greater dignity and freedom!* Do not forget that freedom involves responsibility. A person is defined above all by his responsible behavior toward others and before history (*Gaudium et Spes*). No one should avoid the challenges of the time in which he lives. Take your proper place in the great family of the peoples of this continent and of the world, not as inferiors seeking acceptance, but as men and women possessing a great and rich tradition, the origins of which are found in Christianity. I also wish to speak to you about commitment. Commitment is the courageous response of people who do not want to let life pass them by, but rather seek to shape their own personal history and the history of the society around them. I encourage you to make a concrete commitment, however humble and simple, but one that, if carried out with perseverance, will be the best proof of your love and the best path to personal holiness.

Discourse to the Young People of Cuba, Camagüey, January 23, 1998

Genuine Love

"Love is patient, love is kind, love is not envious or boastful or arrogant or rude. It does not insist on its own way; it is not irritable or resentful.... *It bears all things, believes all things, hopes all things, endures all things"* (1 Cor. 13:4–7). Genuine love, to which the apostle Paul devoted a hymn in his First Letter to the Corinthians, is demanding. But its beauty lies precisely in the demands it makes. Only those able to make demands on themselves in the name of love can then demand love from others. Young people of today need to discover this love, because it is the true and solid foundation of the family. Forcefully reject any of its false substitutes, such as "free love." How many families have been destroyed because of this! Never forget that blindly following the impulse of our emotions often means becoming a slave to our passions.

Discourse to the Young People of Cuba, Camagüey, January 23, 1998

———— ⬥ ————

The Transfiguration: Prelude to the Passion

Peter, James, and John were witnesses of this extraordinary event (the Transfiguration). The Gospel recounts that Jesus took them apart and led them with him up a *high mountain* (Mark 9:2). The disciples' ascent to Tabor spurs us to reflect on the penitential journey of these days. Lent is also an *upward path*. It is an invitation to rediscover the calming and regenerating silence of meditation. It is an effort to purify the heart of the sin that burdens it. It is certainly a demanding journey, but one that leads us toward a goal rich in beauty, splendor, and joy. In the Transfiguration the heavenly Father's voice is heard: *"This is my beloved Son; listen to him"* (Mark 9:7). These words contain the whole program for Lent: we must *listen to Jesus.* He reveals the Father to us, because, as the eternal Son, he is "the image of the invisible God" (Col. 1:15). But at the same time, as true "Son of Man," he reveals what we are, *he reveals man to man* (*Gaudium et Spes*). So let us not be afraid of Christ! In raising us to the heights of his divine life, he does not take away our humanity, but on the contrary, he *humanizes* us, giving our personal and social life full meaning. We are also urged to this ever more invigorating rediscovery of Christ by the prospect of the Great Jubilee, which in this first year of immediate preparation is principally centered on the *contemplation of Christ:* a contemplation that must be nourished by the Gospel and prayer and must always be accompanied by authentic conversion and the constant rediscovery of love as the law of daily life.

Discourse at the Vatican, February 23, 1997

The Greatest Sacrament

The Eucharist is the greatest sacrament of our faith, and everything else is concentrated in it. Our Lord is present in it as Man, Son of God, and Son of Mary; he is present thanks to the power of the words he spoke and, as a result of the institution, he is present under the species which he himself chose as sign of his presence. We know that all this took place during the Last Supper when those species were quite naturally on the table to be shared between those who were eating with him. The words the Apostles heard him say were completely new and full of deep significance. Speaking of the bread, Christ said: "This is my body which is given for you." He then took the cup of wine and said: "This is the cup of my blood which is shed for you" (Luke 22:19–20). This took place on Holy Thursday, but his words already referred to the events of Good Friday.

The Way to Christ

———∞∞∞———

The Cross and Eucharist: The Same Event

The next day it became clear that his real body—the one he had received from his virgin mother—was to be condemned to death and his real blood shed. At that point the truth of those words spoken in the upper room the previous day became clear and certain—just as certain as they are every time we follow Christ's express instructions and transubstantiation takes place, and we say, "Christ has died." These words, which we speak today, have been enriched by two thousand years of tradition, but when they were spoken for the first time by Christ's disciples and Apostles, they still had their immediate, original freshness.

These two events took place at the same time, parallel to one another, the first being, so to speak, concretized in the second. Jesus instituted the sacrament of his death, and the next day he gave himself up to death. Then the disciples celebrated this sacrament, while the living event was still fresh in their minds—the event which is referred to in the words, "This body which is given; this blood which is shed," and which confirmed the truth of these words. And we go on to say: "Christ is risen."

The Way to Christ

———∞∞∞———

As Christians Bear Witness to the Paschal Mystery

We must therefore be witnesses of the reality that comes to us from the Pasch. Jesus when taking leave of his disciples and foretelling the coming of the Holy Spirit had said to them: "You shall be my witnesses in Jerusalem and in all Judea and Samaria and to the end of the earth" (Acts 1:8). Now the disciples' first testimony was precisely that concerning the fact of the *Resurrection.* In the first discourses of the apostles the central part is always dedicated to the testimony concerning Christ's *death and Resurrection.* You also bring to your Christian communities this witness, and you keep before their eyes the glorious figure of the risen Christ, while you repeat in the liturgical assemblies the chant of the Easter Alleluia. (This is the substance and meaning of Lent).

Discourse at the Vatican, April 6, 1988

April 11

At the Foot of the Cross We See God

The history of the covenant, which begins together with the call of Abraham, leads across the mount of the Transfiguration to the mount of the Crucifixion. The Transfiguration prepares the apostles for the experience of Good Friday. *He who will offer his life on the cross* and undergo a shameful death is *the chosen Son* of the Father. In him, God's covenant with man will reach its zenith.... *The covenant is God's initiative with regard to man.* God created man in his image and likeness, and for this reason he has made him capable of accepting his salvific initiative. Man, as God's image, has in himself *the capacity for immortality, which God alone can bestow with his presence,* with his divine life, giving himself to man in the full reality of his divinity. God, who is love, wishes to give himself to man in this way. *Man has in himself the deeply hidden desire to "see" God.*

Discourse at the Parish of Our Lady Mother of the Church, Tor DiValle, Italy,
February 19, 1989

April 12

Lessons of the Cross

In fact, the cross is the symbol of the Christian faith; it is the emblem of Jesus, crucified and risen for us. Therefore the cross must mark the stages of our Lenten journey, to teach us to understand ever better the *gravity* of sin and the *power* of the blood with which the Redeemer has washed and purified us. Let us place ourselves in the school of the Crucified One not merely during the devotion of the *Way of the Cross,* which is characteristic of Lent, but also in our meditation and prayer, until we reach a single mind and an intimate communion with Christ. In fact, as the apostle Peter says, "Rejoice insofar as you share Christ's sufferings, that you may also rejoice and be glad when his glory is revealed" (1 Pet. 4:13).

Discourse at the Parish of Our Lady Mother of the Church, Tor DiValle, Italy,
February 19, 1989

—⟨∞⟩—

The Cross and the Terrorist Attack of September 11, 2001

I join my prayers to those of all assembled in the National Shrine for the Mass of suffrage celebrated for those who lost their lives in last Tuesday's terrorist attack on the Pentagon. I am confident that in this time of trial all Americans will find their religious faith a source of renewed hope and the impetus for an ever more determined resolve to reject the ways of hatred and violence. To those affected by this immense tragedy I hold up the light of the gospel and pray that by the prompting of the Holy Spirit they will be led to an ever closer union with the Lord Jesus Christ in the mystery of his Cross and Resurrection. To all I solemnly repeat the gospel injunction not to be conquered by evil, but to conquer evil with good (Rom. 12:21), to trust in the power of God's grace to transform human hearts, and to work fearlessly to shape a future of justice, peace, and security for the children of our world. Upon you, Archbishop O'Brien, Bishop Loverde, and all the military and civilian personnel who have gathered to commend the departed to the infinite mercy of God our loving Father, I cordially invoke the divine gifts of wisdom, strength, and perseverance in good. To all the faithful I cordially impart my apostolic blessing as a pledge of comfort and peace in the Lord.

Letter of Condolence to Cardinal Theodore E. McCarrick,
Archbishop of Washington, September 15, 2001

April 14

⸺ ∞ ⸺

Forgiveness, the Cry from the Cross:
A Timely Message

No religious leader can condone terrorism, and much less preach it. It is a profanation of religion to declare oneself a terrorist in the name of God, to do violence to others in his name. Terrorist violence is a contradiction of faith in God, the Creator of man, who cares for man and loves him. It is altogether contrary to faith in Christ the Lord, who taught his disciples to pray: *"Forgive us our debts, as we also have forgiven our debtors"* (Matt. 6:12). Following the teaching and example of Jesus, Christians hold that to show mercy is to live out the truth of our lives: we can and must be merciful because mercy has been shown us by a God who is Love (1 John 4:7-12). The God who enters into history to redeem us, is a God of mercy and forgiveness (Ps. 103:3-4, 10-13). Thus Jesus told those who challenged his dining with sinners: "I came not to call the righteous, but sinners" (Matt. 9:13). The followers of Christ must always be men and women of mercy and forgiveness. *But what does forgiveness actually mean? And why should we forgive?* Forgiveness inhabits people's hearts before it becomes a social reality. Forgiveness is above all a personal choice, a decision of the heart to go against the natural instinct to pay back evil with evil. The measure of such a decision is the love of God who draws us to himself in spite of our sin. It has its perfect exemplar in the forgiveness of Christ, who on the Cross prayed: *"Father, forgive them, for they know not what they do"* (Luke 23:34).

World Day of Peace Message, the Vatican, January 1, 2002

April 15

The Parish as a School of Prayer

I especially urge you, dear priests, to foster your personal spiritual progress in this holy season. The faithful draw great benefit for understanding and welcoming the spiritual riches of Lent from the priest's example and witness and rediscover the parish as a "school" of prayer, "where the meeting with Christ is expressed not just in imploring help, but also in thanksgiving, praise, adoration, contemplation, listening and ardent devotion, until the heart truly *'falls in love'"* (*Novo Millennio Ineunte*). Lent is the acceptable time in every community to foster that spirituality of communion that flows from a more intense encounter with the Lord into mutual relations, making it possible to relish "how good and pleasant it is when brothers dwell in unity" (Ps. 133:1). From this standpoint, priestly communion, which is expressed in lived brotherhood between parish priests and curates, between elderly and young priests, and especially with confrères who are ill or in difficulty is decisive. Within the presbyterate, each individual is called to regard others as "those who are a part of me" and to see first what is positive in their brothers, to welcome it and prize it as "a gift for me." "resisting the selfish temptations which constantly beset us and provoke competition, careerism, distrust and jealousy" (*Novo Millennio Ineunte*).... Lent is the acceptable time for our sanctification. It is so for every baptized person and even more so for us priests, who are called to "celebrate each day what we live and to live what we celebrate," the Lord's paschal sacrifice, the first and eternal source of holiness and grace.

Address to the Clergy of Rome, March 1, 2001

April 16

―――∞――――

Through Our Lenten Journey

"God so loved the world that he gave his only Son, so that whoever believes in him should not perish but have eternal life" (John 3:16). Does contemporary man feel the need for this message? At first sight it would seem not, especially since in public expressions and in a certain prevalent culture, we can see the image of a humanity sure of itself, that willingly does without God and claims absolute freedom even from the moral law. But when we look closely at the real situation of each person, forced to confront his own frailty and loneliness, we realize that, more than we think, hearts are weighed down by anguish, by worry about the future, by fear of sickness and death. This explains why so many seek an escape by sometimes taking deviant shortcuts, such as the blind alley of drugs or that of superstition and distressing magical rites. Christianity offers no cheap comforts, demanding as it is in requiring an authentic faith and a strict moral life. But it gives us reason for *hope* by showing us God as a *Father rich in mercy* who has given us his Son, thereby revealing to us his immense love.

Discourse at the Vatican, March 9, 1997

───∞───

The Lord's Supper

In the Gospel we read: *"Now before the Feast of the Passover, when Jesus knew that his hour had come to depart out of this world to the Father, having loved his own who were in the world, he loved them to the end"* (John 13:1). Today we recall the institution of the Eucharist, a gift and inexhaustible source of love. Engraved and rooted in it is the new commandment *"that you love one another"* (John 13:34). Love reaches its peak in the gift the person makes of himself, without reserve, to God and to his brothers and sisters. By washing the apostles' feet, the Teacher presents them with an example of service: *"You call me Teacher and Lord; and you are right, for so I am. If I then, your Lord and Teacher, have washed your feet, you also ought to wash one another's feet"* (John 13:13–14). By this act, Jesus reveals a distinctive feature of his mission: *"I am among you as one who serves"* (Luke 22:27). Thus a true disciple of Christ can only be someone who *"takes part"* in Christ's actions, making himself, as he was, prompt in serving others even with personal sacrifice. Indeed, service, that is, caring for our neighbor's needs, is the essence of any well-ordered authority: to reign is to serve. The priestly ministry, whose institution we celebrate and venerate today, implies an attitude of humble availability, especially to those most in need.

Homily at the Basilica of St. John Lateran, Rome, Italy, April 9, 1998

~~~~~~~~

Proclaim the Mystery of Faith

"We proclaim your Resurrection!" The Church proclaims Christ's Resurrection at the central moment of every Mass, when, after the consecration, the celebrant says aloud: "Let us proclaim the mystery of faith!" The assembly responds with the acclamation: "We proclaim your death, Lord Jesus, until you come in glory." *These words refer to the very heart of the saving event handed down to us in the Gospel.* Today the Church still proclaims Christ crucified as did the apostles; as did St. Paul who considered that he knew nothing "except Jesus Christ, and him crucified" (1 Cor. 2:2). The Church proclaims Christ's death and points to it as the *beginning of the new life.*

Homily in the Cathedral Trent, Italy, April 30, 1995

April 19

Here in Jerusalem

Jesus, "having loved his own who were in the world, loved them to the end" (John 13:1). Here in Jerusalem, in the place where according to tradition Jesus and the Twelve were present for the Passover meal and the institution of the Eucharist, I am deeply moved as I read once again the words with which the Evangelist John introduces the account of the Last Supper. Today, this visit to the Upper Room gives me an opportunity to survey the entire mystery of the Redemption. It was here that Christ gave us the immense gift of the Eucharist. Here too our priesthood was born.

Discourse from Jerusalem, March 23, 2000

———∞———

Letter from the Upper Room

From this Upper Room I would like to address this letter to you, as I have done for more than twenty years, on Holy Thursday, the day of the Eucharist and "our" day *par excellence*. I am indeed writing to you from the Upper Room, thinking back to all that took place within these walls on that evening charged with mystery. Spiritually, I see Jesus and the apostles seated at table with him. I think of Peter especially: it is as if I can see him, with the other disciples, watching in amazement the Lord's actions, listening with deep emotion to his words and, for all the burden of his frailty, opening himself to the mystery proclaimed here and soon to be accomplished. These are the hours of the great battle between the love that gives itself without reserve and the *mysterium iniquitatis* (the mystery of evil), which is imprisoned in hostility. The betrayal of Judas appears emblematic of humanity's sin. "It was night," observes the Evangelist John (John 13:30): the hour of darkness, an hour of separation and of infinite sadness. Yet in the emotion-filled words of Christ the light of dawn already shines forth: "I will see you again and your hearts will rejoice, and no one will take your joy from you" (John 16:22).

Letter from the Cenacle, Jerusalem, March 23, 2000

A Message He Would Never Deliver

In our day human society appears to be shrouded in dark shadows while it is shaken by tragic events and shattered by catastrophic natural disasters. Nevertheless, as *"on the night he was betrayed"* (1 Cor. 11:23), also today Jesus "breaks the bread" (Matt. 26:26) for us in our eucharistic celebrations and offers himself under the sacramental sign of his love for all mankind. This is why I underlined that "the Eucharist is not merely an expression of communion in the Church's life; it is also a project of solidarity for all of humanity" (*Ecclesia de Eucharistia*); it is "bread from heaven" that gives eternal life (John 6:33) and opens the human heart to a great hope. Present in the Eucharist, the same Redeemer who saw the needy crowds and was filled with compassion *"because they were harassed and dejected, like sheep without a shepherd"* (Matt. 9:36), continues through the centuries to show compassion for humanity's poor and suffering.

Message to Have Been Delivered on World Mission Sunday, October 23, 2005;
Prepared and Signed on February 22, 2005, Feast of the Chair of Peter

April 22

⁓⁓⁓

The Priesthood of Christ

To go to the heart of it, we must reflect upon the priesthood of Christ. Certainly, the entire People of God participates in this priesthood by Baptism. But the Second Vatican Council reminds us that, in addition to the participation proper to all the baptized, there exists another specific ministerial participation that, although intimately linked to the first, nonetheless differs from it in essence (*Lumen Gentium*). In the context of the Jubilee of the Incarnation, we can approach the priesthood of Christ from a particular perspective. The Jubilee invites us to contemplate the intimate link between Christ's priesthood and the mystery of his person. The priesthood of Christ is not "incidental," a task that he might or might not have assumed: rather, it is integral to his identity as the Son Incarnate, as God made man. From now on, the relationship between mankind and God passes wholly through Christ: "No one comes to the Father, except through me" (John 14:6). This is why Christ is a priest endowed with an eternal and universal priesthood, of which the priesthood of the first covenant was a prefigurement and a preparation (Heb. 9:9). He has exercised it fully from the moment he took his seat as High Priest "at the right hand of the throne of the Majesty in heaven" (Heb. 8:1). From that time forth, the very nature of human priesthood changed: now there is but one priesthood, that of Christ, which can be shared and exercised in different ways.

Letter from the Cenacle, Jerusalem, March 23, 2000

———∞∞∞———

Festival of Saints

How can we not return ever anew to this mystery, which contains the entire life of the Church? For two thousand years, this sacrament has given nourishment to countless believers. It has been the source of a great river of grace. How many saints have found in it not only the pledge, but as it were the foretaste of heaven! Let us allow ourselves to be carried along by the contemplative impulse, rich in poetry and theology, that inspired St. Thomas Aquinas to sing of the mystery in the words of the hymn *Pange Lingua* ("Sing My Tongue"). Today, in this Upper Room, these words come to me as an echo of the voice of so many Christian communities throughout the world, of so many priests, consecrated persons and lay faithful, who each day pause in adoration of the eucharistic mystery:

Verbum caro, panem verum verbo carnem efficit,
fitque sanguis Christi merum, et, si sensus deficit,
ad firmandum cor sincerum sola fides sufficit.

(Word made flesh, the bread of nature by his word to flesh he turns; wine into his blood he changes: what though sense no change discerns? Only be the heart in earnest, faith its lesson quickly learns.)

Letter from the Cenacle, Jerusalem, March 23, 2000

Prayer in the Garden: Prayer on the Surface of the World

The lack of prayer can never be taken to mean that you do not need prayer. Indeed, the longer we do not pray, the greater the need grows, so that at a certain moment it explodes in the search for some outlet. Not praying does not necessarily mean that we do not feel the need to pray. In this case your prayer needs a more interior basis, a more spiritual attitude, and a deeper orientation; you must simply look for the means of expression and the type of prayer that corresponds with and satisfies … your mature moral personality…. Let us return to the basic question and main subject of today's meditation: Why do we pray? Why does everybody pray—Christians, Muslims, Buddhists, pagans? Why do even those who do not think they are praying pray? The answer is very simple: I pray because God exists. I know that God exists, and this is why I pray. Some people will give this type of frank reply: "I know that God exists." However, others may phrase their answer differently, with somewhat less certainty, "I believe," or maybe even, "I'm searching." In the course of this reflection, I should like you to become more precise in the use of these different expressions, since they describe a variety of different spiritual attitudes.

The Way to Christ

The Stations of the Cross

Christ is God himself, who continues to convert people, even on the Way of the Cross: we see this process in the conversion of Simon of Cyrene, the women of Jerusalem, and Veronica (and the good thief on the cross). The Way of the Cross is the perfect school for contrition. Sometimes our problems with regard to confession spring from the fact that we cannot resolve to resist sin in the future. How can we know if we shall change, when appearances would tend to indicate that we shall remain the same? In fact, we can maybe already feel the forces of evil stirring in us again and urging us back toward sin. The conscience raises us up, and the forces of evil drag us down. My dear children, the resolution not to sin anymore is first and foremost a matter of conversion to God; it is not a matter of being certain that one will not commit the same sin again, but rather of the will not to do so. We should cling to God with our whole will. We would not be capable of bringing about this great transformation on our own, but if we cling to God, if we cling to Christ, it will gradually take place within us.

The Way to Christ

The Cross of Christ

Although he was the light to enlighten all nations, Jesus was destined in his own day and in every age to be a sign disparaged, a sign opposed, a sign of contradiction. This has been true of the prophets of Israel before him. It was true for John the Baptist and would be true of the lives of his future followers.... Crowds flocked to him from everywhere and listened to him carefully because he spoke with authority. And yet he met harsh opposition from those who refused to open their hearts and minds to him. Finally, we find the most tangible sign of this contradiction in his suffering and death on the cross. Simeon's prophecy came true—true regarding the life of Christ, and true regarding the lives of those who followed him, in every land and in every age. So the Cross becomes light; the Cross becomes salvation. Isn't this perhaps the good news for the poor and for all who know the bitter taste of suffering? The cross of poverty, the cross of hunger, the cross of every other suffering can be transformed, since Christ's Cross has become a light in our world. It is the light of hope and salvation. It gives meaning to all human suffering. It brings with it the promise of an eternal life, free from sorrow, free from sin. The Cross was followed by the Resurrection.... And all who are united to the crucified and risen Lord can look forward to sharing in this selfsame victory.

Agenda for the Third Millennium

---∞∞∞---

The Witness of the Empty Tomb

Following the path of salvation history, as narrated in the Apostles' Creed, my Jubilee pilgrimage has brought me to the Holy Land. From Nazareth, where Jesus was conceived of the Virgin Mary by the power of the Holy Spirit, I have reached Jerusalem, where he "suffered under Pontius Pilate, was crucified, died and was buried." Here, in the Church of the Holy Sepulchre, I kneel before the place of his burial: "Behold, the place where they laid him" (Mark 16:6). The tomb is empty. It is a silent witness to the central event of human history: the Resurrection of our Lord Jesus Christ. For almost two thousand years the empty tomb has borne witness to the victory of Life over death. With the apostles and Evangelists, with the Church of every time and place, we too bear witness and proclaim: "Christ is risen! Raised from the dead he will never die again; death no longer has power over him" (Rom. 6:9). *"Mors et vita duello conflixere mirando; dux vitae mortuus, regnat vivus"* (Latin Easter Sequence: *Victimae Pascali Laudes*—"Behold death and life contended together; the Lord of Life was dead, but now living, he reigns). The Lord of Life was dead; now he reigns, victorious over death, the source of everlasting life for all who believe.

Homily at the Church of the Holy Sepulchre, Jerusalem, March 26, 2000

Resurrection

"Destroy this temple and in three days I will raise it up" (John 2:19).
John tells us that, after Jesus rose from the dead, the disciples remembered these words, and they believed (John 2:22). Jesus had spoken
these words that they might be a sign for his disciples. When he and the
disciples visited the Temple, he expelled the money changers and vendors from the holy place (John 2:15). When those present protested,
saying: "What sign have you to show us for doing this?" Jesus replied:
"Destroy this temple and in three days I will raise it up." The Evangelist observes that he "was speaking of the temple of his body" (John
2:18–21). The prophecy contained in Jesus's words was fulfilled at Easter, when "on the third day he rose from the dead." The Resurrection
of our Lord Jesus Christ is the sign that the Eternal Father is faithful
to his promise and brings new life out of death: "the resurrection of
the body and life everlasting." The mystery is clearly reflected in this
ancient Church of the *Anástasis*, which contains both the empty tomb,
the sign of the Resurrection, and Golgotha, the place of the Crucifixion. The good news of the Resurrection can never be separated from
the mystery of the Cross. Christ, who offered himself as an evening
sacrifice on the altar of the Cross (Ps. 141:2), has now been revealed as
"the power of God and the wisdom of God" (1 Cor. 1:24). And in his
Resurrection the sons and daughters of Adam have been made sharers
in the divine life, which was his from all eternity, with the Father, in
the Holy Spirit.

Homily at the Church of the Holy Sepulchre, Jerusalem, March 26, 2000

⎯ ⚬⚬⚬ ⎯

The Resurrection Covenant

The law and the covenant are the seal of the promise made to Abraham. Through the Decalogue and the moral law inscribed on the human heart (Rom. 2:15), God radically challenges the freedom of every man and woman. To respond to God's voice resounding in the depths of our conscience and to choose good is the most sublime use of human freedom. It is to make the choice between life and death (Deut. 30:15). By walking the path of the covenant with the All-Holy God the people became bearers and witnesses of the promise, the promise of genuine liberation and fullness of life. *The Resurrection of Jesus is the definitive seal of all God's promises,* the birthplace of a new, risen humanity, the pledge of a history marked by the messianic gifts of peace and spiritual joy. At the dawn of a new millennium, Christians can and ought to look to the future with steadfast trust in the glorious power of the Risen One to make all things new (Rev. 21:5). By his Resurrection he opens the way to the great Sabbath rest, the Eighth Day, when mankind's pilgrimage will come to its end and God will be all in all (1 Cor. 15:28). Here at the Holy Sepulchre and Golgotha, as we renew our profession of faith in the Risen Lord, can we doubt that in the power of the Spirit of Life we will be given the strength to overcome our divisions and to work together to build a future of reconciliation, unity, and peace? Here, as in no other place on earth, we hear the Lord say once again to his disciples: "Do not fear; I have overcome the world!" (John 16:33).

Homily at the Church of the Holy Sepulchre, Jerusalem: March 26, 2000

—∞∞—

Radiance

Radiant with the glory of the Spirit, the Risen Lord is the Head of the Church, his Mystical Body. He sustains her in her mission of proclaiming the gospel of salvation to the men and women of every generation, until he returns in glory! From this place, where the Resurrection was first made known to the women and then to the apostles, I urge all the Church's members to renew their obedience to the Lord's command to take the gospel to all the ends of the earth. At the dawn of a new millennium, there is a great need to proclaim from the rooftops the good news that "God so loved the world that he gave his only Son, that whoever believes in him should not perish, but have eternal life" (John 3:16). "Lord, you have the words of eternal life" (John 6:68). Today, as the unworthy Successor of Peter, I wish to repeat these words as we celebrate the eucharistic Sacrifice in this, the most hallowed place on earth. With all of redeemed humanity, I make my own the words Peter the Fisherman spoke to the Christ, the Son of the living God: "Lord, to whom shall we go? You have the words of eternal life." *Christós anésti.* Jesus Christ is risen! He is truly risen! Amen.

Homily at the Church of the Holy Sepulchre, Jerusalem, March 26, 2000

May

May 1

⁕

Stay with Us, Lord

"Mane nobiscum, Domine! Stay with us, Lord!" (Luke 24:29). With these words, the disciples on the road to Emmaus invited the mysterious Wayfarer to stay with them, as the sun was setting on that first day of the week when the incredible had occurred. According to his promise, *Christ had risen;* but they did not yet know this. Nevertheless, the words spoken by the Wayfarer along the road made their hearts *burn within them.* So they said to him: "Stay with us." Seated around the supper table, *they recognized him* in the "breaking of bread"—and suddenly he *vanished.* There remained in front of them *the broken bread.* There echoed in their hearts the gentle sound of *his words.* Dear brothers and sisters, the *Word* and the *Bread* of the Eucharist, the mystery and the gift of Easter, remain down the centuries as a constant memorial of the Passion, death, and Resurrection of Christ! On this Easter Day, together with all Christians throughout the world, we too repeat those words: Jesus, crucified and risen, *Stay with us!* Stay with us, faithful friend and sure support for humanity on its journey through history! *Living Word of the Father,* give hope and trust to all who are searching for the true meaning of their lives. *Bread of Eternal Life,* nourish those who hunger for truth, freedom, justice, and peace.

Urbi et Orbi *Message, Easter Sunday, March 27, 2005*

When Threatened with Fratricidal Wars

Stay with us, *Living Word of the Father,* and teach us words and deeds of peace: peace for our world consecrated by your blood and drenched in the blood of so many innocent victims; peace for the countries of the Middle East and Africa, where so much blood continues to be shed; peace for all of humanity, still threatened by fratricidal wars. Stay with us, *Bread of Eternal Life,* broken and distributed to those at table: give also to us the strength to show generous solidarity toward the multitudes who are even today suffering and dying from poverty and hunger, decimated by fatal epidemics or devastated by immense natural disasters. By the power of your Resurrection, may they too become sharers in new life. We, the men and women of the third millennium, we too need you, Risen Lord! Stay with us now, and until the end of time. Grant that the material progress of peoples may never obscure the spiritual values that are the soul of their civilization. Sustain us, we pray, on our journey. In you do we believe, in you do we hope, for you alone have the words of eternal life (John 6:68). *Mane nobiscum, Domine!* (Stay with us, Lord!) Alleluia!

Urbi et Orbi *Message, Easter Sunday, March 27, 2005*

A Resurrection Purity

Dear Brothers, take great care to celebrate the eucharistic Mystery with a pure heart and sincere love. The Lord recommends that we not become branches that are cut off the vine. Preach clearly and simply the right doctrine about the need for the sacrament of Reconciliation before receiving Communion when a person is conscious that he or she is not in God's grace. At the same time, encourage the faithful to receive the Body and Blood of Christ to be purified from venial sins and imperfections, so that celebrations of the Eucharist may be pleasing to God and may unite us in offering the holy and immaculate Victim with a contrite and humble heart, trusting and reconciled. May you be for everyone assiduous, available and competent ministers of the sacrament of Reconciliation, true images of the holy and merciful Christ.

Message to the Participants in the Annual Course on the Internal Forum
Organized by the Tribunal of the Apostolic Penitentiary, March 8, 2005

May 4

Choose God, Choose Life

There is also the possibility of refusing God. It sounds horrifying, but it is true that I, a person, can refuse God. Human history is full of examples of this. The gospel is not the only active force in the lives and actions of humanity and in those of each individual; parallel with it and in opposition to it there is a second force, which I would call the anti-gospel. The anti-gospel maybe has its origins in the words uttered at the beginning of human history: "You shall be as gods" (Gen. 3:5). Now, in the history of mankind and of each individual person—in one's own personal history—this anti-gospel, this opposite of the gospel, takes on certain individual or collective forms with constantly new expressions. Thus we are living in the toils of a contemporary expression or formulation of this anti-gospel. We see it in and around us; we feel it, read about it, and recognize it; it is to be found everywhere.... Christianity is the reality of our choice of God. Choosing God, or choosing Christ, means in some way choosing oneself, choosing one's own self in a new way. We are convinced that being Christians means in some way choosing ourselves. It means a type of existence, a foundation, a lifestyle, and a specific morality.

The Way to Christ

Confirmation of All That Christ Had Done and Taught

All the Church's preaching, from apostolic times down the centuries and spanning the generations, even to the present day, makes its appeal to the Resurrection and draws from it its driving and persuasive force and its vigor. It is easy to understand why. *The Resurrection was first of all the confirmation of all that Christ had done and taught.* It was the divine seal stamped on his word and life. He himself had indicated to his disciples and adversaries this definitive sign of his truth. On the first Easter day the angel told the women at the empty tomb: "He has risen as he said" (Matt. 28:6). If this word and promise of his are revealed as true, then all his other words and promises possess the power of truth that does not pass away, as he himself had proclaimed: "Heaven and earth will pass away, but my words will not pass away" (Matt. 24:35; Mark 13:31; Luke 21:33). No stronger, more decisive, and more authoritative proof than the resurrection from the dead could have been imagined or asked for. All the truths, including those most impenetrable to the human mind, find their justification, even from the rational point of view, in the fact that the risen Christ gave the definitive proof, promised beforehand, of his divine authority: *thus, the truth of Christ's divinity itself is confirmed in the Resurrection.*

Discourse at the Vatican, March 8, 1989

May 6

―∞∞∞―

Building a New Culture of Love

"A large group of people followed Jesus, including many women who mourned and lamented him" (Luke 23:27). A sharing that consists only in the compassion of words, or even in tears, is not enough; each one must be aware of one's own responsibility in the drama of suffering, especially of innocent suffering. This leads us to assume our own share in making an effort to relieve it. The words of Jesus do not indulge in sterile sentimentalism, but invite one to the realistic reading of the history of individuals and communities. *"For if these things are done when the wood is green, what will happen when it is dry?"* (Luke 23:31). If the innocent one *par excellence* is struck down in this way, what will happen to those that are responsible for the evil that comes about in the history of individuals and nations? May Jesus's sorrowful journey, the *Via Crucis* (the Way of the Cross), be for us the spiritual reminder to recognize the value of our daily suffering, a lesson not to evade it with opportunistic pretext or useless deceptions, but rather an incentive to make of it a gift to the One who has loved us (Rom. 8:37), in the certainty that we are thereby building a new culture of love and collaborating in the divine work of salvation.

Discourse at the Vatican, March 5, 1989

———∞∞∞———

The Queen of the Resurrection

Regina coeli laetare! (Queen of Heaven, rejoice!) Behold, precisely today, on this first day after the Sabbath, *the women* went to the tomb, where the body of your Son had been laid, having been taken down from the cross, and they found the stone rolled away and the tomb empty. From within the tomb they heard a voice: "Do not be amazed; you seek Jesus of Nazareth, who was crucified. *He has risen, he is not here*" (Mark 16:6). Rejoice, Queen of Heaven! Rejoice, Mother of Christ. *Regina coeli laetare.* "But go, tell his disciples and Peter" (Mark 16:7). Then *Mary of Magdala* ran to tell the apostles: "They have taken the Lord out of the tomb, and we do not know where they have laid him" (John 20:2). *Peter and John* went at once to the place, and they found that it was as the women had said. He is not here. He is not here, in the place where they laid him, in the tomb. He is not here—he has risen. Rejoice, Queen of Heaven! *Regina coeli laetare!*

Easter Message, St. Peter's Basilica, the Vatican, 1988

May 8

The Timelessness of It All

"This is the day of Christ the Lord!" we sang in the liturgy of Easter Sunday. However, Easter Sunday continues; rather, it is now endless. It is the day of Christ's definitive victory over the devil, over sin, and over death. It is the day that opens onto the temporal cycle, the endless perspective of eternal life where the sacrificial Lamb still offers himself continually to the Father for us, for love of us. For this reason the liturgy celebrates in this octave the unique day of the Pasch. In the mystery of the *ogdoade*, of the octave—as the pastors and teachers of the ancient Church explained—the whole mystery of salvation is summarized; in it is included the onward course of time into eternity, of the corruptible into incorruption, of the mortal into immortality. Everything is new, everything is holy, because Christ, our Pasch, is sacrificed. In this *day* of the Pasch there is anticipated the eternal *day* of Paradise. These ideas are marvelously expressed in poetic form by the ancient *stichira* (hymn) of the Byzantine liturgy, which were sung also in Rome in the ninth century in the presence of the pope on Easter Sunday. This year they were again sung in the Vatican Basilica.

> Today a divine Pasch has been revealed to us,
> a new and holy Pasch, a mysterious Pasch, a most solemn Pasch.
> A Pasch, Christ the Redeemer, a great and immaculate Pasch,
>   a Pasch of the believers.
> A Pasch which opens to us the gates of Paradise.

Discourse at the Vatican, April 6, 1988

May 9

May 9

Finding Comfort in the Cross

I join you in the invocation, so rich in meaning: *Adoramus te, Christe, et benedicimus tibi, quia per sanctam crucem tuam redemisti mundum* (We adore you O Christ, and we bless you; because by your Holy Cross, you have redeemed the world). Yes, we adore and bless the mystery of the Cross of the Son of God, because it was from his death that new hope for humanity was born. The adoration of the Cross directs us to a commitment that we cannot shirk, the mission that St. Paul expressed in these words: *"In my flesh I complete what is lacking in Christ's afflictions for the sake of his body, that is, the Church"* (Col. 1:24). I also offer my sufferings so that God's plan may be completed and his Word spread among the peoples. I, in turn, am close to all who are tried by suffering at this time. I pray for each one of them. *O crux, ave spes unica!* "Hail, O Cross, our only hope!" Give us patience and courage and obtain peace for the world!

Message at the Colosseum, Rome, Italy, March 25, 2005

The Mystery of Evil

Sixty years have passed since the liberation of the prisoners of the Auschwitz-Birkenau death camp. This anniversary calls us to ponder once again the drama that took place there, the final, tragic outcome of a program of hatred. In these days we must remember the millions of persons who, through no fault of their own, were forced to endure inhuman suffering and extermination in the gas chambers and ovens. I bow my head before all those who experienced this manifestation of the *mysterium iniquitatis* (the mystery of evil). When, as pope, I visited the Auschwitz-Birkenau camp in 1979, I halted before the monuments dedicated to the victims. There were inscriptions in many languages: Polish, English, Bulgarian, Romanian, Czech, Danish, French, Greek, Hebrew, Yiddish, Spanish, Flemish, Serbo-Croatian, German, Norwegian, Russian, Hungarian, and Italian. All these languages spoke of the victims of Auschwitz: real, yet in many cases completely anonymous men, women, and children. I stood somewhat longer before the inscription written in Hebrew. I said: "This inscription invites us to remember the people whose sons and daughters were doomed to total extermination. This people has its origin in Abraham, our father in faith (Rom. 4:11–12), as Paul of Tarsus has said. This, the very people that received from God the commandment, 'You shall not kill,' itself experienced in a special measure what killing means. No one is permitted to pass by this inscription with indifference."

Address on the Holocaust, the Vatican, January 15, 2005

May 11

The Shoah

No one is permitted to pass by the tragedy of the Shoah, the Holocaust. That attempt at the systematic destruction of an entire people falls like a shadow on the history of Europe and the whole world; it is a crime that will forever darken the history of humanity. May it serve, today and for the future, as a warning: there must be no yielding to ideologies that justify contempt for human dignity on the basis of race, color, language, or religion. I make this appeal to everyone, and particularly to those who would resort, in the name of religion, to acts of oppression and terrorism. These reflections have remained with me, especially when, during the Great Jubilee of the Year 2000, the Church celebrated the solemn penitential liturgy in St. Peter's, and I journeyed as a pilgrim to the holy places and went up to Jerusalem. In *Yad Vashem*—the memorial to the Shoah—and at the foot of the Western Wall of the Temple I prayed in silence, begging forgiveness and the conversion of hearts. That day in 1979 when I was in Auschwitz, I also remember stopping to reflect before two other inscriptions, written in Russian and in *Romanian*. The history of the Soviet Union's role in that war was complex, yet it must not be forgotten that in it the Russians had the highest number of those who tragically lost their lives. The *Romanians* were also doomed to total extermination in Hitler's plan. *One cannot underestimate the sacrifice of life that was imposed on these, our brothers and sisters in the Auschwitz-Birkenau death camp. For this reason, I insist once more that no one is permitted to pass by those inscriptions with indifference.*

Address on the Holocaust, the Vatican, January 15, 2005

May 12

A Time to Remember the Second World War

During my visit to Auschwitz-Birkenau, I also said that one should halt before every one of the inscriptions. I myself did so, passing in prayerful meditation from one to the next, and commending to the Divine Mercy all the victims from all those nations, which experienced the atrocities of the war. I also prayed that, through their intercession, the gift of peace would be granted to our world. I continue to pray unceasingly, trusting that everywhere, in the end, there will prevail *respect for the dignity of the human person* and for the right of every man and women to seek the truth in freedom, to follow the moral law, to discharge the duties imposed by justice and to lead a fully human life. In speaking of the victims of Auschwitz, I cannot fail to recall that, in the midst of that unspeakable concentration of evil, there were also heroic examples of commitment to good. Certainly there were many persons who were willing, in spiritual freedom, to endure suffering and to show love, not only for their fellow prisoners, but also for their tormentors. Many did so out of love for God and for man; others in the name of the highest spiritual values. Their attitude bore clear witness to a truth, which is often expressed in the Bible: even though man is capable of evil, and at times boundless evil, evil itself will never have the last word. In the very abyss of suffering, love can triumph. The witness to this love shown in Auschwitz must never be forgotten. It must never cease to rouse consciences, to resolve conflicts, to inspire the building of peace.

Address on the Holocaust, the Vatican, January 15, 2005

May 13

~∞∞∞~

An Important Personal Anniversary

In Rome a dying pope, in Poland mourning (after the assassination attempt in St. Peter's Square, of May 13, 1981).... In Krakow the university students organized a demonstration, the "White March." When I went to Poland, I said, "I have come to thank you for the White March." I also went to Fatima to thank Our Lady. O dear Lord! It was a hard experience. I didn't wake up until the following day, toward noon. And I said to Fr. Stanislaw: "Yesterday I didn't say compline." I knew nothing of what Fr. Stanislaw knew. They hadn't told me how serious the situation was. Besides, I was simply unconscious for quite some time. When I awoke, my morale was reasonably good. At least initially.... As you see, I have quite a strong constitution.

Memory and Identity

———∞∞∞———

A Pontiff Reflects

It was all a testimony to divine grace. I see here a certain similarity to the trials suffered by Cardinal Wyszynski during his imprisonment. The experience of the Primate of Poland, though, lasted more than three years, while my own lasted rather a short time, just a few months. Agca knew how to shoot, and he certainly shot to kill. Yet it was if someone was guiding and deflecting that bullet.... Yes, I remember that journey to the hospital. For a short time I remained conscious. I had a sense that I would survive. I was in pain, and this was a reason to be afraid, but I had a strange trust. I said to Fr. Stanislaw that I had forgiven my assailant. What happened at the hospital, I do not remember.... Again I have become indebted to the Blessed Virgin and to all the patron saints. Could I forget that the event in St. Peter's Square took place on the day and at the hour when the first appearance of the Mother of Christ to the poor little peasants has been remembered for over sixty years at Fatima in Portugal? For in everything that happened to me on that day, on that very day, I felt that extraordinary Motherly protection and care, which turned out to be stronger than the deadly bullet.

Memory and Identity

I Visit My Attacker

Around Christmas 1983 I visited my attacker in prison. We spoke at length. Ali Agca, as everyone knows, was a professional assassin. This means that the attack was not his own initiative; it was someone else's idea; someone else had commissioned him to carry it out. In the course of our conversation it became clear that Ali Agca was still wondering how the attempted assassination could have failed. He had planned it meticulously, attending to every tiny detail. And yet his intended victim had escaped death. The interesting thing was that his perplexity had led him to the religious question. He wanted to know about the secret of Fatima, and what the secret actually was; more than anything else he wanted to know this. Perhaps those insistent questions showed that he had grasped something really important. *Ali Agca had probably sensed that over and above his own power, over and above the power of shooting and killing, there was a higher power.* He then began to look for it. I hope and pray that he found it.

Memory and Identity

Prayer by the Church

It is difficult for me to think about all of this without emotion, without deep gratitude to everyone, to all those who gathered in prayer for the day of May 13, and to all those who persevered in it.... I am grateful to Christ the Lord and to the Holy Spirit, who, through this event, which took place in St. Peter's Square on May 13 at 5:17 PM, inspired so many hearts to come in prayer. And thinking of this great prayer, I cannot forget the words of the Acts of the Apostles referring to Peter: *"Earnest prayer was made for him to God by the Church"* (12:5).

Memory and Identity

My Vocation, My Mission, My Ministry

I am constantly aware that in everything I say and do, in fulfillment of my vocation, my mission, my ministry, what happens is not just my own initiative. I know that it is not I alone who act in what I do as the Successor of Peter. Let us take the example of the Communist system. As I said earlier, a contributory factor in its demise was certainly its deficient economic doctrine, but to account for what happened solely in terms of economic factors would be a rather naive simplification. On the other hand, it would obviously be ridiculous to claim that the pope brought down Communism single-handedly. I think that the explanation can be found in the Gospel. When the first disciples returned to their master, having been sent out on a mission, they said: "Lord, even the demons are subject to us in your name" (Luke 10:17). Christ replied to them: "Do not rejoice in this, that the spirits are subject to you, but rejoice that your names are written in heaven" (Luke 10:20). And on another occasion he adds: "Say: we are unworthy servants, we have only done what was our duty" (Luke 17:10). Unworthy servants ... The sense of being an "unworthy servant" is growing in me—in the midst of all that happens around me—and I think I feel at ease with this.

Memory and Identity

—∞∞∞—

The Final Convulsions of Arrogant Ideologies

Let us return to the assassination attempt. I think it was one of the final convulsions of the arrogant ideologies unleashed during the twentieth century. Both Facism and Nazism eliminated people. So did Communism. Here in Italy, the practice of elimination continued, justifying itself by similar arguments. The Red Brigade killed innocent and honest men. In rereading the transcriptions of those conversations of some years ago, I would note that the manifestations of violence from the so-called *anni di piombo* (years of lead) have been significantly reduced. Yet in recent years the world has seen the rise of so-called terror networks that place the lives of millions of innocent people under constant threat. Striking confirmation of this was provided by the destruction of the Twin Towers in New York (September 11, 2001), the bomb blast in Atocha station in Madrid (March 11, 2004), and the slaughter at Beslan in North Ossetia (September 1–3, 2004). Where are these new eruptions of violence leading? The demise first of Nazism and then of the Soviet Union signaled a failure. It revealed the utter absurdity of the large-scale violence that formed part of the theory and practice of those systems. Will we be able to learn from the dramatic lessons of history? Or will we be prey once more to the passions at work in the human spirit, yielding yet again to the evil promptings of violence?

Memory and Identity

May 19

The Hope for Good Also Grows

Believers know that the presence of evil is always accompanied by the presence of good, by grace. As St. Paul wrote: "The free gift is not like the trespass. For if the many died through the one man's trespass, much more surely have the grace of God and the free gift in the grace of the one man, Jesus Christ, abounded for the many" (Rom. 5:15). These words retain their relevance today. Redemption is ongoing. Where evil grows, there the hope for good also grows. In our times evil has grown disproportionately, operating through perverted systems which have practiced violence and elimination on a vast scale. I am not speaking here of evil committed by individuals for personal motives or through individual initiatives. The evil of the twentieth century was not a small-scale evil; it was not simply "homemade." It was an evil of gigantic proportions, an evil which availed itself of state structures in order to accomplish its wicked work, an evil built up into a system.

Memory and Identity

"My God, My God, Why Have You Forsaken Me?"

In hearing Jesus crying out his *"why"* (from the cross) we learn indeed that those who suffer can utter this same cry, but with those same dispositions of filial trust and abandonment of which Jesus is the teacher and model. In the *"why"* of Jesus, there is no feeling or resentment leading to rebellion or desperation. There is no semblance of a reproach to the Father, but the expression of the experience of weakness, of solitude, of abandonment to himself made by Jesus in our place. Jesus thus became the first of the "smitten and inflicted," the first of the abandoned, the first of the *desamparados* (as the Spanish call "the forsaken"). At the same time, he tells us that the benign eye of Providence watches over all the poor children of Eve.

Discourse at the Vatican, November 30, 1988

───❦───

A Conversation with God Begins

The human body in history dies more often and earlier than the tree.
Man endures beyond the doors of death in catacombs and crypts.
Man who departs endures in those who follow.
Man who follows endures in those departed.
Man endures beyond all coming and going
  in himself
  and in you.

The history of men, such as I, always looks for the body
  you will give them.
Each man in history loses his body and goes toward you.
In the moment of departure
  each is greater than history
  although but a part
  (a fragment of a century or two,
  merged into one life).

Easter Vigil and Other Poems

May 22

—∞∞∞—

A Pope Teaches Prayer

Prayer can truly change your life, for it turns your attention away from yourself, and directs your mind and your heart toward the Lord. If we look only at ourselves, with our own limitations and sins, we quickly give way to sadness and discouragement. But if we keep our eyes fixed on the Lord, then our hearts are filled with hope, our minds are washed in the light of truth and we come to know the fullness of the gospel with all its promise and life.

Address at the Institut Catholique, Paris, France, June 1, 1980

May 23

From Out of My Own Youth

What are young people of today like, what are they looking for? It could be said that they are the same as ever. There is something in man which never changes.... This is true especially in the young. But today's youth are also different from those who came before. In the past, the younger generations were shaped by the painful experience of war, of concentration camps, of constant danger. This experience allowed young people—I imagine all over the world, although I have Polish youth in mind—to develop *traits of great heroism.* I think of the Warsaw uprising in 1944—the desperate revolt of my contemporaries, who sacrificed everything. They laid down their young lives. They wanted to demonstrate that they could live up to their great and demanding heritage. I was a part of that generation and I must say that *the heroism of my contemporaries helped me to define my personal vocation.* Fr. Konstanty Michalski, one of the great professors at the Jagiellonian University in Krakow, wrote the book *Between Heroism and Brutality* after returning from the Sachsenhausen concentration camp. The title of this book captures the climate of the times. Referring to Friar Albert Schmielowski, Michalski recalled the words of the Gospel about the need "to give up one's life" (John 15:13). Precisely in that period of absolute contempt for man, when the price of human life had never been considered so cheap, precisely then, each life became precious, acquiring the value of a free gift.

Crossing the Threshold of Hope

May 24

Perennial Youth

Today's young people certainly grow up in a different context; they do not carry within them the experiences of the Second World War. Furthermore, many of them have not known—or do not remember—the struggle against Communism, against the totalitarian state. They live in freedom, which others have won for them, and have yielded in large part to the consumer culture. This is, in broad terms, the *status of the present situation.* All the same, it is difficult to say that the young have rejected traditional values, that they have left the Church. The experiences of teachers and pastors *confirm, today no less than yesterday, the idealism present in young people,* even if nowadays it tends to be expressed mostly in the form of criticism, whereas before it would have translated more simply into duty. In general, the younger generations grow up *in an atmosphere marked by a new positivism,* whereas in Poland, when I was a boy, *romantic traditions prevailed.* The young people with whom I came into contact after I was ordained as a priest believed in these traditions. In the Church and in the gospel they saw a point of reference which helped them to focus their inner strength, to lead their lives in a way that made sense. I still remember my conversations with those young people who spoke of their relationship with the faith in precisely these terms.

Crossing the Threshold of Hope

—∞∞∞—

The Fundamental Importance of Youth

My most memorable experience of the period when my pastoral activities concentrated above all on the young was *the discovery of the fundamental importance of youth*. What is youth? It is not only a period of life that corresponds to a certain number of years; it is also *a time given by Providence to every person and given to him as a responsibility.* During that time he searches, like the young man in the Gospel, for answers to basic questions; he searches not only for the meaning of life but also for a concrete way to go about living his life. This is the most fundamental characteristic of youth. Every mentor, beginning with parents, let alone every pastor, must be aware of this characteristic and must know how to identify it in every boy and girl. I will say more: *he must love this fundamental aspect of youth.* If at every stage of his life man desires to be his own person, to find love; during his youth he desires it even more strongly.

Crossing the Threshold of Hope

—∞—

Mentoring

The desire to be one's own person must not be understood as a license to do anything, without exception. The young do not want that at all—they are willing to be corrected, they want to be told yes or no. *They need guides,* and they want them close at hand. If they turn to authority figures, they do so because they see in them a wealth of human warmth and a willingness to walk with them along the paths they are following.

Crossing the Threshold of Hope

May 27

The Fundamental Problem of Youth

Clearly, then, *the fundamental problem of youth is profoundly personal.* In life, youth is when we come to know ourselves. It is also a time of *communion.* Young people, whether boys or girls, know that they must live for and with others, they know that their life *has meaning to the extent that it becomes a free gift for others.* Here is the origin of all vocations—whether to priesthood or religious life, or to marriage and family. The call to marriage is also a vocation, a gift from God. *I will never forget a young man, an engineering student in Krakow, who everyone knew aspired with determination to holiness.* This was his life plan. He knew he had been "created for greater things," as St. Stanislaus Kostka once expressed it, and at the same time, he had no doubt that his vocation was neither to priesthood nor to religious life. He knew that he was called to remain in the secular world. Technical work, the study of engineering, was his passion. He sought a companion for his life and sought her on his knees, in prayer. I will never forget the conversation in which, after a special day of retreat, he said to me: "I think that this is the woman who should be my wife, that it is God who has given her to me." It was almost as if he were following not only the voice of his own wishes, but above all the voice of God himself. He knew that all good things come from him, and he made a good choice. I am speaking of Jerzy Ciesielski, who died in a tragic accident in the Sudan, where he had been invited to teach at the university. The cause for his beatification is already under way.

Crossing the Threshold of Hope

One of the Fundamental Themes of My Priesthood

It is the vocation to love that naturally allows us to draw close to the young. As a priest I realized this very early. I felt almost an inner call in this direction. It is necessary to prepare young people for marriage; it is necessary to teach them love. Love is not something that is learned, and yet there is nothing else that is as important to learn. As a young priest *I learned to love human love.* This has been one of the fundamental themes of my priesthood—my ministry in the pulpit, in the confessional, and also in my writing. If one loves human love, there naturally arises the need to commit oneself completely to the service of "fair love," because love is fair, it is beautiful. After all, young people are always searching for the beauty in love. They want their love to be beautiful. If they give in to weakness, following models of behavior that can rightly be considered a "scandal in the contemporary world" (and these are widely diffused models), in the depths of their hearts they still desire a beautiful and pure love. This is true of boys as it is of girls. Ultimately, they know that only God can give them this love. As a result, they are willing to follow Christ, without caring about the sacrifices this may entail.

Crossing the Threshold of Hope

World Youth Day

As a young priest and pastor I came to this way of looking at young people and at youth and it has remained constant all these years. It is an outlook that allows me to meet young people wherever I go. Every parish priest in Rome knows that my visits to the parish must conclude with a meeting between the Bishop of Rome and the young people of the parish. And not only in Rome, but anywhere the Pope goes, *he seeks out the young and the young seek him out. Actually, in truth, it is not the Pope who is being sought out at all. The one being sought out is Christ,* who knows "that which is in every man" (John 2:25), especially in a young person, and who can give true answers to his questions! And even if they are demanding answers the young are not afraid of them; more to the point, they even await them. This also explains the idea of holding World Youth Days.... *No one invented the World Youth Days. It was the young people themselves who created them.... It is not true that the Pope brings the young from one end of the world to the other. It is they who bring him.* Even though he is getting older, they urge him to be young; they do not permit him to forget his experience, his discovery of youth and its great importance for the life of every man. I believe this explains a great deal.

Crossing the Threshold of Hope

———⁂———

Basic Lesson of Christianity

This is the confession I wish to make again in your presence today, dear brothers in the episcopate. *Indeed, we serve together!* I shall never forget the words of the Primate Cardinal Wyszynski, who during the celebrations for the millennium of the Baptism of Poland, in a period of great tension with the Communist authorities, said at Lublin: *"I serve here! I do not command, but I serve!"*

Message Broadcast to the Basilica of St. Mary Major, May 19, 1994

Some Thoughts for a Feast of Mary

Dear brothers, allow me to think back to what happened ... years ago in St. Peter's Square. We all remember that moment during the afternoon when *some pistol shots were fired at the pope* with the intention of killing him. The bullet that passed through his abdomen is now in the shrine of Fatima; his sash, pierced by this bullet, is in the *shrine of Jasna Gora*. It was a motherly hand that guided the path of the bullets, and the agonizing pope, rushed to the Gemelli Polyclinic, halted at the threshold of death.... Thanks to the gift of her divine Motherhood, the Blessed Virgin became, as St. Ambrose and other Fathers taught, *a figure of the Church in the order of faith, love, and perfect union with Christ.* This is precisely why the Church itself is called *Mother and Virgin.* In contemplating the unique holiness of Mary and imitating her charity in faithfully fulfilling the Father's will, *the Church also becomes a mother,* when by preaching the gospel and administering Baptism, she brings forth to new life sons and daughters conceived by the Holy Spirit and begotten of God. *The Church herself is a virgin,* because she keeps in its entirety and purity the faith she pledged to her Spouse, imitating the mother of her Lord; and by the power of the Holy Spirit, she keeps intact her faith, firm hope, and sincere charity.

Message Broadcast to the Basilica of St. Mary Major, May 19, 1994

June

June 1

The Month of the Sacred Heart

Today begins the month of June, dedicated to the Sacred Heart of Jesus, that divine heart pierced by a lance on the cross, so that the treasures of grace would flow from it for all men. It is an everlasting source from which every believer and the whole Church draw the ever new vigor of faith, hope, and charity. Devotion to Christ's heart cannot be separated from the Eucharist, the sacrament of the Lord's Body and Blood, whose solemn feast occurs precisely tomorrow. Here in Rome it will be celebrated with the traditional, moving procession from St. John Lateran to St. Mary Major.

Discourse at the Vatican, June 1, 1994

---∞∞∞---

The Coming of the Holy Spirit

The Church is celebrating the Solemnity of Pentecost, which recalls the miraculous outpouring of the Holy Spirit upon Mary and the apostles in the Upper Room. Fifty days after Easter, what Christ had promised the disciples came to pass: that they would be baptized with the Holy Spirit (Acts 1:5) and would thus be clothed in power from on high (Luke 24:49) to have the strength to proclaim the gospel to all the nations. Inspired by the fire of the Spirit, the apostles came out of the Upper Room and began to speak about the dead and risen Christ to the faithful from every country who had arrived in Jerusalem; each one heard them speaking in his or her own native language. With Pentecost, God fulfilled the plan he had revealed to Abraham to give life to a new people. The Church was born, the Mystical Body of Christ, scattered across the world. She is made up of men and women of every race and culture, gathered together in faith and in the love of the Most Blessed Trinity to be a sign and an instrument of the unity of the whole human race (*Lumen Gentium*). Conformed by the Holy Spirit to Christ the new man, believers become his witnesses, sowers of hope, and artisans of mercy and of peace.

Discourse for Pentecost Sunday, May 30, 2004

Jesus Also Calls Children to Be His Witnesses

Dear boys and girls, the faith you have in Jesus and your love for him, joined with the enthusiasm and imagination typical of children, enable you to "color the world" to make it more beautiful and more just, conquering poverty, disease, and hatred, which unfortunately cause so much suffering among children as well. I know that every year you pool what you have and take material and spiritual care of the world's children. The Church is very happy about this: that children and young people help each other. *It is very good that in the family brothers and sisters love one another from childhood.* I praise you for this: be missionaries always and everywhere! Jesus calls every individual to be his witness: some in their homeland, others in distant countries, but all must feel that they are missionaries!

Message to the Pontifical Society of the Missionary Childhood, Gemelli Clinic,
Rome, Italy, May 20, 1994

—⟶∞⟵—

The Bond Between the Church in America and the Apostolic See

I am grateful for the deep affection that American Catholics have traditionally felt for the *Successor of Peter*, as well as their sensitivity and generosity to the needs of the Holy See and the universal Church. The bishops of the United States have always shown a great love for the one in whom the Lord established "the lasting and visible source and foundation of the unity both of faith and of communion" (*Lumen Gentium*). Your abiding loyalty to the Roman pontiff has led you to seek ways to strengthen the bond linking the Church in America with the Apostolic See. These devoted sentiments are a fruit of the *hierarchical communion* linking all members of the episcopal college with the pope. At the same time, they constitute *a great spiritual resource for the renewal of the Church in the United States*. In encouraging your people to deepen their fidelity to the magisterium and their union of mind and heart with the Successor of Peter, you offer them the inspirational leadership that is needed to carry them forward into the third millennium.

Message to the Bishops of New York on their Ad Limina Visit, *Rome, Italy, October 8, 2004*

June 5

God Is Father and Mother:
A Reflection for the Family

I would like to draw your attention to a basic aspect of conjugal love: its intrinsic *openness to life*. The *Catechism of the Catholic Church* stresses this when it points out that the spouses' love "naturally tends to be fruitful. A child does not come from outside as something added on to the mutual love of the spouses, but springs from the very heart of that mutual giving, as its fruit and fulfillment." Grasping the mysterious greatness of this event is of fundamental importance. As I wrote in the *Letter to Families,* "*God himself is present* in human fatherhood and motherhood.... Indeed, God alone is the source of that 'image and likeness' which is proper to the human being, as it was received at creation. Begetting is the continuation of the creation."

Discourse at Castel Gandolfo, July 17, 1994

Parents: God's Co-workers

The Church's teaching about responsible parenthood is based on the essential anthropological and ethical foundation (of fidelity and responsibility). Unfortunately, *Catholic thought is often misunderstood* as if the Church supported an ideology of fertility at all costs, urging married couples to procreate indiscriminately and without thought for the future. But one need only study the pronouncements of the magisterium to know that this is not so. Truly, in begetting life the spouses fulfill one of the highest dimensions of their calling: they are *God's co-workers.* Precisely for this reason they must have an extremely responsible attitude. In deciding whether or not to have a child, they must not be motivated by selfishness or carelessness, but by a prudent, conscious generosity that weighs the possibilities and circumstances, and especially gives priority to the welfare of the unborn child.

Discourse at Castel Gandolfo, July 17, 1994

June 7

Power Through Weakness

In the Letter to the Romans, the apostle Paul deals still more fully with the theme of the "birth of power in weakness," the spiritual tempering of man in the midst of trials and tribulations, which is the particular vocation of those who share in Christ's sufferings. "More than that, we rejoice in our sufferings, knowing that suffering produces endurance, and endurance produces character, and character produces hope, and hope does not disappoint us, because God's love has been poured into our hearts through the Holy Spirit which has been given to us" (5:3–5). Suffering, as it were, contains a special call to the virtue that man must exercise on his own part. And this is the virtue of perseverance in bearing whatever disturbs and causes harm. In doing this, the individual unleashes hope, which maintains in him the conviction that suffering will not get the better of him, that it will not deprive him of his dignity as a human being, a dignity linked to awareness of the meaning of life. And indeed this meaning makes itself known together with the working of God's love, which is the supreme gift of the Holy Spirit. The more he shares in this love, man rediscovers himself more and more fully in suffering: he rediscovers the "soul" he thought he had "lost" because of suffering.

Apostolic Letter Salvifici Doloris, *February 11, 1984*

―∞∞∞―

A Message to Colombia

In fact, holiness is the goal and the basic program of all pastoral action. "It would be a contradiction to settle for a life of mediocrity, marked by a minimalist ethic and a shallow religiosity" (*Novo Millennio Ineunte*). For these very reasons, the visit of the relics of St. Thérèse of the Child Jesus to Colombia is an opportunity to become aware that we are all called to holiness, a fundamental objective of the Church's mission.

Address to the Bishops of Colombia on their Ad Limina *Visit, Rome, Italy,*
September 30, 2004

A Sense of Moral Reality

In analyzing the situation of the Church and of Colombian society, you noted the increase in the truly disturbing phenomenon of moral deterioration. It appears in many different forms and affects the most varied contexts of personal, family, and social life, undermining the intrinsic importance of moral rectitude and seriously threatening the very authenticity of the faith, which "gives rise to and calls for a consistent life commitment; it entails and brings to perfection the acceptance and observance of God's commandments" (*Veritatis Splendor*). It is a phenomenon that is partly due to ideologies that prevent the human being from clearly recognizing good in order to put it into practice. More often, however, it is a matter of a blurred conscience or one that deceitfully seeks to justify the person's conduct, aided by an atmosphere that dazzlingly displays false values that tend to mask or denigrate the supreme good to which individuals aspire in the depth of their hearts. Moreover, it is a very significant challenge that entails various types of pastoral action modeled on Jesus, the Good Shepherd, who came precisely to call sinners (Matt. 9:13), coming close to many of them and urging them to change their way of life (Luke 19:8).

Address to the Bishops of Colombia on Their Ad Limina *Visit, Rome, Italy,*
September 30, 2004

---⊶∞⊷---

A Sense of Moral Responsibility

Jesus's mercy and compassion for human frailty did not prevent him from clearly pointing out what conduct to follow or which activities are most in tune with the divine will, and he often demolished the subtle arguments of his adversaries; this earned him the admiration of the people, "for he taught them as one who had authority, and not as their scribes" (Matt. 7:29). Nor did the Lord shrink from denouncing hypocrisy or abuse. Following his teachings, the apostles never ceased in their preaching to insist on the ethical demands of those called to live "in true righteousness and holiness" (Eph. 4:24). As his successors, it is the duty of bishops to teach "that worldly things and human institutions are ordered, according to the plan of God the Creator, towards the salvation of men" (*Christus Dominus*). Proclaiming justice, truth, fidelity, and love of neighbor with all their concrete implications is inherent in proclaiming the gospel in its integrity. This proclamation contributes to the formation of an upright conscience and enlightens all people of goodwill: thus, "They will listen, and every one turn from his evil way" (Jer. 26:3).

Address to the Bishops of Colombia on Their Ad Limina *Visit, Rome, Italy,*
September 30, 2004

Look at the Face of Christ

In the midst of the *Year of the Rosary,* I issued the encyclical letter *Ecclesia de Eucharistia* with the intention of shedding light on the mystery of the Eucharist in its inseparable and vital relation to the Church. I urged all the faithful to celebrate the eucharistic Sacrifice with due reverence, offering to Jesus present in the Eucharist, both within and outside Mass, the worship demanded by so great a Mystery. Above all, I suggested once again the need for a eucharistic spirituality and pointed to Mary, "woman of the Eucharist," as its model. *The Year of the Eucharist* takes place against *a background that has been enriched by the passage of the years,* while remaining ever rooted in the theme of Christ and the contemplation of his face. In a certain sense, it is meant to be a year of synthesis, *the high point of a journey in progress.*

Apostolic Letter Mane Nobiscum Domine, *October 7, 2004*

The Mission of the Son

The whole New Testament expresses the truth of the sending of the Son by the Father. This truth is made concrete in the messianic message of Jesus Christ. In this regard, of particular importance are the numerous texts of John's Gospel, to which we must first of all refer (John 8:16; 18:18; 7:28–29) and, ..."My food is to do the will of him who sent me and to accomplish his work" (4:34). As is seen in John's Gospel, Jesus often speaks of himself in the first person as one sent by the Father. In a special way, the same truth will emerge in the priestly prayer, where Jesus, recommending his disciples to the Father, emphasizes, "They ... know in truth that I have come from you; and they have believed that you have sent me" (17:8). And continuing this prayer on the eve of his Passion, Jesus says, "As you sent me into the world, so I have sent them into the world" (17:18). As though referring directly to the High-Priestly Prayer (of the Last Supper) the first words addressed to the disciples on the evening of the day of the Resurrection are: "As the Father has sent me, even so I send you" (20:21).

Discourse at the Vatican, June 24, 1987

June 13

≈≈≈

The Heart's Deepest Longing

When the disciples on the way to Emmaus asked Jesus to stay "with" them, he responded by giving them a much greater gift: through the sacrament of the Eucharist he found a way to stay "in" them. Receiving the Eucharist means entering into a profound communion with Jesus. "Abide in me, as I in you" (John 15:4). This relationship of profound and mutual "abiding" *enables us to have a certain foretaste of heaven on earth.* Is this not the greatest of human yearnings? Is this not what God had in mind when he brought about in history his plan of salvation? God has placed in human hearts a "hunger" for his word (Amos 8:11), a hunger that will be satisfied only by full union with him. Eucharistic communion was given so that we might be "sated" with God here on earth, in expectation of our complete fulfillment in heaven.

Apostolic Letter Mane Nobiscum Domine, *October 7, 2004*

———ↂ———

"Solidarity" the Preferred Word for Communion

The Eucharist is not merely an expression of communion in the Church's life; it is also a *project of solidarity* for all of humanity. In the celebration of the Eucharist the Church constantly renews her awareness of being a "sign and instrument" not only of intimate union with God but also of the unity of the whole human race. Each Mass, even when celebrated in obscurity or in isolation, always has a universal character. The Christian who takes part in the Eucharist learns to become a *promoter of communion, peace, and solidarity* in every situation. More than ever, our troubled world, which began the new millennium with the spectre of terrorism and the tragedy of war, demands that Christians learn to experience the Eucharist as *a great school of peace,* forming men and women who, at various levels of responsibility in social, cultural and political life, can become promoters of dialogue and communion, at *the service of the least.*

Apostolic Letter Mane Nobiscum Domine, *October 7, 2004*

June 15

---oggo---

A Church of Martyrs

"At the end of the second millennium, the Church has once again become a Church of martyrs" (*Tertio Millennio Adveniente*). The witness of the Trappists of Notre-Dame de l'Atlas is linked to that of Bishop Pierre Lucien Claverie of Oran and the many children of the African continent who in this period have given their lives for God and for their brothers and sisters, beginning with those who persecuted and killed them. Their witness is the victory of the Cross, the victory of God's merciful love, which saves the world. Brother Christian de Cherge's testimony has offered everyone a key to interpreting his own and his confreres' tragedy, whose ultimate meaning is the gift of life in Christ. "My life," he wrote, "was given to God and this country."

Message to the Cistercians of the Strict Observance, Rome, Italy,
October 12, 1996

Enough War, Enough Violence

I am in solidarity with this step of yours (an open-table discussion regarding terrorism and violence held by all of the Christian leaders of Lebanon), dear brothers, and with you I feel united with all those in your country who experience anguish and the temptation to despair. We make our own the psalmist's appeal, "In my distress I called to the Lord, and he heard my prayer" (Ps. 120:1). And we ardently await the blessed day when weapons will be silent forever, when the wounded can be cared for, when the dead will be given a dignified burial, when all people can find the minimum of tranquility that will allow them to build a home, to earn their daily bread, and to give their children an appropriate upbringing. All of this without having to fear that blind violence will emerge again to wipe out so many persistent and often heroic efforts.... How I would like to erase from the children's eyes those horrible sights of blood and destruction, to express my compassion to all parents who must care for children or adults who have been handicapped for life because of their injuries! And most of all to pray with you that the Lord may remove from every heart all feelings of hatred, violence, and revenge!

Message to His Beatitude Nasrallah Pierre Sfeir, Patriarch of
Antioch of the Maronites, May 25, 1990

———— ⊛ ————

The Significance of Blessed Pier Giorgio Frassati

"Sanctify Christ as Lord in your hearts. Always be ready to give an explanation to anyone who asks you for a reason for your hope" (1 Pet. 3:15). In our century, *Pier Giorgio Frassati*, whom I have the joy of declaring Blessed, ... *incarnated these words of St. Peter in his own life.* The power of the spirit of truth, united to Christ, made him a modern witness to the hope that springs from the gospel and to the grace of salvation, which works in human hearts. Thus he became *a living witness and courageous defender of this hope in the name of the Christian youth* of the twentieth century. *Faith and charity, the true driving force of his existence,* made him active and diligent in the milieu in which he lived, in his family and school, in the university and society; they transformed him into a joyful, enthusiastic apostle of Christ, a passionate follower of his message and charity. Certainly at a superficial glance, Pier Giorgio Frassati's lifestyle, that of a modern young man who was full of life, does not present anything out of the ordinary. This, however, is the originality of his virtue, which invites us to reflect upon it and impels us to imitate it.

Beatification Homily at the Vatican, May 20, 1990

———∞∞∞———

The Problem of Suffering

Suffering is always a trial—at times a very hard one—to which humanity is subjected. The gospel paradox of weakness and strength often speaks to us from the pages of the Letters of St. Paul, a paradox particularly experienced by the Apostle himself and together with him experienced by all who share Christ's sufferings. Paul writes: "I will all the more gladly boast of my weaknesses, that the power of Christ may rest upon me" (2 Cor. 12:9). Also we read: "And therefore I suffer as I do. But I am not ashamed, for I know whom I have believed" (2 Tim. 1:12). And to the Philippians he will even say: "I can do all things in him who strengthens me" (4:13). Those who share in Christ's sufferings have before their eyes the Paschal Mystery of the Cross and Resurrection, in which Christ descends, in a first phase, to the ultimate limits of human weakness and impotence: indeed, he dies nailed to the cross. But if at the same time in this weakness there is accomplished his lifting up, confirmed by the power of the Resurrection, then this means that the weaknesses of all human sufferings are capable of being infused with the same power of God manifested in Christ's Cross. In such a concept, to suffer means to become particularly susceptible, particularly open to the working of the salvific powers of God, offered to humanity in Christ. In him God has confirmed his desire to act especially through suffering, which is man's weakness and emptying of self, and he wishes to make his power known precisely in this weakness and emptying of self.

Apostolic Letter Salvifici Doloris, *February 11, 1984*

June 19

The Issue of Health

Believers are called to develop the insight of faith, as they look at the sublime and mysterious value of life, even when it seems frail and vulnerable. "This outlook does not give in to discouragement when confronted by those who are sick, suffering, outcast, or at death's door. Instead, in all these situations it feels challenged to find meaning, and precisely in these circumstances it is open to perceiving in the face of every person a call to encounter, dialogue and solidarity" (*Evangelium Vitae*). This task especially involves health professionals: doctors, pharmacists, nurses, chaplains, men and women religious, administrators, and volunteer workers who, by virtue of their profession, are called in a special capacity to be guardians of human life. However, it also calls into question every other human being, starting with the relatives of the sick person. They know that "the request which arises from the human heart in the supreme confrontation with suffering and death, especially when faced with the temptation to give up in utter desperation, is above all a request for companionship, sympathy, and support in the time of trial. It is a plea for help to keep on hoping when all human hopes fail" (*Evangelium Vitae*).

Message for the World Day of the Sick, Castel Gandolfo, August 6, 1999

An Ecology Worthy of Man

The proposed model of health requires that the Church and society create an ecology worthy of man. The environment, in fact, is connected with the health of the individual and of the population: it constitutes the human being's "home" and the complex of resources entrusted to his care and stewardship, the garden to be tended and the field to be cultivated. But the external ecology of the person must be combined with an interior, moral ecology, the only one that is fitting for a proper concept of health. Considered in its entirety, human health thus becomes an attribute of life, a resource for the service of one's neighbor and openness to salvation.

Message for the World Day of the Sick, Castel Gandolfo, August 6, 1999

June 21

A Visit by God

Only in Christ, the incarnate Word, Redeemer of mankind and victor over death, is it possible to find satisfactory answers to fundamental questions about illness. In the light of Christ's death and Resurrection, illness no longer appears as an exclusively negative event; rather, it is seen as a "visit by God," an opportunity "to release love, in order to give birth to works of love toward neighbor, in order to transform the whole of human civilization into a civilization of love" (*Salvifici Doloris*). The history of the Church and of Christian spirituality offers very broad testimony to this. Over the centuries shining pages have been written of heroism in suffering accepted and offered in union with Christ. And no less marvelous pages have been traced out through humble service to the poor and the sick, in whose tormented flesh the presence of the poor, crucified Christ has been recognized. The World Day of the Sick—in its preparation, realization, and objectives—is not meant to be reduced to a mere external display centering on certain initiatives, however praiseworthy they may be, but is intended to reach consciences to make them aware of the valuable contribution that human and Christian service to those suffering makes to better understanding among people and, consequently, to building real peace. Indeed, peace presupposes, as its preliminary condition, that special attention be reserved for the suffering and the sick by public authorities, national and international organizations, and every person of goodwill.

Discourse from the Vatican for the First Annual World Day of the Sick,
October 21, 1992

Shrouded in Dark Shadows

In our day human society appears to be shrouded in dark shadows while it is shaken by tragic events and shattered by catastrophic natural disasters. Nevertheless, as "on the night he was betrayed" (1 Cor. 11:23), also today Jesus "breaks the bread" (Matt. 26:26) for us in our eucharistic celebrations and offers himself under the sacramental sign of his love for all humankind. This is why I underlined that "the Eucharist is not merely an expression of communion in the Church's life; it is also a project of solidarity for all of humanity" (*Mane Nobiscum Domine*); it is "bread from heaven," which gives eternal life (John 6:33) and opens the human heart to a great hope. Present in the Eucharist, the same Redeemer who saw the needy crowds and was filled with compassion "because they were harassed and dejected, like sheep without a shepherd" (Matt. 9:36) continues through the centuries to show compassion for humanity, poor and suffering. And it is in his name that pastoral workers and missionaries travel unexplored paths to carry the "bread" of salvation to all. They are spurred on by the knowledge that, united with Christ, they "center not just on the history of the Church, but also on the history of humanity" (Eph. 1:10; Col. 1:15–20; *Mane Nobiscum Domine*). It is possible to meet the deepest longings of the human heart. Jesus alone can satisfy humanity's hunger for love and thirst for justice; he alone makes it possible for every human person to share in eternal life. . . .

Letter for Mission Sunday, February 22, 2005

Our Personal Untiring Cooperation

Jesus Christ, sent by the Father, the first Missionary, is the only Savior of the world. He is the Way, the Truth, and the Life; as he was yesterday, he is today and will be tomorrow, until the end of time, when all things will be united in him. The salvation brought by Jesus penetrates the intimate depth of the human person, freeing us from the Evil One, from sin and from eternal death. Salvation is the coming of "new life" in Christ. It is a gratuitous gift of God, who seeks our free adhesion: in fact, it must be won, day after day, "through abnegation and the Cross" (*Evangelii Nuntiandi*). This calls for *our personal untiring cooperation* through the will's docile acceptance of God's plan. This is the way to reach the safe and definitive haven, which Christ won through his Cross. There is no alternative liberation through which we may obtain true peace and joy, which can only come from an encounter with God-Truth: "You will learn the truth and the truth will make you free" (John 8:32). This, in brief, is the good news that Christ was sent to bring to the "poor," to the captives of so many forms of slavery in this world, to the "afflicted" of every era and latitude, to all people, since this salvation is for every person, and every man and woman on earth has the right to be told about it: it is a matter of our eternal destiny. "Everyone who calls upon the name of the Lord will be saved" (Rom. 10:13), St. Paul reminds us. No one, however, can invoke Jesus, believe in him, unless they are told about him, unless they hear his name (Rom. 10:14–15).

Discourse from the Vatican for World Mission Sunday, October 19, 1997

June 24

⎯⎯ ∞∞∞ ⎯⎯

The Modern Movement of Peoples

In this complex phenomenon, numerous elements come in: the tendency to foster the political and juridical unity of the human family, the noteworthy increase in cultural exchanges, interdependence among States, the liberalization of trade and, above all, of capital, the multiplication of multinational enterprises, the imbalance between rich and poor countries, the development of the means of communication and transportation. The interplay of such factors produces the movement of masses from one area of the globe to another. The vastness and complexity of the phenomenon calls for a profound analysis of the structural changes that have taken place, namely the globalization of economics and of social life. The convergence of races, civilizations, and cultures within one and the same juridical and social order, poses an urgent problem of cohabitation. We are witnessing a profound change in the way of thinking and living, which cannot but present ambiguous aspects together with the positive elements. The sense of temporariness induces one to prefer what is new to the detriment of stability and a clear hierarchy of values. At the same time, the spirit becomes more curious and open, more sensitive and ready for dialogue. In this climate, people may be induced to deepen their own convictions, but also to indulge in superficial relativism. Mobility always implies an uprooting from the original environment, often translated into an experience of marked solitude accompanied by the risk of fading into anonymity. This situation may lead to a rejection of the new environment, but also to accepting it acritically, . . .

Address from the Vatican for the World Day of Migration, November 9, 1997

—⊶∞⊷—

The Perennial Problem of "Inculturation"

For many, going to a foreign country means encountering ways of life and thinking that are foreign, that produce different reactions. Cities and nations increasingly present multiethnic and multicultural communities. This is a great challenge for Christians too. A serene reading of this new situation highlights many values that merit to be greatly appreciated. The Holy Spirit is not conditioned by ethnic groups or cultures. He enlightens and inspires people through many mysterious ways. Through various paths, he brings everyone close to salvation, to Jesus, the Word incarnate, who is "the fulfillment of the yearning of all the world's religions and, as such, he is their sole and definitive completion" (*Tertio Millennio Adveniente*). This reading will surely help the non-Christian migrants see their own religiosity as a strong element of cultural identity, and at the same time it will make it possible for them to discover the values of the Christian faith. To this end, the collaboration of the local churches and missionaries who know the immigrants' culture will be more useful than ever. This means establishing links between the community of migrants and those of the countries of origin, and at the same time informing the communities of arrival regarding the cultures and the religions of the immigrants and the reasons that have caused them to emigrate. It is important to help the community of arrival be open not only to charitable hospitality, but also to meeting, collaboration, and exchange.

Address from the Vatican for the World Day of Migration,
February 2, 2001

Freedom: The Constitutive Element of Faith

Enriching intercultural and interreligious dialogue presupposes a climate that is permeated with mutual trust and respects religious freedom. Among the sectors to be illuminated by the light of Christ, therefore, is freedom, particularly religious freedom, which is still at times limited or restricted. It is the premise and guarantee of every other authentic form of freedom. "Religious freedom"—I wrote in *Redemptoris Missio*—"is not a question of the religion of the majority or the minority, but of an inalienable right of each and every human person." Freedom is a constitutive dimension of the Christian faith itself, since it is not a transmission of human traditions or a point of arrival of philosophical discussion, but a free gift of God, which is communicated with due respect for the human conscience. It is the Lord who acts efficaciously through his Spirit; it is he who is the true protagonist. People are instruments that he uses, to each of whom he assigns a singular role. The gospel is for everyone. No one is excluded from the possibility of participating in the joy of the divine Kingdom. The mission of the Church today is exactly that of giving every human being, regardless of culture or race, the concrete possibility of meeting Christ. I wholeheartedly wish that this possibility be offered to all migrants and for this, I assure my prayers.

Angelus Message, Krakow, Poland, August 18, 2002

⚘

Pastoral Concern for the Problem of Alcoholism

Particularly worrisome is the effect that the abuse of alcohol has had on the young people of modern society. Many factors come into play in this social evil, not the least of which are peer pressure and group involvement in surroundings that are unwholesome and that prevent young people from maturing and becoming happy and healthy human beings. The ready availability of alcohol as compared to other drugs makes the percentage of users very high among the young, and this too is cause for serious concern. Likewise, the economic conditions existing in society, such as high rates of poverty and unemployment, can contribute to a young person's sense of restlessness, insecurity, frustration, and social alienation and can draw that person to the fantasy world of alcohol as an escape from the problems of life. However significant these factors may be, it is the family that most powerfully influences young people in the area of alcohol. The example given by parents in all things, including the abuse of alcohol, is foremost in the formation of the young. The child is watchful and alert in observing how the father and mother cope with the pressures of life. The child can be easily led to imitate behavior patterns that have been learned at home. Parents must take special care to provide a positive example in this regard, lest the temptation to resort to unhealthy ways of psychological escape be communicated to their children.

Address from the Vatican to the International Institute for the Prevention and Treatment of Alcoholism, June 7, 1985

———— ∞ ————

The Family and the Alcoholic

Parents should perceive as important the fostering of family values, that is, forming the family into a true community of persons, where husband and wife, parents and children live in relationships of genuine love for each other. Love is the point of departure and the final goal of the family. Love is the inner dynamism that leads the family to ever deeper and more intense communion (*Familiaris Consortio*). The example that parents offer to their children in showing that love, which implies mutual respect, forgiveness, and moderation in their own behavior, will mark the path for their children to follow. I wish to offer my encouragement to all who work toward a solution to the problem of alcohol abuse. In particular, I would like to thank all those who, in the name of fundamental human solidarity, strive to assist people who suffer from alcoholism. I am thinking of those experts, doctors, nurses, and other individuals as well as the institutions especially established for this purpose, who perform an incalculable service to their suffering neighbors. The compassion that motivates this activity, reminiscent of the spirit of the Good Samaritan, is a beautiful testimony to the concern of people today to pay closer attention to the sufferings of their neighbors and to seek to deal with them with ever greater skill.

Address from the Vatican to the International Institute for the Prevention and Treatment of Alcoholism, June 7, 1985

The Significance of Peter and Paul

The Church is celebrating the feast day of the holy apostles Peter and Paul: the fisherman of Galilee who first professed faith in Christ, and the teacher and doctor who proclaimed salvation to the Gentiles. Through the design of divine Providence they both came to Rome, where they suffered martyrdom within a few years. From that time, the city that had been the capital of a great empire was called to a very different glory: to be the home of the Apostolic See that presides over the universal mission of the Church to spread throughout the world the gospel of Christ, Redeemer of humanity and of history. This year, today's Solemnity is gladdened by the presence of His Holiness Bartholomew I, Ecumenical Patriarch of Constantinople, whom I have just had the joy of welcoming and greeting. His welcome visit has a special reason. Forty years ago, to be precise, in January 1964, Pope Paul VI and Patriarch Athenagoras I met in Jerusalem and exchanged a fraternal embrace. That embrace has become the symbol of the longed-for reconciliation between the Catholic Church and the Orthodox churches, as well as a prophecy of hope on the journey toward full unity among Christians. I have invited Patriarch Bartholomew I to take part in Holy Mass at 6 PM later today in St. Peter's Square, at which I will preside. Together we will give the homily and proclaim the common profession of faith.

Angelus Address for the Feast of the Holy Apostles Peter and Paul,
June 29, 2004

Christ: The Good Samaritan

It is a question of fighting the indifference that makes individuals and groups withdraw selfishly into themselves. The example of Jesus, the Good Samaritan, not only spurs one to help the sick, but also to do all one can to reintegrate him in society. For Christ, in fact, healing is also this reintegration: just as sickness excludes the human being from the community, so healing must bring him to rediscover his place in the family, in the Church and in society. I extend a warm invitation to those involved professionally or voluntarily in the world of health to fix their gaze on the divine Samaritan, so that their service can become a prefiguration of definitive salvation and a proclamation of new heavens and a new earth "in which righteousness dwells" (2 Pet. 3:13). Jesus did not only treat and heal the sick, but he was also a tireless promoter of health through his saving presence, teaching and action. His love for man was expressed in relationships full of humanity, which led him to understand, to show compassion and bring comfort, harmoniously combining tenderness and strength. He was moved by the beauty of nature, he was sensitive to human suffering, he fought evil and injustice. He faced the negative aspects of this experience courageously and, fully aware of the implications, communicated the certainty of a new world. In him, the human condition showed its face redeemed and the deepest human aspirations found fulfillment. He wants to communicate this harmonious fullness of life to people today.

Message from Castel Gondolfo for the World Day of the Sick, August 6, 1999

July

———— ∞∞∞ ————

July 1

If You Have Accepted Christ, Proclaim It with the Pronoun "I"

If you have met Christ, live Christ, live with Christ! Proclaim it in the first person, as genuine testimony: *"For me life is Christ."* That is true liberation: to proclaim Christ Jesus, free of ties, present in men and women, transformed, made new creatures. Why instead at times does our testimony seem useless? Because we present Jesus without the full seductive power of his person, without revealing the treasures of the sublime ideal inherent in following him; and because we are not always successful in demonstrating conviction, translated into living terms, regarding the extraordinary value of the gift of ourselves to the ecclesial cause we serve.... In prayer, it is in that trusting contact with God our Father that we can discern better what our strengths and weaknesses are, because the Spirit comes to our aid. The same Spirit speaks to us and slowly immerses us in the divine mysteries, in God's design for humanity, which he realizes through our willingness to serve him.

Discourse at the Vatican, January 26, 1979

On Pilgrimage: The One Truth of Sinai

On the mountain of the Transfiguration, God speaks from the cloud, as he had done on Sinai. But now he says: "This is my beloved Son; listen to him" (Mark 9:7). He commands us to listen to his Son, because "no one knows the Father except the Son . . ." (Matt. 11:27). And so we learn that the true name of God is Father! The name that is beyond all other names: Abba! (Gal. 4:6). And in Jesus we learn that our true name is son, daughter! We learn that the God of the Exodus and the Covenant sets his people free because they are his sons and daughters, created not for slavery but for "the glorious liberty of the children of God" (Rom. 8:21). So when St. Paul writes that we "have died to the law through the body of Christ" (Rom. 7:4), he does not mean that the law of Sinai is past. He means that the Ten Commandments now make themselves heard through the voice of the Beloved Son. Persons delivered by Jesus Christ into true freedom are aware of being bound not externally by a multitude of prescriptions, but internally by the love that has taken hold in the deepest recesses of their hearts. The Ten Commandments are the law of freedom: not the freedom to follow our blind passions, but the freedom to love, to choose what is good in every situation, even when to do so is a burden. It is not an impersonal law that we obey; what is required is loving surrender to the Father through Christ Jesus in the Holy Spirit (Rom. 6:14; Gal. 5:18). Sinai stands at the very heart of the truth about man and his destiny.

Homily from St. Catherine's Monastery, Mt. Sinai, Egypt, February 26, 2000

July 3

On Pilgrimage: Encountering the Ten Commandments

The encounter of God and Moses on the Mountain enshrines at the heart of our religion the mystery of liberating obedience, which finds its fulfillment in the perfect obedience of Christ in the Incarnation and on the Cross (Phil. 2:8; Heb. 5:8–9). We too shall be truly free if we learn to obey as Jesus did (Heb. 5:8). The Ten Commandments are not an arbitrary imposition of a tyrannical Lord. They were written in stone; but before that, they were written on the human heart as the universal moral law, valid in every time and place. Today as always, the Ten Words of the Law provide the only true basis for the lives of individuals, societies, and nations. Today as always, they are the only future of the human family. They save man from the destructive force of egoism, hatred, and falsehood. They point out all the false gods that draw him into slavery: the love of self to the exclusion of God, the greed for power and pleasure that overturns the order of justice and degrades our human dignity and that of our neighbor. If we turn from these false idols and follow the God who sets his people free and remains always with them, then we shall emerge like Moses, after forty days on the Mountain, "shining with glory" (St. Gregory of Nyssa, *The Life of Moses*), ablaze with the light of God! To keep the commandments is to be faithful to God, but it is also to be faithful to ourselves, to our true nature and our deepest aspirations.

Homily from St. Catherine's Monastery, Mt. Sinai, Egypt, February 26, 2000

———∞∞∞———

On Pilgrimage: The Monastery of St. Catherine

In pursuit of this truth, the monks of this monastery pitched their tent in the shadow of Sinai. The Monastery of St. Catherine bears all the marks of time and human turmoil, but it stands indomitable as a witness to divine wisdom and love. For centuries monks from all Christian traditions lived and prayed together in this monastery, listening to the Word, in whom dwells the fullness of the Father's wisdom and love. In this very monastery, St. John Climacus wrote *The Ladder of Divine Ascent*, a spiritual masterpiece that continues to inspire monks and nuns, from East and West, generation after generation. All this has taken place under the mighty protection of the Great Mother of God. As early as the third century Egyptian Christians appealed to her with words of trust: "We flee to your protection, O Holy Mother of God!" *Sub tuum praesidium confugimus, sancta Dei Genetrix!* Through the centuries, this monastery has been an exceptional meeting place for people belonging to different Churches, traditions, and cultures. *I pray that in the new millennium the Monastery of St. Catherine will be a radiant beacon calling the Churches to know one another better and to rediscover the importance in the eyes of God of the things that unite us in Christ.*

Homily from St. Catherine's Monastery, Mt. Sinai, Egypt, February 26, 2000

On Pilgrimage: Egypt, Cradle of Christianity

Egypt has been home to the Church from the beginning. Founded upon the apostolic preaching and authority of St. Mark, the Church of Alexandria soon became one of the leading communities in the early Christian world. Venerable bishops like St. Athanasius and St. Cyril bore witness to faith in the Triune God and in Jesus Christ, True God and True man, as defined by the first ecumenical councils. It was in the desert of Egypt that monastic life originated, in both its solitary and communal forms, under the spiritual fatherhood of St. Anthony and St. Pachomius. Thanks to them and to the great impact of their spiritual writings, monastic life became part of our common heritage. During recent decades that same monastic charism has flourished anew, and it irradiates a vital spiritual message far beyond the borders of Egypt. Today we give thanks to God that we are ever more aware of our common heritage, in faith and in the richness of sacramental life. We also have in common that filial veneration of the Virgin Mary, Mother of God, for which the Coptic and all the Eastern Churches are renowned. And "when we speak about a common heritage, we must acknowledge as part of it, not only the institutions, rites, means of salvation, and the traditions which all the communities have preserved and by which they have been shaped, but first and foremost this reality of holiness" (Encyclical Letter *Ut Unum Sint*).

Speech at the Cathedral of Our Lady of Egypt, Cairo, February 25, 2000

On Pilgrimage: The Action of the Spirit

From the beginning, this common apostolic tradition and heritage has been transmitted and explained in various forms, which take account of the specific cultural character of peoples. As far back as the fifth century, however, theological and nontheological factors, combined with a lack of fraternal love and understanding, led to painful divisions in the one Church of Christ. Mistrust and hostility arose between Christians, in contradiction with the fervent desire of our Lord Jesus Christ who prayed "that they may all be one" (John 17:21). The Holy Spirit has brought the Christian Churches and communities closer together in a movement of reconciliation. I recall the meeting between Pope Paul VI and His Holiness Pope Shenouda III (of the Coptic Church) in 1973, and the *Common Christological Declaration* which they signed on that occasion. I repeat what I wrote in my Encyclical Letter *Ut Unum Sint*, that whatever relates to the unity of all Christian communities clearly forms part of the concerns of the primacy of the Bishop of Rome. I renew the invitation to all "Church leaders and their theologians to engage with me in a patient and fraternal dialogue on this subject, a dialogue in which, leaving useless controversies behind, we could listen to one another, keeping before us only the will of Christ for his Church." I ask the Holy Spirit to shine his light upon us, enlightening all the Pastors and theologians of our Churches, that we may seek together the forms in which this ministry may accomplish a service of love.

Speech at the Cathedral of Our Lady of Egypt, Cairo, February 25, 2000

July 7

On Pilgrimage: Common Witness

Our communion in the one Lord Jesus Christ, in the one Holy Spirit, and in one baptism already represents a deep and fundamental reality. This communion enables us to bear common witness to our faith in a whole range of ways, and indeed it demands that we cooperate in bringing the light of Christ to a world in need of salvation. This common witness is all the more important at the beginning of a new century and a new millennium, which present enormous challenges to the human family. For this reason too, *there is no time to lose!* As a basic condition for this common witness, we must avoid anything that might lead, once again, to distrust and discord. We have agreed to avoid any form of proselytism or methods and attitudes opposed to the exigencies of Christian love and what should characterize the relationship between Churches (see the *Common Declaration* of Pope Paul VI and Pope Shenouda III, 1973). And we recall that true charity, rooted in total fidelity to the one Lord Jesus Christ and in mutual respect for each one's ecclesial traditions and sacramental practices, is an essential element of this search for perfect communion.

Speech at the Cathedral of Our Lady of Egypt, Cairo, February 25, 2000

On Pilgrimage: Let Us Find Ways to Meet

We do not know each other sufficiently: let us therefore find ways to meet! Let us seek viable forms of spiritual communion, such as joint prayer and fasting, or mutual exchanges and hospitality between monasteries. Let us find forms of practical cooperation, especially in response to the spiritual thirst of so many people today, for the relief of their distress, in the education of the young, in securing humane conditions of life, in promoting mutual respect, justice, and peace, and in advancing religious freedom as a fundamental human right. At the beginning of the Week of Prayer for Christian Unity, on January 18, I opened the holy door of the Basilica of St. Paul-Outside-the-Walls and crossed its threshold together with representatives of many Churches and Ecclesial Communities. Together with me, His Excellency Amba, Bishop of the Coptic Church, and representatives of the Orthodox Church and of the Lutheran Church raised the Book of the Gospels to the four cardinal points. This was a deeply symbolic expression of our common mission in the new millennium: together we have to bear witness to the gospel of Jesus Christ, the saving message of life, love, and hope for the world. During that same liturgy, the Apostles' Creed was proclaimed by three representatives of different Churches and Ecclesial Communities. Afterward, we offered one another the sign of peace, and for me that joyful moment was a foreshadowing and a foretaste of the full communion we are striving to achieve among all Christ's followers.

Speech at the Cathedral of Our Lady of Egypt, Cairo, February 25, 2000

———∞∞∞———

On Pilgrimage: The Meaning of My Visit

I wish to express my gratitude to you, in your capacity as Chairman of the Islamic Supreme Committee, for receiving me within the Haram al-Sharif, which is connected with the memory of Abraham, who for all believers is a model of faith and submission to Almighty God. This visit of mine, as you are aware, is essentially a religious and spiritual pilgrimage. Pilgrimage to holy places is a feature common to many religious traditions, especially to the three Abrahamic religions. I thank the God revered by Jews, Christians, and Muslims. Jerusalem is the Holy City *par excellence.* It forms part of the common patrimony of our religions and of the whole of humanity. May the Almighty grant peace to the whole of this beloved region, so that all the people living in it may enjoy their rights, live in harmony and cooperation, and bear witness to the One God in acts of goodness and human solidarity. Thank you, all!

Greeting to Sheikh Akram Sabri, the Grand Mufti of Jerusalem,
March 26, 2000

—⚬⚬⚬—

On Pilgrimage: My Prayer at the Western Wall of the Temple

God of our fathers,
you chose Abraham and his descendants
to bring your Name to the nations:
we are deeply saddened by the behavior of those
who in the course of history
have caused these children of yours to suffer,
and asking your forgiveness, we wish to commit ourselves
to genuine brotherhood
with the people of the Covenant.
We ask this through Christ our Lord.
Amen

Prayer at Jerusalem, March 26, 2000

The Two Civilizations

Dear families, the question of responsible fatherhood and motherhood is an integral part of the "civilization of love," which I now wish to discuss with you. From what has already been said it is clear that *the family is fundamental to what Pope Paul VI called the "civilization of love,"* an expression that has entered the teaching of the Church and by now has become familiar. Today it is difficult to imagine a statement by the Church or about the Church that does not mention the civilization of love. The phrase *is linked to the tradition of the "domestic church" in early Christianity,* but it has a particular significance for the present time. Etymologically the word "civilization" is derived from *civis,* "citizen," and it emphasizes the civic or political dimension of the life of every individual. But the most profound meaning of the term "civilization" is not merely political, but rather pertains to human culture. Civilization belongs to human history because it answers man's spiritual and moral needs. Created in the image and likeness of God, man has received the world from the hands of the Creator, together with the task of shaping it in his own image and likeness. The fulfillment of this task gives rise to civilization, which in the final analysis is nothing else than the "humanization of the world."

Letter to Families, February 2, 1994

Civilization Means the Same Thing as Culture

In a certain sense "civilization" means the same thing as "culture," and so one could also speak of the *"culture of love,"* even though it is preferable to keep to the now familiar expression the "civilization of love," inspired by the words of the Pastoral Constitution *Gaudium et Spes:* *"Christ ... fully discloses man to himself and unfolds his noble calling."* And so we can say that the civilization of love originates in the revelation of the God who "is love," as John writes (1 John 4:8, 16); it is effectively described by Paul in the hymn of charity (1 Cor. 13:1–13). This civilization is intimately linked to the love "poured into our hearts through the Holy Spirit which has been given to us" (Rom. 5:5), and it grows as a result of the *constant cultivation* that the Gospel allegory of the vine and the branches describes in such a direct way: "I am the true vine, and my Father is the vinedresser. . . ." (John 15:1–2). In the light of these and other texts of the New Testament it is possible to understand what is meant by the "civilization of love" and why the *family is organically linked to this civilization.* If the first "way of the Church" is the family, the civilization of love is also the "way of the Church," which journeys through the world and summons families to this way; it summons also other social, national, and international institutions because of families and through families. *The family in fact depends on the civilization of love* and finds therein the reasons for its existence as family. At the same time *the family is the center and the heart of the civilization of love.*

Letter to Families, February 2, 1994

July 13

⊶⊷

God Is Love

There is no true love without an awareness that "God is Love"—and that man is the only creature on earth God has called into existence "for its own sake." Created in the image and likeness of God, man cannot fully "find himself" except through the sincere gift of self. Without such a concept of man, of the person, and the "communion of persons" in the family, there can be no civilization of love; similarly, without the civilization of love it is impossible to have *such a concept of person and of the communion of persons.* The family constitutes the fundamental "cell" of society. But Christ—the "vine" from which the "branches" draw nourishment—is needed, so that this cell will not be exposed to the threat of a kind of *cultural uprooting* that can come both from within and from without. Indeed, although there is on the one hand the "civilization of love," there continues to exist on the other hand *the possibility of a destructive "anti-civilization,"* as so many present trends and situations confirm. Who can deny that our age is one marked by a great crisis that appears above all as a profound *crisis of truth?* A crisis of truth means, in the first place, a *crisis of concepts.* Do the words "love," "freedom," "sincere gift," and even "person" and "rights of the person" really convey their essential meaning? Only if the truth about freedom and the communion of persons in marriage and in the family can regain its splendor, will the building of the civilization of love truly begin.

Letter to Families, February 2, 1994

July 14

Catholics and Politics

Catholics must not remain on the fringes of social and political life. Indeed, they can and must make a significant contribution, inspired by the Church's social teaching and without ever taking refuge in preconceived or one-sided positions, which are often sterile if not harmful. In this area, mutual respect is as important as ever according to the old golden rule: *In necessariis unitas, in dubiis libertas, in omnibus caritas (In necessities unity, in doubt liberty, but in all things charity)....* Europe is going through a delicate time in its history: Christians together with people of goodwill, are called to offer that *supplement of soul* referred to by my venerable predecessor, the Servant of God Paul VI: a supplement of faith, hope, and love, the supplement of truth, freedom, justice, and peace.

Discourse at the Vatican to Slovak Pilgrims, November 9, 1996

July 15

The Family: The Font of Joy

The contemporary family, like families in every age, *is searching for "fairest love."* A love that is not "fairest," but reduced only to the satisfaction of concupiscence (1 John 2:16) or to a man and a woman's mutual "use" of each other, makes persons *slaves to their weaknesses.* Do not certain modern "cultural agendas" lead to this enslavement? There are agendas that "play" on man's weaknesses and thus make him increasingly weak and defenseless. *The civilization of love evokes joy:* joy, among other things, for the fact that a man has come into the world (John 16:21) and consequently because spouses have become parents. The civilization of love means "rejoicing in the right" (1 Cor. 13:6). But a civilization inspired by a consumerist, antibirth mentality is not and cannot ever be a civilization of love. If the family is so important for the civilization of love, it is because of the particular *closeness and intensity of the bonds* that come to be between persons and generations within the family. However, the family remains *vulnerable* and can easily fall prey to dangers that weaken it or actually destroy its unity and stability. As a result of these dangers families cease to be witnesses of the civilization of love and can even become a negation of it, a kind of *countersign.* A broken family can, for its part, consolidate a specific form of "anticivilization," destroying love in its various expressions, with inevitable consequences for the whole of life in society.

Letter to Families, February 2, 1994

Love and the Ego

Subjectivism is the soil in which egoism grows. Both subjectivism and egoism are inimical to love—in the first place, because love has an objective orientation toward the person and the good of the person and, in the second place, because love is altruistic, is directed toward another human being. Subjectivism, on the contrary, is exclusively concerned with the subject and the "authenticity" of the subject's feelings, the affirmation of love through those feelings alone. *The egoist is preoccupied to the exclusion to all else with his own "I," his ego, and so seeks the good of that "I" alone, caring nothing for others.* Egoism precludes love, as it precludes any shared good, and hence also the possibility of reciprocity, which always presupposes the pursuit of a common good. Putting your own ego first, keeping your eyes fixed on it alone—and this is characteristic of egoism—always means an exaggerated concern with the subject.

Love and Responsibility

———∞∞∞———

The Development of the Person

The development of thought, knowledge, and intellectual ability takes place on a deeper level in the person. A great deal of growth takes place between the first words and the first childish ideas, the first naive questions which sometimes concern important subjects, and later stages of study, when the mind comes to understand trigonometry, literary analysis, philosophical reflection, or mathematical logic. All this is part of human development. We must view each individual person from this angle. Even the less gifted people with whom we sometimes meet belong to this great human reality of the person in development. The person is in fact conscience; and if we do not grasp this central factor of conscience, it is impossible to examine or discuss human development. The conscience provides the basis for the definitive structure and defines me as that unique and unrepeatable self, or *I*.

The Way to Christ

July 18

The Dark Side of the Ego

One's own "I," considered primarily as a subject, becomes egoistic when we cease to seek correctly *its objective position among other beings,* its connections and its interdependence with them. A second form of subjectivism in particular, subjectivism of values, cannot in the nature of things be anything except egoism. If the only value involved in a man and a woman's relationship to each other is pleasure, there can be no question of reciprocity or of the union of persons. The fixation of pleasure as their purpose restricts each of them to the confines of his or her "I." There can therefore be no reciprocity, but only "bilateralism": there exists a quantum of pleasure deriving from the association of two persons of different sex that must be so skillfully shared between them that each obtains as much as possible. Egoism excludes love, but permits calculation and compromise—even though there is no love there can be a bilateral accommodation between egoisms.

Love and Responsibility

July 19

The Good Shepherd at Cana

At Cana in Galilee, where Jesus was invited to a marriage banquet, his Mother, also present, said to the servants: "Do whatever he tells you" (John 2:5). Mary says the same words to us. What Christ tells us, in this particular moment of history, constitutes a forceful call to a great prayer with families and for families. The Virgin Mother invites us to unite ourselves through this prayer to the sentiments of her Son, who loves each and every family. He expressed this love at the very beginning of his mission as Redeemer with his sanctifying presence at Cana in Galilee, a presence that still continues. Let us pray, through Christ, with him and in him, to the Father "from whom every family in heaven and on earth is named" (Eph. 3:15).... Everywhere the Good Shepherd is with us. Even as he was at Cana in Galilee, *the Bridegroom in the midst of the bride and groom* as they entrusted themselves to each other for their whole life, so the Good Shepherd is also with us today as the reason for our hope, the source of strength for our hearts, the wellspring of ever new enthusiasm, and the sign of the triumph of the "civilization of love." Jesus, the Good Shepherd, continues to say to us: *Do not be afraid. I am with you.* "I am with you always, to the close of the age" (Matt. 28:20). What is the source of this strength? What is the reason for our certainty that you are with us, even though they put you to death, O Son of God, and you died like any other human being? What is the reason for this certainty? The Evangelist says: "He loved them to the end" (John 13:1).

Letter to Families, February 2, 1994

Love Is Demanding

The love that the Apostle Paul celebrates in the First Letter to the Corinthians—the love that is *"patient"* and *"kind"* and *"endures all things"* (1 Cor. 13:4, 7)—is certainly *a demanding love*. But this is precisely the source of its beauty: by the very fact that it is demanding, it builds up the true good of man and allows it to radiate to others. The good, says St. Thomas (Aquinas), is by its nature "diffusive." Love is true when *it creates the good of persons and of communities*; it creates that good and *gives it* to others. Only the one who is able to be demanding with himself in the name of love can also demand love from others. Love is demanding. It makes demands in all human situations; it is even more demanding in the case of those who are open to the gospel. Is this not what Christ proclaims in "his" commandment? Nowadays people need to rediscover this demanding love, for it is the truly firm foundation of the family, a foundation able to "endure all things." According to the Apostle, love is not able to "endure all things" if it yields to "jealousies," or if it is "boastful … arrogant or rude" (1 Cor. 13:5–6). True love, St. Paul teaches, is different: "Love believes all things, hopes all things, endures all things" (1 Cor. 13:7). This is the very love that "endures all things." At work within it is the power and strength of God himself, who "is love" (1 John 4:8, 16). At work within it is also the power and strength of Christ, the Redeemer of man and Savior of the world.

Letter to Families, February 2, 1994

———∞∞∞———

The Dangers Faced by Love

The dangers faced by love are dangers for the civilization of love, because they promote everything capable of effectively opposing it. Here one thinks first of *selfishness*, not only selfishness of individuals, but also of couples or, more broadly, of social selfishness, that of class or nation (nationalism). Selfishness in all its forms is directly and radically opposed to the civilization of love. But is love to be defined simply as "anti-selfishness"? This would be a very impoverished and ultimately a purely negative definition, even though it is true that different forms of selfishness must be overcome in order to realize love and the civilization of love. It would be more correct to speak of "altruism," which is the opposite of selfishness. But far richer and more complete is the concept of love illustrated by St. Paul. The hymn to love in the First Letter to the Corinthians remains the *Magna Carta* of the civilization of love. In this concept, what is important is not so much individual actions (whether selfish or altruistic), so much as the radical acceptance of the understanding of man as a person who "finds himself" by making a sincere gift of self. A gift is, obviously, "for others": this is *the most important dimension* of the civilization of love. We thus come to the very heart of the gospel truth about *freedom*. Freedom cannot be understood as a license to do *absolutely anything*: it means a *gift of self*. Even more: it means an *interior discipline of the gift*. The idea of gift contains not only the free initiative of the subject, but also the aspect of *duty*. All this is made real in the "communion of persons."

Letter to Families, February 2, 1994

The Ethos of Personalism Is Altruistic

We *come now to the antithesis between individualism and personalism*. Love, the civilization of love, is bound up with personalism. Why with personalism? And *why does individualism threaten the civilization of love?* We find a key to answering this in the Second Vatican Council's expression a "sincere gift." Individualism presupposes a use of freedom in which the subject does what he wants, in which he himself is the one to "establish the truth" of whatever he finds pleasing or useful. He does not tolerate the fact that someone else "wants" or demands something from him in the name of an objective truth. He does not want to "give" to another on the basis of truth; he does not want to become a "sincere gift." Individualism thus remains egocentric and selfish. The real antithesis between individualism and personalism emerges not only on the level of theory, but even more *on that of "ethos."* The "ethos" of personalism is altruistic: it moves the person to become a gift for others and to discover joy in giving himself. This is the joy about which Christ speaks (John 15:11; 16:20, 22). What is needed then is for human societies, and the families who live within them, often in a context of struggle between the civilization of love and its opposites, to seek their solid foundation in a correct vision of man and of everything that determines the full "realization" of his humanity.

Letter to Families, February 2, 1994

—⊗⊗⊗—

The Phenomenology of Love

Love is a phenomenon peculiar to the world of human beings. In the animal world *only* the sexual instinct is at work. Love is not, however, merely a biological or even a psycho-physiological chrystallization of the sexual urge, but is something fundamentally different from it. For although love grows out of the sexual urge and develops on that basis and in the conditions which the sexual urge creates in the psycho-physiological lives of concrete people, it is nonetheless given its definitive shape by *acts of will at the level of the person.*

Love and Responsibility

July 24

———∞∞∞———

Do Not Be Afraid

The Apostles, overcoming their initial fears even about marriage and the family, grew in courage. They came to understand that marriage and family are a true vocation, which comes from God himself and is an apostolate: the apostolate of the laity. Families are meant to contribute to the transformation of the earth and the renewal of the world, of creation and of all humanity. Dear families, you too should be fearless, ever ready to give witness to the hope that is in you (1 Pet. 3:15), since the Good Shepherd has put that hope in your hearts through the Gospel. You should be ready to follow Christ toward the pastures of life, which he himself has prepared through the Paschal Mystery of his Death and Resurrection. *Do not be afraid* of the risks! God's strength is always far more powerful than your difficulties!

Letter to Families, February 2, 1994

—⨯⨯⨯—

The Fact of Concupiscence

Concupiscence does not mean only the natural faculty of carnal desire, that is to say, orientation toward those values to which, in the context of sex, the senses respond. Concupiscence is a consistent tendency to see persons of the other sex through the prism of sexuality alone, "as objects of potential enjoyment." Concupiscence, then, refers to a latent inclination of human beings to invert the objective order of values, for the correct way to see and "desire" a person is through the medium of his or her value as a person. We should not think of this manner of seeing and desiring as "asexual," as blind to the value of "the body and sex"; it is simply that this value must be correctly integrated with love of the person—love in the proper and full sense of the word. Concupiscence, however, looks upon a person as "a potential object for use" precisely because of this value of "the body and sex" (whereas the body as a component of the person should itself be an object of love, only because of the value of the person); *hence the distinction between "love of the body" and "carnal love."*

Love and Responsibility

————— ∞ —————

Man's Duty Is to Love

Concupiscence is then in every man, the terrain on which two attitudes toward a person of the other sex contend for mastery. The object of the struggle is "the body," which because of its sexual value ("body and sex") arouses an appetite for enjoyment, whereas it should awaken love because of the value of the person, since it is after all the body of a person. Concupiscence itself means a constant tendency merely to "enjoy," whereas man's duty is to "love." This is why the view formulated in our analysis of love—that sensuality and emotion furnish the "raw material" of love—needs some qualification. This happens only to the extent that sensual and emotional reactions are not swallowed up by concupiscence, but absorbed in true love. This is difficult, especially where sensual reactions are concerned, for, as we have said, these are spontaneous, and they urge us in the same direction as concupiscence—so much so that sensual reactions are, in some measure, the cause of concupiscence. Sensuality is the capacity to react to the sexual value connected to the body as a "potential object of enjoyment," while concupiscence is a permanent tendency to experience desire caused by sensual reactions.

Love and Responsibility

July 27

The Mission of the Media: Everybody's Mission

"Go into the whole world and proclaim the gospel to every creature" (Mark 16:15). This is certainly not an easy mission in an age such as ours, in which there exists the conviction that the time of certainties is irretrievably past. Many people, in fact, believe that humanity must learn to live in a climate governed by an absence of meaning, by the provisional and by the fleeting. In this context, the communications media can be used "to proclaim the gospel or to reduce it to silence within men's hearts" (Pastoral Instruction, *Ae tatis novae*, February 22, 1992). This poses a serious challenge for believers, especially for parents, families, and all those responsible for the formation of children and young people. Those individuals in the Church community particularly gifted with talent to work in the media should be encouraged with pastoral prudence and wisdom, so that they may become professionals capable of dialoguing with the vast world of the mass media. The appreciation of the media is not reserved only to those already adept in the field, but to the entire Church community. If, as has already been noted, the communications media take into account different aspects of the expression of faith, Christians must take into account the media culture in which they live: from the liturgy, the fullest and fundamental expression of communication with God and with one another, to catechesis, which cannot prescind from the fact of being directed to people immersed in the language and the culture of the day.

Apostolic Letter on Communications, January 24, 2005

Expressing an Opinion

There cannot be forgotten the great possibilities of mass media in promoting dialogue, becoming vehicles for reciprocal knowledge, of solidarity and of peace. They become a powerful resource for good if used to foster understanding; a destructive "weapon" if used to foster injustice and conflicts. John XXIII prophetically warned humanity of such potential risks in *Pacem in Terris*. The reflection upon the role "of public opinion in the Church" and "of the Church in public opinion" aroused great interest. In a meeting with the editors of Catholic publications, Pius XII stated that something would be missing from the life of the Church were it not for public opinion. This same idea has since been repeated on other occasions, and in the code of canon law there is recognized, under certain conditions, the right to the expression of one's own opinion. Although it is true that truths of the faith are not open to arbitrary interpretations, and that respect for the rights of others places intrinsic limits upon the expression of one's judgments, it is no less true that there is still room among Catholics for an exchange of opinions in a dialogue that is respectful of justice and prudence. Communication both within the Church community and between the Church and the world at large requires openness and a new approach toward facing questions regarding the world of media. This communication must tend toward a constructive dialogue, so as to promote a correctly informed and discerning public opinion within the Christian community.

Apostolic Letter on Communications, January 24, 2005

July 29

———⌘———

The Good Shepherd Makes the Journey

Two thousand years have passed since the Son of God was made man and came to dwell among us. Today as then, the salvation brought by Christ is continually being offered to us that it may bear abundant fruits of goodness in keeping with the plan of God, who wishes to save all his children, especially those who have gone away from him and are looking for the way back. The Good Shepherd is always going in search of the lost sheep, and when he finds them he puts them on his shoulders and brings them back to the flock. Christ is in search of every human being, whatever the situation! This is because Jesus wants to save each one—and with a salvation that is offered, not imposed. What Christ is looking for is trusting acceptance, an attitude that opens the mind to generous decisions aimed at rectifying the evil done and fostering what is good. Sometimes this involves a long journey, but always a stimulating one, for it is a journey not made alone, but in the company of Christ himself and with his support. Jesus is a patient traveling companion, who respects the seasons and rhythms of the human heart. He never tires of encouraging each person along the path to salvation.

Message from the Vatican to Encourage Prisoners, June 24, 2000

The Priority of the Dignity and Fundamental Rights of Human Beings

According to God's plan, all must play their part in helping to build a better society. Obviously, this includes making a great effort in the area of crime prevention. In spite of everything, criminal actions are committed. For all to play their part in building the common good they must work, in the measure of their competence, to ensure that prisoners have the means to redeem themselves, both as individuals and in their relations with society. Such a process is based on growth in the sense of responsibility. None of this should be considered utopian. Those who are in a position to do so must strive to incorporate these aims in the legal system. In this regard, therefore, we must hope for a change of attitude leading to an appropriate adjustment of the juridical system. Clearly this presupposes a strong social consensus and the relevent professional skills. A strong appeal of this kind comes from the countless prisons throughout the world, in which millions of our brothers and sisters are held. Above all they call for a review of prison structures and in some cases a revision of penal law. *Regulations contrary to the dignity and fundamental rights of the human person should be definitively abolished from national legislation, as should laws that deny prisoners religious freedom.* There will also have to be a review of prison regulations where they give insufficient attention to those who have serious or terminal illnesses. Likewise, institutions offering legal protection to the poor must be further developed.

Message from the Vatican to Encourage Prisoners, June 24, 2000

July 31

ᴏᴈᴈᴏ

The Health of the Whole Person

A duty that Christians cannot shirk concerns the promotion of health worthy of the human being. In our society there is a risk of making health an idol to which every other value is subservient. The Christian vision of the human being opposes a notion of health reduced to pure, exuberant vitality and satisfaction with one's own physical fitness, far removed from any real consideration of suffering. This view, ignoring the person's spiritual and social dimensions, ends by jeopardizing his true good. Precisely because health is not limited to biological perfection, life lived in suffering also offers room for growth and self-fulfillment and opens the way to discovering new values. This vision of health based on an anthropology that respects the whole person, far from being identified with the mere absence of illness, strives to achieve a fuller harmony and healthy balance on the physical, psychological, spiritual, and social level. In this perspective, the person himself is called to mobilize all his available energies to fulfill his own vocation and for the good of others.

Message for the World Day of the Sick, Castel Gandolfo, August 6, 1999

August

The Warsaw Insurrection

It is not possible to understand Warsaw, capital of Poland, which in 1944 engaged in an unequal battle with the aggressor, a battle in which it was abandoned by the Allied Powers, a battle in which it was buried under its own ruins, if one does not recall that under those same ruins there was also Christ the Savior with his cross, which stands before the church at Krakowskie Przedmiescle. I recall these words spoken in Victory Square in Warsaw during my first pilgrimage to my fatherland, in 1999. I recall them today *on the fortieth anniversary of the Insurrection of Warsaw* to render homage to all its heroes, both fallen and still alive. At the same time *I entrust to Divine Providence, through Our Lady of Jasna Gora, my fatherland and the nation,* which in the terrible struggles of the Second World War spared no sacrifice to confirm its *right to independence* and to decide for itself in its own native land. The Insurrection of Warsaw was its extreme expression. May the eloquence of this anniversary cease not to speak *to the conscience* of the contemporary world.

Discourse at St. Peter's Square, August 1, 1984

———— ∞∞∞ ————

Speak Well

The freedom of public expression of one's own views is a great good for society, but it does not assure freedom of expression. Freedom of speech does not count for much, if the word uttered is not free, if it is a slave to selfishness, lies, deceit, or maybe even hate or contempt for others—for those who differ in nationality, religion, or point of view. The benefit of public speech and expression will not be very great if the words are going to be used not to seek truth and share that truth, but only to win a discussion and defend one's own opinion—perhaps even mistaken ones. Words may sometimes express truth in a degrading manner. It may happen that a person says some sort of truth in order to substantiate his own lie. Man brings great confusion to our mortal earth, when he tries to use truth in the service of lies. For many people, it is then more difficult to recognize that this is God's world. Truth is also degraded when it is devoid of love for itself and for man. In general, it is impossible to follow the Eighth Commandment—at least on the level of society—if it lacks goodwill, a firm trust, and a respect for all the differences, which enrich our social life.

Discourse at Olsztyn, Poland, June 6, 1991

---∞∞∞---

The Priestly Heart

In all these years I have always started my day with the celebration of the Eucharist, the pivot and heart of every priestly life, discovering each time with immense gratitude that it is the mysterious and essential bond that ties every priest to Christ the Redeemer. At the school of Jesus, priest and victim, I came increasingly to understand that the priest does not live for himself, but for the Church and for the sanctification of the People of God.

Angelus Address, St. Peter's Basilica, October 30, 1996

Love and Morality

The great moral force of true love lies precisely in the desire for the happiness, for the true good, of another person. This is what makes it possible for a man to be reborn because of love, makes him aware of the riches within him, his spiritual fertility and creativity: I am capable of desiring the good for another person, therefore I am, in general, capable of desiring the good. True love compels me to believe in my own spiritual powers even when I am "bad"; if true love awakens in me, it bids me seek the true good where the object of my love is concerned. In this way, affirmation of the worth of another person is echoed in affirmation of the worth of one's own person—for it is awareness of the value of the person, not of sexual values, that makes a man desire the happiness of another "I." When love attains its full dimensions, it introduces into relationship not only a "climate" of honesty between persons, but a certain awareness of the "absolute," a sense of contact with the unconditional and the ultimate. Love is indeed the highest of moral values. But one must know how to transfer it to the ordinary affairs of everyday life. This is where the problem of educating love arises.

Love and Responsibility

August 5

The Education of Love

Man is being condemned, so to speak, to create. Creativity is a duty in the sphere of love too. We find that what develops from "promising" raw material in the form of emotions and desires is often not true love, and often indeed sharply opposed to it, whereas a truly great love sometimes develops from modest material. But such great love can only be the work of persons and—let us add here to complete the picture—the work of divine grace.... But the operation of grace is implicit in these efforts, for they are the contribution of the invisible Creator, who is himself love and has the power to fashion any love, including that which in its natural development is based on the values of sex and the body—provided that human beings are willing to be his conscious cocreators. There is no need to be dismayed if love sometimes follows tortuous ways. Grace has the power to make straight the paths of human love.

Love and Responsibility

August 6

∞∞∞

The Transfiguration

Today's liturgy invites us to gaze to the face of the Son of God, who is transfigured on the mountain before Peter, James, and John, while the Father's voice proclaims from the cloud: "This is my beloved Son; listen to him" (Mark 9:7). St. Peter will recall the event with emotion, saying, "We were eyewitnesses of his majesty" (2 Pet. 1:16). In our era, pervaded by the image culture, the desire to be able to fill one's eyes with the figure of the divine Master becomes more intense, but it is appropriate to recall his words: "Blessed are those who have not seen and yet believe" (John 20:29). It was precisely with his eyes of faith fixed on the face of Christ, a true man and true God, that the revered Paul VI lived. Contemplating him with impassioned love, he said, "Christ is beauty, human and divine. Beauty, the beauty of reality, of truth, of life" (Discourse, January 13, 1971). And he added: "The figure of Christ presents over and above the charm of his merciful gentleness, an aspect which is grave and strong, formidable, when dealing with cowardice, hypocrisy, injustice, and cruelty, but never lacking a sovereign aura of love" (Discourse, January 27, 1971). As we approach the altar with grateful hearts, we also wish, like the disciples, to turn our gaze to the radiant face of the Son of God, to be illumined by it. Let us ask God through the intercession of Mary, Teacher of faith and contemplation, to enable us to receive within us the light that shines brightly on the face of Christ, so that we may reflect its image on everyone we meet.

Discourse at the Vatican, August 6, 2000

———— ∞∞∞ ————

A Letter to Altar Servers

I greet you affectionately, dear young people. Your commitment to the altar is not only a duty, but a great honor, a true holy service. Regarding this service, I would like to suggest some points for your reflection. The *vestments* worn by altar servers are very *special*. They recall a garment that everyone puts on when he is welcomed, in Jesus Christ, into the community. I am referring to the baptismal garment, whose deep meaning is explained by St. Paul: "For as many of you as were baptized into Christ have put on Christ" (Gal. 3:27). Even if you no longer fit into your baptismal garment, dear altar servers, you have put on that of an altar server. Yes, Baptism is the starting point of your "authentic liturgical service," which puts you beside your bishops, priests, and deacons. The altar server has a *privileged place in liturgical celebrations.* Those who serve at Mass present themselves to a community. They experience from close at hand that Jesus Christ is present and active in every liturgy. Jesus is present whenever the community gathers to pray and give praise to God. Jesus is present in the words of Sacred Scripture. Jesus is present above all in the Eucharist, under the appearances of bread and wine. He acts for the priest who celebrates Holy Mass and administers the sacraments *in persona Christi* (in the person of Christ).

Undated Letter to Altar Servers, 2002

The Importance of a Candle

In the liturgy you altar servers are far more than mere helpers of the parish priest. Above all, you are servants of Jesus Christ, the eternal High Priest. Thus you especially are called to be young friends of Jesus. Strive to deepen and foster this friendship with him. You will discover that in Jesus you have found a true friend for life. The altar server often holds a *candle* in his hand. How can we not think of what Jesus said in the Sermon on the Mount: "You are the light of the world" (Matt. 5:14)? Your service cannot be restricted to the inside of a church. It must shine out in your everyday life, at school, in the family, and in the different social contexts, for those who want to serve Jesus Christ in a church must be his witnesses everywhere. Dear young people, your contemporaries are awaiting the true "light of the world" (John 1:9). Do not hold your candlestick only inside the church, but take the light of the gospel to all who live in darkness and are going through a difficult time in their lives.

Undated Letter to Altar Servers, 2002

Hope Is Our Future

Dear young people, your statements and questions would require a long discussion. All the problems you have mentioned to me are serious ones and reveal your concern for the world and for the Church of today and tomorrow. I cannot reply to all this in a short time, but I hope that our dialogue will be continued with those responsible for your various organizations, with your catechists, your priests, and your bishops.... The future of the world seems rather gloomy to you. Unemployment, famine, violence, the threat to humanity from the stockpiling of armaments capable of terrible destruction, the economic disparity between north and south, the spiritual poverty that comes with the consumer society in many countries are many causes of anxiety and worry. *To you, young people I say: "Do not allow yourselves to be discouraged* by defeatism and discouragement!" You are "tomorrow's world." The future depends primarily on you. From us, the elders, you inherit a world, which can deceive you; but it has its riches and its miseries, its values and its countervalues. The extraordinary progress of science and technology is *ambivalent*. It can be used for good and for evil. It can save human lives and destroy them. It can allow a better and more equitable distribution of the world's goods or, on the contrary, allow a growth of their accumulation by small groups while increasing the misery of the masses. It can favor peace or, on the contrary, threaten humanity with frightful destruction.

Discourse to the Youth of Fribourg, Switzerland, June 13, 1984

———∞———

A Change of Heart

Everything depends on the use that is made of the progress of science and technology. Ultimately, everything depends on the hearts of men. *It is the hearts of men that must be changed.* Various systems that foster injustice and suffering must certainly be modified, but the hearts of men must be transformed at the same time. Here, dear young people, is the vast project for the world to which you must commit yourselves. Together, work with *your hands,* your heart, your intelligence, and your faith to build *a new world* where it will really be possible for all to grow and to live in an atmosphere of security and mutual confidence. *The future of humanity is not built on hatred, on violence, on oppression,* whatsoever this may be. *The future of humanity is not built on the triumph of individual or collective selfishness. The future of humanity cannot be built on a false conception of liberty that does not respect the freedom of others.* The consumer society in which we live and the fear of an uncertain future drive one to seek immediate gratification for oneself. One becomes introverted, falling back on one's small personal happiness, on one's emotions, in a circle where aroused feeling is incessantly on the lookout for new sensations, which quickly fade away, where there is no reference but to self and to one's pleasures. This is no way to live. This is not the world you want: it would be a world without hope, one that empties man's life of all meaning.

Discourse to the Youth of Fribourg, Switzerland, June 13, 1984

Precious in the Eyes of the Lord

Suffering, sickness, and death itself are part of the mystery of life. But although they remain a mystery, they need not be without meaning. In Christ and through his Passion and Resurrection, all creation has been redeemed, including all human experience. In fact, in his Passion, Christ used suffering and death to express, in the fullest way, his obedient love for the Father. And now, in union with Christ, our sufferings can become an act of love for the Father, a loving act of surrender to the providence of God. People often tell me that they are offering their prayers and sacrifices for me and for my intentions. I am deeply grateful for this gesture of solidarity and devotion, and I am humbled by the goodness and generous love of those who suffer. May you never doubt that the willing acceptance of your suffering and union with Christ is of great value for the Church. If the salvation of the world was accomplished by the suffering and death of Jesus, then we know that important contributions to the mission of the Church are made by the sick and elderly, by persons confined to hospital beds, by invalids in wheelchairs, by those who fully share in the Cross of our saving Lord. As St. Paul said of his own sufferings: "In my flesh I complete what is lacking in Christ's afflictions" (Col. 1:24).

Discourse at the Shrine at Huronia, Sainte Marie, Canada,
September 15, 1984

With a Good Heart

Today let us heed the severe but hopeful admonition that comes to us from the word of God in the liturgy. The Gospel calls us to a faithful and correct observance of the Lord's precepts, without neglecting God's commandments in order to observe human traditions (Mark 7:7). Jesus's strong rebuke is addressed to a people who "honor me with their lips, but their hearts are far from me" (Mark 7:6). The Lord asks us to be faithful to the law of God in truth and sincerity of conscience; however, at the same time he shows us where we can find the true and inalienable source of the authentic observance of the law: *"in the heart of each person!"* The roots of moral evil, of nonfulfillment, or rejection of the law can nestle in hearts for "wicked designs come from deep recesses of the heart" (Mark 7:21); likewise from the heart are born good proposals, desires for good, the decisive commitment of the upright conscience. It is necessary, however, to work with *good heart* that is, in sincerity and truth. In the *good heart* is the foundation of our relationship with God. "Humbly welcome the Word that has taken root in you" (James 1:21). The Lord insists in asking us for true conversion, accepting his Word with a pure conscience. To accept, in fact, means to make the Word our own, to act in such a way that it enters into the dynamics of our liberty, following a conscience open to the light that comes from that Word.

Discourse at the Vatican, August 28, 1988

———∞∞∞———

Maximilian Kolbe

The Franciscan Order spread far beyond the borders of Italy and soon reached my own country of Poland, where it flourishes no less than in other countries and continents. When I was bishop of Krakow I lived near a very old Franciscan Church where I used to pray and make the Stations of the Cross (a particularly Franciscan devotion to the Passion of Jesus) and visit the chapel of Our Lady of Sorrows (whom I took as my spiritual mother). It is a place I shall never forget, and we must remember too that the Blessed (now Saint) Maximilian Kolbe (1894–1941; Poland's modern Franciscan martyred hero whose example we are now celebrating), a special patron of our troubled times, was an offspring of that noble branch of Franciscan spirituality.

Private diary of Pope John Paul II, Undated

——∞——

The Vigil of the Assumption

A prayer: Mother, you were present with the apostles in the Upper Room in Jerusalem on the day of Pentecost. Mother, you who are present in Jasna Gora, in this particular upper room of our history, we pray you that the Holy Spirit may descend on all of us.... May he particularly come in our era as the *Parakletos*—the Consoler—*that he may convict us "in regard to sin, righteousness, and condemnation"* (John 16:8). He convicts us in regard to sin not to accuse people and to condemn them, but in order to convert them, purify them, raise them up spiritually, and liberate them. We need such a salvific "conviction." Each and every one of us needs it. The whole society needs it for a renewal of the spirit, a moral renewal. This is also indicated by the words the Polish bishops chose as the leitmotif of the papal visit to the homeland: "Give thanks to God—*do not quench the Spirit*" (1 Thess. 5:18–19). May the most dangerous sin not take root in you; according to the words of Christ, it is *the sin against the Holy Spirit* (Matt. 12:31). Therefore, we pray you, All-Virgin Mother of God,... help us *"be guided by the Holy Spirit"* (Gal. 5:18).

Meditation at the Vatican, May 22, 1991

The Church Believes in Mary's Assumption

The dogma of the Assumption affirms that Mary's body was glorified after her death. In fact, although for other human beings the resurrection of the body will take place at the end of the world, for Mary the glorification of her body was anticipated by a special privilege. How can we not see that the Assumption of the Blessed Virgin has always been part of the faith of the Christian people, who, by affirming Mary's entrance into heavenly glory, have meant to proclaim the glorification of her body? The first trace of belief in the Virgin's Assumption can be found in the apocryphal accounts entitled *Transitus Mariae*, whose origin dates to the second and third centuries. These are popular and sometimes romanticized depictions that in this case, however, pick up an intuition of faith on the part of God's people. Later, there was a long period of growing reflection on Mary's destiny in the next world. This gradually led the faithful to believe in the glorious raising of the Mother of Jesus, in body and soul, and to the institution in the East of the liturgical feasts of the Dormition and Assumption of Mary. Belief in the glorious destiny of the body and soul of the Lord's Mother after her death spread very rapidly from East to West and has been widespread since the fourteenth century. In our century, on the eve of the definition of the dogma it was a truth almost universally accepted and professed by the Christian community in every corner of the world.

Discourse at the Vatican, July 2, 1997

Pope John XXIII: Prophet of the New World Order

Humanity, Pope John XXIII wrote (in 1963), had entered a new stage of its journey. The end of colonialism and the rise of newly independent states, the protection of workers' rights, the new and welcome presence of women in public life all testified to the fact that the human race was indeed entering a new phase of its history, one characterized by *"the conviction that all men are equal by reason of their natural dignity"* (*Pacem in Terris*). The pope knew that that dignity was still being trampled upon in many parts of the world. Yet he was convinced that the world was becoming increasingly *conscious of certain spiritual values* and increasingly open to the meaning of those *pillars of peace*—truth, justice, love, and freedom. Seeking to bring these values into local, national, and international life, men and women were becoming more aware that their relationship with God, the source of all good, *must* be the solid foundation and supreme criterion of their lives, as individuals and in society. This evolving spiritual intuition would, the pope was convinced, have profound public and political consequences. What was later to happen in central and eastern Europe would confirm his insight. The road to peace lay in the defense and promotion of basic human rights, which every human being enjoys not as a benefit given by a different social class or conceded by the state but simply because of our humanity.

Message for World Day of Peace, January 1, 2003

———— ∞∞∞ ————

The Kingship of Christ

Through the old covenant, in the consciousness of the people of Israel, the Messiah-King receives his form. It is God himself who, especially through the prophets, reveals to the Israelites his will to gather them as a shepherd does his flock, so that they will live in freedom and peace in the Promised Land. To this end, he will send his Anointed One, in Greek the "Christ," to redeem the people from sin and to introduce them into the Kingdom. Jesus of Nazareth *brings this mission to fulfillment in the Paschal Mystery.* He does not come to reign as the kings of the world do, but to establish the divine power of Love in the heart of the *human person,* of *history,* and of the *cosmos.* In this regard, the Second Vatican Council pointed out the special responsibility of the *lay faithful* in virtue of their Baptism and Confirmation: they participate in the *prophetic mission* of Christ. As a consequence they are called "to seek the Kingdom of God by engaging in temporal affairs and by ordering them according to the plan of God"; they "have their own role to play in the mission of the whole People of God in the Church and in the world ... by their activity for evangelization and for the sanctification of people" (*Novo Millennio Ineunte*).

Angelus Message, November 24, 2002

————⌘————

Jesus's Affection for His Mother

St. Germanus maintains in a richly poetic text that it is Jesus's affection for his Mother that requires Mary to be united with her divine Son in heaven: "Just as a child seeks and desires its mother's presence and a mother delights in her child's company, it was fitting that you, whose motherly love for your Son and God leaves no room for doubt, should return to him. And was it not right, in any case, that this God who had a truly filial love for you, should take you into his company?" In another text, the venerable author combines the private aspect of the relationship between Christ and Mary with the saving dimension of her motherhood, maintaining that "the mother of Life should share the dwelling place of Life." According to some of the Church Fathers, another argument for the privilege of the Assumption is taken from Mary's sharing in the work of Redemption. St. John Damascene underscores the relationship between her participation in the Passion and her glorious destiny: "It was right that she who had seen her Son on the Cross and received the sword of sorrow in the depths of her heart ... should behold this Son seated at the right hand of the Father." In the light of the Paschal Mystery, it appears particularly clear that the Mother should also be glorified with her Son after death.

Discourse at the Vatican, July 9, 1997

The Role of Woman in the Economy of Salvation

Looking at the mystery of the Blessed Virgin's Assumption, we can understand the plan of Divine Providence for humanity: after Christ, the incarnate Word, Mary is the first human being to achieve the eschatological ideal, anticipating the fullness of happiness promised to the elect through the resurrection of the body. In the Assumption of the Blessed Virgin we can also see the divine will to advance woman. In a way analogous to what happened at the beginning of the human race and of salvation history, in God's plan the eschatological ideal was not to be revealed in an individual, but in a couple. Thus in heavenly glory, beside the risen Christ there is a woman who has been raised up, Mary: the new Adam and the new Eve, the firstfruits of the general resurrection of the bodies of all humanity. Despite their brevity, these notes enable us to show clearly that Mary's Assumption reveals the nobility and dignity of the human body. In the face of the profanation and debasement to which modern society frequently subjects the female body, the mystery of the Assumption proclaims the supernatural destiny and dignity of every human body, called by the Lord to become an instrument of holiness and to share in his glory.

Discourse at the Vatican, July 9, 1997

The Song of Mary

The word *Magnificat,* the Latin version of a Greek word with the same meaning, celebrates the greatness of God. He reveals his omnipotence through the angel's message, surpassing the expectations and hopes of the people of the covenant, and even the noblest aspirations of the human soul. In the presence of the powerful and merciful Lord, Mary expressed her own sense of lowliness: "My soul magnifies the Lord and my spirit exults in God my savior, for he has regarded the low estate of his handmaid" (Luke 1:47–48). The Greek word *tapeinosis* (a state of degradation) is probably borrowed from the Song of Hannah, Samuel's mother. It calls attention to the "humiliation" and "misery" of a barren woman (1 Sam. 1:11), who confides her pain to the Lord. With a similar expression, Mary made known her situation of poverty and her awareness of being little before God, who by a free decision looked upon her, a humble girl from Nazareth, to become the Mother of the Messiah. The words, "Henceforth all generations will call me blessed" (Luke 1:48) arise from the fact that Elizabeth was the first to proclaim Mary "Blessed" (Luke 1:45). Not without daring, the song predicts that the same proclamation will be extended and increased with relentless momentum. At the same time it testifies to the special veneration of the Mother of Jesus, which has been present in the Christian community from the first century. The Magnificat is the firstfruit of the various forms of devotion, passed on from one generation to the next, in which the Church has expressed her love for the Virgin of Nazareth.

Discourse at the Vatican, November 6, 1996

August 21

━━━━ ∽∞∾ ━━━━

Push Out into Deep Water

To realize fully such a demanding mission (to communicate holiness), it is above all necessary to maintain constant communion with Jesus, untiringly contemplating his face in prayer, to serve him energetically in our brothers and sisters. For this reason, I desire to repeat to you the Lord's exhortation, "to put out into the deep water" (Luke 5:4), which I directed to the entire Christian people in the apostolic letter *Novo Millennio Ineunte.* Yes! Put out into the water and confidently throw the nets in the name of the Redeemer. In an era marked by a disturbing culture, empty and "lacking direction," proclaim categorically the primacy of God, who always hears the cry of the oppressed and the afflicted. The foundation of every apostolic commitment and the antidote to dangerous spiritual fragmentation is personal holiness coming from a docile listening to the Spirit, who frees and transforms the heart. Holiness is your essential and primary mission. It is the best contribution you can make to the new evangelization and the guarantee of a genuinely evangelical service for the benefit of the neediest.

Discourse to the Silesian Sisters, November 8, 2002

———∞∞∞———

Charity and Justice Together

He (Frederick Ozanam—1818–53—Founder of St. Vincent de Paul Society) observed the real situation of the poor and sought to be more and more effective in helping them in their human development. He understood that charity must lead to efforts to remedy injustice. Charity and justice go together. He had the clear-sighted courage to seek a front-line social and political commitment in a troubled time in the life of this country, for no society can accept indulgence as if it were a simple fatality without damaging its honor. So it is that we can see in him a precursor of the social doctrine of the Church, which Pope Leo XIII would develop some years later in the encyclical *Rerum Novarum*.

Beatification Homily, Notre Dame Cathedral, Paris, August 22, 1997

———∞∞∞———

The Existential Character of Christianity

More than ever, the world today needs to rediscover the meaning of life and death in the perspective of eternal life. Outside it, modern culture, born to exalt the human person and his dignity, is paradoxically transformed into a culture of death, because, without the horizon of God, the person finds himself a prisoner in the world, overwhelmed by fear, and gives way to many collective and personal pathologies. I am happy on this topic to quote a text of St. Charles Borromeo (my personal patron). He wrote in a homily of September 5, 1583: "May my soul never cease to praise the Lord who never ceases to lavish gifts. It is a gift of God if, from being a sinner, you are called to justice; a gift of God if you are sustained so that you do not fall; a gift of God that you are given the strength to persevere until the end; the resurrection of your dead body will be a gift of God, so that not a hair of your head will be lost; the glorification after the resurrection will be a gift of God; and, finally, it will also be a gift of God to be able to praise him continually in eternity."

Angelus Message, November 3, 2002

———∞∞∞———

The Word of God

Our first impression may be that the Gospels are only a book, and this is the form in which we hold it in our hands, read it with our eyes, and hear its words with our ears. The Church systematically proclaims sections of the Gospels to us day by day at Mass.... It is a truly unique book. It has been translated into almost every language in the world and even into various dialects, but it loses nothing of its initial freshness and even a certain Semitic flavor. This regional flavor, which is derived from the fact that Jesus taught in Aramaic and lived in Palestine, in no way diminishes its universality. Its unique content strikes and affects people everywhere. God speaks of himself in such a way that he is found within this information. In the Gospels the most important thing is not the words, but the content or reality. It is clearly a form of written language, but language used simply as a means to reveal this reality to us: God speaks of himself ... telling us and revealing to us who he is—who he is in his divinity and deepest reality. He says that he is love and tells us how he is love. He is love because he is Father, Son, and Holy Spirit, and in this way he is, in himself, love. Further, not only does he speak of himself, but through the Gospels he tells us what he wants. He tells us what he wants *from us*, but first and foremost he tells us what he wants *for us*, and this is why he tells us who he is and says that he is love. He says that he wants to draw each and every one of us into his love and involve us in it. This is both a great self-revelation and a great offer!

The Way to Christ

—∞∞∞—

Looking Inside

It is necessary for us to be able to distinguish between good and evil. Conversion means breaking away from evil, breaking away from sin. We see that it has very deep roots in human history. In each of us it has its "original" dimension. The beginning of sanctifying grace, which we receive through Baptism, does not make us sinless. *In each person an inclination to sin continues to exist*—what St. John calls the concupiscence of the eyes, concupiscence of the flesh, and the pride of life (1 John 2:16); this continues to be in us. All sin comes from this inclination. Personal sin is that for which I alone am responsible, that which is "my sin." It is necessary that we call this sin by name, presenting ourselves before God as King David did: "Against you only have I sinned, and done what is evil in your sight.... Have mercy on me, O God" (Ps. 51:4, 3). The Second Vatican Council tells us: "Sin brought man to a lower state, forcing him away from the completeness that is his to attain" (*Gaudium et Spes*). It also says that sin is the source of internal division, and that all of human life (individual and social) "shows itself to be *a struggle and a dramatic one between good and evil,* between light and darkness."

Discourse at the Vatican, March 13, 1991

---∞∞∞---

The Simplicity of Virtue

Today I want to say to you: may you be able to embody in yourselves the virtues that made St. Francis of Paola great, so that with strength you may weaken the social evil that, in the eyes of many, often obscures the image of your country. If you are able to be open and sincere among yourselves, if you have the courage to erase *omertà* (the conspiracy to silence) that binds so many people in a kind of squalid complicity dictated by fear, then relations between families will improve, the tragic chain of vendetta will be broken, serene society will begin to flourish again, and this generous land will appear to be what it is—the land of St. Francis, the land in which charity and forgiveness flourish.

Discourse at Paola, Calabria, Italy, October 5, 1984

August 27

---~∞∞∞~---

The Task of the Consecrated

Thirst for God is widespread: it is up to the members of religious institutes to channel this need, reviving in their daily witness the joy of living with God and by God, which does not alienate the spirit and does not take away freedom, but which enriches the soul and makes it free to savor his presence. Is this not the experience that you have when, with complete readiness, you are able to follow Christ, chaste, poor, and obedient to the Father? Do you not find in this the secret of true peace of your soul? Share this style of life with your brothers and sisters, strongly emphasizing the joy of being together, "of one heart and of one mind" in the generous sharing of all your goods (Acts 4:32). Do not be afraid of feeling that you are not understood: Christ is with you to instill hope and strengthen you that you may carry it enthusiastically to your brothers and sisters. The world can well distinguish your evangelical witness from any other: not for nothing does it set its ideology and its fleeting values against you. Today, to live in union with God with an emphasized spirit of prayer is an obligatory passage of religious life: the Church needs consecrated souls who live the interior life of relationship with God and affirm God's primacy before the world, that the world may understand that it is not material goods, success, or pleasures that give man serenity, but the degree of union with Christ, man's true hope.

Discourse at Paola, Calabria, Italy, October 5, 1984

———— ∞∞∞ ————

The Contemplative Dimension

Allow me to return to a fundamental point,... the contemplative dimension, the commitment to prayer. The religious is a man or woman consecrated to God, by means of Christ, in the charity of the Spirit. This is an ontological *datum* that demands to emerge to consciousness and to orientate life. This is for the benefit of the individual, but also for the advantage of the community, which, in consecrated souls, experiences and enjoys in a quite special way the life-bringing presence of the divine Bridegroom! Remind your confreres frequently that a pause for true worship has greater value and spiritual fruit than the most intense activity, were it apostolic activity itself. This is the most urgent contention that religious must oppose in a society in which efficiency has become an *idol*, on the altar of which human dignity itself is not infrequently sacrificed.... The soul that lives in habitual contact with God and moves within the warm range of his love can easily protect itself from the temptation of particularisms and oppositions that create painful divisions. It can interpret in the right evangelical light the option for the poorest and every victim of human selfishness without surrendering to sociopolitical radicalizations, which in the long run turn out to be inopportune, self-defeating, and often causes of new forms of tyranny. It can approach people and take its place in their midst without questioning its own religious identity or dimming that "specific originality" of its own vocation, which derives from the peculiar "following of Christ"—poor, chaste, and obedient.

Discourse at the Vatican, November 24, 1978

———— ∞ ————

The Poor: God's Chosen Ones

The pope loves you because you are God's favorites. He himself, on founding his family, the Church, kept poor and needy humanity in mind. To redeem it, he sent precisely his son, who was born poor and lived among the poor in order to make us rich with his poverty (2 Cor. 8:9). As a consequence of this Redemption, carried out in him who became one of us, we are now no longer poor servants, we are sons who can call God "Father" (Gal. 4:4–6). We are no longer abandoned, since, we are all sons of God, we are also heirs to the goods he offers abundantly to those who love him. Could we doubt that a father gives good things to his children (Matt. 7:7ff.)? Jesus himself, our Savior, waits for us in order to relieve us when we are weary (Matt. 11:28). At the same time, he counts on our personal collaboration to make us more and more worthy, being the architects of our own human and moral elevation. At the same time, faced with your own overwhelming situation, I call with all my strength on those who have means and who feel they are Christians to renew their minds and their hearts in order that, promoting greater justice and even giving something of their own, no one will lack proper food, clothing, housing, culture, and work—all that gives dignity to the human person. The image of Christ on the cross, the price of the Redemption of humanity, is a pressing appeal to spend our lives in putting ourselves in the service of the needy, in harmony with charity, which is generous and which does not sympathize with injustice, but with truth (1 Cor. 13:2ff.).

Homily at Barrio Santa Cecilia, Guadalajara, Mexico, January 30, 1979

Solitude and Joy

But the Lord Jesus tells us to do something more. When he says, "Go into your room and shut the door" (Matt. 6:6), he indicates an ascetic effort of the human spirit that must not end in man himself. That shutting-in of oneself is, at the same time, the deepest opening of the human heart. It is indispensable for the purpose of meeting the Father and must be undertaken for this purpose. "Your Father who sees in secret will reward you." Here it is a question of acquiring again the simplicity of thought, of will, and of heart that are indispensable to meet God in one's own "self," and God is waiting for that in order to approach man, who is absorbed interiorly and at the same time open to his word and his love! God wishes to communicate himself to the soul thus disposed. He wishes to give it truth and love, which have their real source in him.

Discourse at the Vatican, February 28, 1979

August 31

The Parish as Family

I encourage you to rediscover the true image of the parish, that is, the very mystery of the Church living and acting. Before ever being a structure, the parish is "a family home, fraternal and welcoming, in which the baptized and those who are confirmed are aware of being God's people. Therein the bread of true doctrine and the Bread of the Eucharist are abundantly broken before them.... From it, daily, they are sent out on their apostolic mission into all the work places of the world's life" (*Catechesi Tradendae*). The last synod of bishops expressed the wish that the parishes would more resolutely renew themselves by encouraging the participation of laity in pastoral responsibilities. The action of laity is, in fact, so necessary in the parishes that without it the apostolate of pastors cannot have its full effect. We return to the theme of ecclesiology of communion. Because they are diverse and complementary, ministries and charisms have their proper part to play in the growth of the Church. The parish, the Church's presence amid human dwellings, provides the possibility of experiencing and cultivating, day after day, more fraternal relations between the faithful of diverse origins and circumstances. It is the first place for community celebration of the Lord's presence acknowledged in faith. It is the pole of the apostolate, and it awaits missionary drive toward the unbeliever or the half believer. It is open to everyone—to take up a phrase of John XXIII—it is the "village foundation" to which all come to slake their thirst.

Discourse at Saint-Dénis, Reunion, May 1, 1989

September

September 1

———— ∞ ————

The Dignity of Labor

Sharing the daily work of the most common activities with Joseph and Mary, Jesus enlightens us about the fact that all work, no matter if it is humble and hidden, *draws a person closer to the mystery of the Cross:* it is a redemptive activity; it is a necessity and a liberation; it is a manifestation of the opportunity the human person has to subdue the earth. Work makes life more human when it helps to build a new, more perfect world. As such, work makes implicit the proclamation that *humanity is journeying toward the new heavens and a new earth* foretold by Christ's Resurrection. I want to remind the workers present here of all this—all those in this region who constantly strive to promote new and better living conditions: to those who work the land and those who work in small or large industries, to those who work in the trades, and those who practice ancient and traditional arts, to those who are searching for work, and to migrants, to those who have traditional work places, and to those who use the most modern technologies. I want to remind everyone that work, which is sometimes seen as condemnation and servitude, has rather been assumed by Christ *as a moment of redemption and the proclamation of liberation.* It is the path to personal sanctification and salvation. It is the constructive moment of fraternal solidarity. Every profession can thus be understood as a particular vocation that confers on human work a superior dignity and a transcendent value because of the spiritual union with Christ.

Discourse at Camerino–San Severino Marche, Italy, March 18, 1991

The Family and Work

The carpenter of Nazareth, the husband of the Mother of God and the guardian of the Son of the Most High, is filled with *meaning for the Church,* a community called to live fully the mystery of mankind, a fullness that is fulfilled only in Christ. Thus, *the Mother of Jesus along with St. Joseph in a special way draws the mystery of the incarnate Word closer to the fundamental problems of human existence.* It is a question of two realities—the family and work—two realities that are distinct, but are connected to one another in a mutual relationship.... In light of the gospel and the Church's tradition, which are expressed not only in the continuity of her teaching but also in Christian morality, these two important human realities shed light on *the proper hierarchy of values.* They emphasize that *the primacy belongs to the human being as a person and as a community of persons: in the first place, therefore, to the family.* All work, and especially physical labor, binds the person to the world of things, to the whole "order" of things. The world has been given to mankind as a task by the creator, as an earthly job: "Subdue the earth!" The words from Genesis (1:28) indicate precisely this *subordination of things to the person. The visible world is "for man." Things are for people.... May this order be understood and respected: may it never be violated, and even less so upset!* Modern progress has such a danger in itself. *The "progressive" culture, with the exception of those projects that have the person as their true reference, all too easily becomes a culture of things rather than of people.*

Discourse at Fabriano, Italy, March 19, 1991

True Maturity Is Christ

Today, then, the Church finds itself in a new missionary situation. Not only the meeting with non-Christian religions and with the cultures influenced by them, but also the spread of atheistic cultures opens new and vast fields to the Church's mission. Among the numerous tasks of the missiology specialists, I would like to mention a few with regard to which the Church expects from you special attention in research and academic formation. The theology of mission should study Christology in a special way. Christ, the Redeemer of mankind, is the key to missionary theology just as he who, through his spirit, animates and enlightens missionary service. While studying non-Christian cultures and religions and during the constant dialogue with them, always keep his person and his role in mind. He will be the one to enlighten, as if from within, the reality of man, since Jesus Christ, "by the revelation of the mystery of the Father and his love, fully reveals man to man himself" (*Gaudium et Spes*).

Address at the Gregorian University, Rome, Italy, November 29, 1983

⸺⊗⊗⊗⸺

Life Among the Catacombs

The catacombs were rediscovered as a subject for study and spiritual reflection toward the end of the sixteenth century, when a group of scholars formed an active cultural circle around the great personality of St. Philip Neri. The "Christopher Columbus of the Roman catacombs," as he was called, was the Maltese archaeologist Antonio Bosio, who identified at least thirty of the sixty Christian burial places in the city.... By visiting these monuments, one comes into contact with the evocative traces of early Christianity and one can, so to speak, tangibly sense the faith that motivated those ancient Christian communities. Walking through the underground passages of the catacombs, one frequently glimpses many signs of the iconography of faith: the *fish*, a symbol of Christ; the *anchor*, an image of hope; the *dove*, which represents the believing soul; and next to the names on the tombs one often sees the greeting *"In Christo."* They are also testimonies of the spiritual zeal that motivated the first Christian generations. By entering that world, today's Christians can draw beneficial encouragement for their life and a far more effective commitment to the new evangelization.

Discourse at the Vatican for the Pontifical Commission for
Sacred Archaeology, June 7, 1996

September 5

---- ✿ ----

Women Are Bearers of the Good News

It is impossible to think of the worldwide task of evangelization without the vital and specific contribution of women religious. The witness of your religious consecration is a source of abundant new life in the younger churches and a necessary antidote to the "secularization of salvation," which too often occurs in more developed societies. To this urgent task you bring the deep inner experience of your following of Christ in spousal love and your complete readiness to serve the human family through "all the *manifestations of the feminine 'genius',*... all the charisms which the Holy Spirit distributes to women ... the victories which (the Church) owes to their faith, hope, and charity" (*Mulieris Dignitatem*).

Discourse to the International Union of Superiors General, Rome, Italy,
May 16, 1991

Run Like the Women at the Tomb

Women religious, partners in evangelization, it is as women that you are such. You are like the women who, with the apostles, followed Jesus and assisted them from their resources (Luke 8:1–3). You are such especially like Mary Magdalene, the *apostola apostolorum* (the apostle of the apostles), manifesting as she did, through your privileged relationship with Jesus, your acceptance of his word and your fidelity to his message. You are like the Samaritan woman who became a bearer of the good news after recognizing the one who was speaking to her as the expected Messiah (John 4:7–30).

Discourse to the International Union of Superiors General, Rome, Italy,
May 16, 1991

———∞———

Dimensions of Femininity

Partners in evangelization, you are such according to the "two particular dimensions of the fulfillment of the female personality," virginity and motherhood, two dimensions that explain and complement one another in woman's vocation. If "motherhood in the bio-physical sense appears to be passive, . . . at the same time in its personal-ethical sense, [it expresses a very important creativity]" (*Mulieris Dignitatem*). It is this creativity that women religious are called to use in the service of evangelization. Motherhood of others, as the Gospel reveals it to us, is "not only of 'flesh and blood': it expresses a profound 'listening to the Word of the living God' and a readiness to safeguard this Word, which is 'the Word of eternal life'" (*Mulieris Dignitatem*).

Discourse to the International Union of Superiors General, Rome, Italy,
May 16, 1991

———∞∞∞———

Virginity Bespeaks Intense Love

As for virginity, which it is impossible to understand correctly without referring to married love, that is, to a love in which a person becomes a gift for the other, it is open to the experience of motherhood in a new sense: motherhood "according to the Spirit." Indeed, we must not forget that St. Paul himself felt the need to have recourse to that which is feminine in nature to express the truth of his apostolic service when he addressed the Galatians as "my children, for whom I am again in labor" (Gal. 4:19). Many other aspects could be recalled to shed greater light on the dignity of woman and her vocation, but I wanted simply to mention those that seemed to me to be more closely connected to the service of evangelization.

Discourse to the International Union of Superiors General, Rome, Italy,
May 16, 1991

———— ◦∞◦ ————

Moral Values in Youth: Toward the Civilization of Love

In today's world, more than ever, ... people cherish deep hopes and aspirations particularly for peace and respect for human rights. Justifiably, each one wishes to be recognized as a person, along with his culture and his particular spiritual approach, and at the same time as part of a social body in which he can take the place that is his due. You know the Holy See's conviction and commitment to an ever broader understanding between peoples. *Peace is the desire to live together* for the good of all, especially for the good of the young generations, for whom we must prepare a better future. Those who today work to instill in young people a conviction that every individual is our brother and for this reason is deserving of our attention and respect are peacemakers. In this spirit, to be trained in brotherhood and in human, civic, moral, and spiritual values is a contribution to building a civilization of love, which we all need on the threshold of the third millennium.

Discourse at the Vatican, October 4, 1996

———❧———

The Pope Must Come Here

I am here today *at Auschwitz* as a pilgrim. It is well known that I have been here many times. So many times! And many times I have gone down to Maximilian Kolbe's death cell, and stopped in front of the execution wall, and passed among the ruins of the cremation furnaces of Brzezinka. *It was impossible for me not to come here as pope.* I have come to pray with all of you who have come here today, and with the whole of Poland, and the whole of Europe. *Christ wishes that I, who have become the Successor of Peter, should give witness before the world to what constitutes the greatness and misery of contemporary man, to what is his defeat and victory.*

Visit to Auschwitz, June 7, 1979

———— ⊶⊷⊶ ————

Remembering the Tragedy

One month since the inhumane terrorist attacks that occurred in different parts of the United States of America, we again recommend to the eternal mercy of the God of our Fathers the numerous innocent victims. We ask for consolation and comfort for their family and relatives, burdened by pain; we invoke strength and courage for the many who continue their work in the places struck by this terrible disaster; we implore for tenacity and perseverance by all men of goodwill continuing on the paths of justice and peace. May the Lord remove from the heart of man every trace of resentment, of hostility and of hate, and open him to reconciliation, to solidarity and to peace. Let us pray, so that the "culture of love" may be established all over the world.... O God, Almighty and Merciful Father, he who sows discord cannot understand You; he who loves violence cannot welcome You: watch over us in our painful human condition tried by the brutal acts of terrorism and death. Comfort your children and open our hearts to hope, that our time may again know days of serenity and peace, through Christ our Lord.

Hora Tertia *for the One-Month Memorial for the Terrorist Attacks of*
September 11, 2001; Rome, Italy, October 11, 2001

September 12

⎯⎯∞⎯⎯

Victory Through Faith and Love

In this site of the terrible slaughter that brought death to four million people of different nations, Fr. Maximilian voluntarily offered himself for death in the starvation bunker for a brother, and so won a spiritual *victory like that of Christ himself.* This brother still lives today in the land of Poland. But was Fr. Maximilian Kolbe the only one? Certainly he won the victory that was immediately felt by his companions in captivity and is still felt today by the Church and the world. However, there is no doubt that many other similar victories were won. I am thinking, for example, of the death in the gas chamber of a concentration camp of the Carmelite sister Benedicta of the Cross, whose name in the world was Edith Stein, an illustrious pupil of Husserl who became one of the glories of contemporary German philosophy, and who was a descendant of a Jewish family living in Wroclaw. Where the dignity of man was so horribly trampled on, victory was won through faith and love.

Visit to Auschwitz, June 7, 1979

The Radicalness of Love

"Having loved his own who were in the world, Jesus loved them to the end" (John 13:1). In contrast to the synoptic Gospels, the Gospel of John does not relate the institution of the Eucharist, of which Jesus had already spoken at length in Capernaum (John 6:26–65); instead, it dwells upon the washing of the feet (John 13:1–11). Even more than an example of humility offered for our imitation, this action of Jesus, so disconcerting to Peter, is a revelation of the radicalness of God's condescension toward us. In Christ, God has "stripped himself" and has taken on "the form of a slave" even to the utter abasement of the Cross (Phil. 2:7), so that humanity might have access to the depths of God's very life. The great speeches that in John's Gospel follow the washing of the feet and are in some way commentaries upon it serve as an introduction to the mystery of trinitarian communion to which we are called by the Father, who makes us sharers in Christ by the gift of the Spirit. This communion must be lived in compliance with the new commandment: "Love one another as I have loved you" (John 13:34). It is not by chance that the priestly prayer is the culmination of this "mystagogy," since it shows us Christ in his oneness with the Father, ready to return to him through the sacrifice of himself, and wanting only that the disciples come to share his unity with the Father: "As you, Father, are in me and I in you, may they too be one in us" (John 17:21).

Letter from the Cenacle, Jerusalem, March 23, 2000

———∞———

Listening to God

We are called to examine our practical acceptance of the gospel, knowing that even before it offers us a plan of life, it is news, indeed, as the very word "gospel" says, *good news.* It is the news that God loves us and in his incarnate Son has shown us his solidarity, redeeming us from sin and death. Thus the gospel is a message of liberation, joy, and fullness of life. But whoever takes this message seriously must also make *the commitment to a new life* inspired by gospel values. It is a question of moving from a superficial life to deep interiority, from selfishness to love, of striving to live according to the model of Christ himself. Prayer can have many expressions, personal and communal. But we must above all live its essence, listening to God who speaks to us, conversing with us as children in a "face-to-face" dialogue filled with trust and love.

Discourse at the Vatican, February 16, 1997

—⚬⚬⚬—

Transform the World to Renew the Family of Man

Brothers and sisters in Christ, I desire to direct my words, my greeting, and my blessing to the Catholic laity in every country of Africa. I want to reach beyond the boundaries of language, geography, and ethnic origin, and, without distinction, to entrust each one to Christ the Lord. Thus I ask every one of you who hears my message of fraternal solidarity and pastoral instruction to pass it on. I ask you to make my message travel from village to village, from home to home. Tell your brothers and sisters in the faith that the pope loves you all and embraces you in the peace of Christ. You who are laypersons in the Church and who possess faith, the greatest of all resources—you have a unique opportunity and crucial responsibility. *Through your lives in the midst of your daily activities in the world, you show the power that faith has to transform the world and to renew the family of man.* Even though it is hidden and unnoticed like the leaven or the salt of the earth spoken of in the Gospel, your role as laity is indispensable for the Church in the fulfillment of her mission from Christ. This was clearly taught by the Fathers of the Second Vatican Council when they stated: "The Church is not truly established and does not fully live, nor is she a perfect sign of Christ among people, unless there exists a laity worthy of the name, working alongside the hierarchy. For the Gospel cannot be deeply imprinted on the mentality, life, and work of any people without the active presence of laypeople" (*Lumen Gentium*).

Homily at Accra, Ghana, May 8, 1980

———— ∞∞∞ ————

Coventry! The Cathedral of Peace

We are close to the city of Coventry, a city devastated by war, rebuilt in hope. We pray: "Send your Spirit, Lord, renew the face of the earth." We call upon God to enable us to bring about reconciliation and peace not simply in symbol, but in reality too. The ruins of the old Cathedral constantly remind our society of its *capacity to destroy.* Today that capacity is *greater than ever.* Yet people everywhere long for peace. Men and women of goodwill desire to make common cause in their search for a worldwide community of brotherhood and understanding. They long for justice filled with mercy. What is this peace, symbolized by the new Cathedral of Coventry? Peace is not the absence of war. It involves mutual respect and confidence between peoples and nations. It involves collaboration and binding agreements. *Like a cathedral, peace has to be constructed* patiently and with unshakeable faith. The Cathedral of Peace is built of many small stones. Each person has to become a stone in that beautiful edifice. All people must deliberately and resolutely commit themselves to the pursuit of peace. Mistrust and division between nations begin in the heart of individuals. Work for peace starts when we listen to *the urgent call of Christ: "Repent and believe in the Gospel"* (Mark 1:15). We must turn from domination to service; we must turn from violence to peace; we must turn from ourselves to Christ, who alone can give us a new heart. Each individual is destined to hear this call from Christ. Each person's response leads to death or to life.

Homily at Coventry, England, May 30, 1982

September 17

The Mystery of Evil

The World Day of Peace this year is being celebrated in the shadow of the dramatic events of September 11 last. On that day, a terrible crime was committed: in a few brief hours thousands of innocent people of many ethnic backgrounds were slaughtered. Since then, people throughout the world have felt a profound personal vulnerability and a new fear for the future. Addressing this state of mind, the Church testifies to her hope, based on the conviction that evil, the *mysterium iniquitatis* (the mystery of evil), does not have the final word in human affairs. The history of salvation, narrated in Sacred Scripture, sheds clear light on the entire history of the world and shows us that human events are always accompanied by the merciful Providence of God, who knows how to touch even the most hardened of hearts and bring good fruits even from what seems utterly barren soil. This is the hope that sustains the Church at the beginning of 2002: that, by the grace of God, a world in which the power of evil seems once again to have taken the upper hand will in fact be transformed into a world in which the noblest aspirations of the human heart will triumph, a world in which true peace will prevail.

Message for the World Day of Peace, January 1, 2002

September 18

⎯⎯⎯⎯∞∞∞⎯⎯⎯⎯

The Work of Justice and Love

Recent events, including the terrible killings [of September 11, 2001], move me to return to a theme that often stirs in the depths of my heart when I remember the events of history that have marked my life, especially my youth. The enormous suffering of peoples and individuals, even among my own friends and acquaintances, caused by Nazi and Communist totalitarianism has never been far from my thoughts and prayers. I have often paused to reflect on the persistent question: *How do we restore the moral and social order subjected to such horrific violence?* My reasoned conviction, confirmed in turn by biblical revelation, is that the shattered order cannot be fully restored except by a response that combines justice with forgiveness. *The pillars of true peace are justice and the form of love that is forgiveness.* But in the present circumstances, how can we speak of justice and forgiveness as the source and condition of peace? *We can and we must,* no matter how difficult this may be, a difficulty that often comes from thinking that justice and forgiveness are irreconcilable. But forgiveness is the opposite of resentment and revenge, not of justice. In fact, true peace is "the work of justice" (Isa. 32:17). As the Second Vatican Council put it, peace is "the fruit of that right ordering of things with which the divine founder has invested human society and which must be actualized by man thirsting for an ever more perfect reign of justice" (*Gaudium et Spes*).

Message for the World Day of Peace, January 1, 2002

———— ∞ ————

The Globalization of Solidarity

My presence here among you is meant as a further sign that the Catholic Church wants to enter ever more deeply into dialogue with the religions of the world. She sees this dialogue as an act of love that has its roots in God himself. "God is love," proclaims the New Testament, "and whoever remains in love remains in God and God in him.... Let us love, then, because he loved us first.... No one who fails to love the brother whom he sees can love God, whom he has not seen" (1 John 4:16, 19–20). It is a sign of hope that the religions of the world are becoming more aware of their shared responsibility for the well-being of the human family. This is a crucial part of the *globalization of solidarity,* which must come if the future of the world is to be secure. This sense of shared responsibility increases as we discover more of what we have in common as religious men and women. Which of us does not grapple with the mystery of suffering and death? Which of us does not hold life, truth, peace, freedom, and justice to be supremely important values? Which of us is not convinced that moral goodness is soundly rooted in the individual's and society's openness to the transcendent world of the Divinity? Which of us does not believe that the way to God requires prayer, silence, asceticism, sacrifice, and humility? Which of us is not concerned that scientific and technical progress should be accompanied by spiritual and moral awareness? And which of us does not believe that the challenges now facing society can only be met by building a civilization of love . . . ?

Discourse with the Religious Leaders of India, New Delhi, November 7, 1999

―∞―

Listen to Your Inner Voice

All of you are bidden to give hope to humanity by transforming it from within by the force of the gospel. Some of you will fulfill this call by founding a Christian home, which will become a missionary cell. Others will feel drawn to live in chastity, poor and available to others in the religious life, to radiate the Beatitudes. Others again will be ready to consecrate their life as deacons or as priests to lead the people of God on its journey. Today, to each one of you, the Virgin addresses an important piece of advice, as she did at Cana when the wine ran low at the wedding: "Whatever he tells you, do it" (John 2:5). So that your life may retain a taste of the feast, be dynamic and joyful in the service of others. Seek to carry out what Christ asks of you; answer with Mary's "fiat": "I am the servant of the Lord" (Luke 1:38).

Radio Address to a Pilgrimage to Lourdes, France, August 15, 1988

––––– ∞∞∞ –––––

Challenge of the New Millennium: The Culture of Dialogue

As we survey the situation of humanity, is it too much to speak of *a crisis of civilization?* We see great technological advances, but these are not always accompanied by great spiritual and moral progress. We see as well a growing gap between the rich and poor—at the level of individuals and of nations. Many people make great sacrifices to show solidarity with those suffering want or hunger or disease, but there is still lacking the collective will to overcome scandalous inequalities and to create new structures that will enable all peoples to have a just share in the world's resources. Then there are the many conflicts continually breaking out around the world—wars between nations, armed struggles within nations, conflicts that linger like festering wounds and cry out for a healing that seems never to come. Inevitably it is the weakest who suffer most in these conflicts, especially when they are uprooted from their homes and forced to flee. Surely this is not the way humanity is supposed to live. Is it not therefore right to say that there is indeed a crisis of civilization, which can be countered only by *a new civilization of love* founded on the universal values of peace, solidarity, justice, and liberty?

Discourse at St. Peter's, October 28, 1999

We Are a Resurrection and Ascension People

Christ returns to the glory that has always been his as Son of God, consubstantial with the Father, but he returns with the *human nature* taken from Mary, bringing with him the glorious marks of his Passion. Indeed, he ascends to the Father as the Redeemer of man, to send us the gift of the Spirit, who gives life. Therefore, the Ascension is a great message of *hope.* Contemporary man, who, despite the technical and scientific achievements of which he is justly proud, risks losing the ultimate meaning of life, finds an indication of his destiny in this mystery. The glorified humanity of Christ is also *our humanity:* in his person Jesus linked God forever to the history of man and man to the heart of the heavenly Father. "And behold, I am with you always, until the end of the age" (Matt. 28:20). Thus the Lord assures us, and this promise of his *invigorates the apostolic commitment of Christians.* After two thousand years of history, the Church still feels *young* today; with her early enthusiasm, she wishes to bring the proclamation of God's love to the world.

Discourse at the Vatican, May 15, 1994

———∞———

An Expression of the Person

Still, man cannot be authentically free, cannot totally realize his humanity, if he does not recognize and does not live the transcendence of his own being over the world and his rapport with God. To the uplifting of man belongs not only the promotion of his humanity, but also the opening of his humanity to God. Culture implies giving to man, to every man and to the community of man, a human and divine dimension that springs from the depths of the spirit from the clearness of thought and the generous disinterestedness of love. As I have previously said: Where freedom does not exist we cannot have culture. It is because of this that the true culture of a people, its full humanization, cannot develop within the constraints of political or economic power, but must be helped by the one and the other by every form of public and private initiative that conforms to true humanism, to the tradition and authentic spirit of a people. Culture that is born from freedom should then spread in a regime of freedom such as your work, your dedication, your professionalism are constantly committed to defend.

Discourse to the Officers of the Italian Army, July 9, 1984

———◆◆◆———

Always on the Way

Before all and above all, I exhort you to turn your attention toward the divine Master, from whom you will obtain light for this work. The Gospel can also be read as a report on the work of Jesus in regard to his disciples. Jesus proclaims from the beginning the "good news" of the fatherly love of God, but then he gradually teaches the profound riches of this message, and he gradually reveals himself and the Father, with infinite patience, beginning over again if necessary: "After I have been with you all this time, you still do not know me?" (John 14:9). We can also read the Gospel to discover the method Jesus used to give his disciples the basic formation, their initial training. The "continuous formation" as it is called, will come later, and the Holy Spirit will complete it. This will bring the apostles to an understanding of how much Jesus had taught them, will help them to arrive at the fullness of the truth, to deepen it in their lives, and to follow in the way of the freedom of the sons of God (John 14:26; Rom. 8:14ff.). From this look at Jesus and his lesson comes the confirmation of an experience that we have all had: none of us has reached the perfection to which we are called, each of us is always in formation, is always on the way.

Address to the Participants of the Third World Congress of Secular Institutes,
Domus Mariae, Rome, Italy, August 28, 1984

The Gospel of Love and Work

All sowers of the Word, Christ, derive strength for their service from that ineffable mystery of the unification of God as Word with human nature in each man once and for all (so says the last council, *Gaudium et Spes*). The words of the Gospel fall on the good soil of human souls, but it was *the eternal Word,* begotten in the Virgin Mother by the Holy Spirit, that has become the *source of life for human souls.* In the parable (Mark 4:1–9) Christ draws particular attention to the soil of human souls and consciences. He points out what happens to the word of God, depending on the quality of that exceptional soil. We *hear about the seed* that was trampled upon, devoured by the birds of the air, and *never bore fruit in the human heart,* because man had succumbed to the Evil One and failed to understand the Word. We hear about the seed that fell upon rock, upon barren soil and *could not take root,* so it did not pass even the first stage. We then heard about the seed that fell among thistles and thorns and *withered away* as soon as it sprang up (these thistles and thorns are the illusions of temporal life and of passing prosperity). Only the seed that fell on good fertile soil "sprang up and bore fruit." Who is the *good soil? He who listens to the word and understands it.* He hears and understands. It is not sufficient to hear; one must also embrace what one hears with one's mind and heart.

Homily at the Cathedral of Łomża, Poland, June 4, 1991

Making Use of One's Freedom

The moral order in the life of a person and society is united in substance with this inalienable right that is the norm that clearly distinguishes good from evil. Following this norm, the individual and every human community as well—society, the nation—*make correct use of its freedom*. They work in a suitable way to *fulfill their human dignity*. "You shall know the truth, and the truth will set you free" (John 8:32), says the Christ. This is *the key* to all moral order. On this way alone can human behavior, in all its dimensions, be free from relativism, utilitarianism, and egoism, which represent different forms of reduction to moral slavery.

Discourse at the Vatican, May 8, 1991

———∞———

A Poetic Prayer

The undulating wood slopes down
To the rhythm of mountain streams ...
If you want to find the source, you have to go up, against the current.
Break through, search, don't yield,
You know it must be here somewhere.
Where are you? ... Source, where are you?!

Silence ...
Stream, woodland stream,
Tell me the secret
Of your origin!

(Silence—why are you silent? With what care you have hidden the mystery
    of your origin!)

Let me wet my lips
In spring water, to feel its freshness,
Its life-giving freshness.

Roman Triptych: The Poetry of John Paul II

The Level of Moral Value

So we find ourselves here at a crucial moment, when at every step time and eternity meet at a level that is proper to man. It is the level of the conscience, *the level of moral values:* the conscience is the most important dimension of time and history. For history is written not only by the events that in a certain sense happen "from inside"; it is written first of all "from within": it is the *history* of human consciences, of moral victories and defeats. Hereto the essential greatness of man finds its foundation: his authentically human dignity. This is that interior treasure whereby man "continually goes beyond himself" in the direction of eternity. If it is true that "it is established that people would die only once," it is also true that man carries with him the treasure of conscience, the deposit of good and evil, across the frontier of death in order that *in the sight of him who is holiness itself,* he may find the ultimate and definitive truth about his whole life: "after that comes judgment." This is just what happens in the conscience: in the interior truth of our acts, in a certain sense, there is constantly present the dimension of eternal life. And simultaneously the same conscience, through moral values, imprints the most expressive seal upon the life of the generations, upon the history and culture of human environments, societies, nations, and of all humanity.

Apostolic Letter to the Youth of the World, March 31, 1985

September 29

The Tradition of Mt. Carmel

As you may recall in the apostolic letter I formerly addressed to your religious family (the Carmelite friars) on the occasion of the fourth centenary of the death of St. John of the Cross, I emphasized the necessity of giving new life to the faith by advancing "the new evangelization, beginning with a re-evangelization of believers, opening them more and more to the teachings and light of Christ." Jesus represents the heart of contemplation and service typical of the spirituality of St. Teresa of Jesus and of St. John of the Cross and the other great masters of your Carmelite tradition. It is to God and to him alone that you must tend, dear brothers, with the ease and freedom of heart proper to those who love the Most High above everything and everybody and who run directly and decisively toward the essential. *You renounce everything in order to give everything.* You discover the *"nothing"* of the creature and the *"everything"* of God in a total progressive abandonment of the Lord's will. Following your spiritual masters, you will walk toward the mountain of holiness, thirsting for the "one thing necessary" (Luke 18:22), desiring the Absolute, firm in the faith, and with a spirit open to the limitless horizons of Christ's love. Yours will certainly be a *journey of joy and holiness,* a witness of purity and authentic inner perfection. You will be guides to asceticism and holiness and will lead souls to contemplate and possess God.

Discourse to the Discalced Carmelites, Rome, Italy, April 22, 1991

⟁

Communion with Christ and One's Neighbor

God's love is not limited to just a few people, but is addressed to all. It *embraces and includes everyone,* inviting them to form one family. The Apostle Peter confirms this when he speaks about evangelization to the many people gathered together in the house of Cornelius the centurion: "God," he affirmed, "does not have favorites, but anybody of any nationality who fears God and does what is right is acceptable to him" (Acts 10:34–35). There are no limits to God's love for mankind: it does not recognize barriers of race or culture; it is universal; it is for everyone. It only asks us to be open to it and to welcome it: it only asks for honest and willing human soil to fertilize. Finally, it is a concrete love, made up of words and gestures that touch man in different situations, even in suffering and oppression, because it is love that frees and saves, that offers friendship and creates communion. All of this comes from the gift of the spirit poured out as a gift of love into the hearts of believers to enable them to glorify God and announce his wonders to all peoples.

Discourse at the Parish of St. Maria del'Olivo, Rome, Italy, May 5, 1991

October

—⚬⚬⚬—

October 1

───※───

Being Loved by God

The contemplation of God's love demands a response and a commitment. But which ones? We must ask ourselves. God's word, which we have just heard, fulfills our expectations. First of all man is asked to *let himself be loved by God.* This happens when one believes in his love and takes it seriously, when one accepts the gift of love into one's own life so that one is transformed and formed by it, especially in the relationship of solidarity and brotherhood, which unites people. Jesus Christ asks those who have been touched by the Father's love *to love one another and to love everyone as he loved them.* The originality and novelty of his commandment lies in the word "as," which means freely given, universal openness, concreteness of words and actions, a capacity to give even to the supreme sacrifice of oneself. In this way his love can spread itself, transform the human heart, and make of all a community gathered in his love. Jesus again asks his people to *abide in his love,* that is, to live firmly in communion with him in a constant relationship of friendship and dialogue. This is in order to experience full joy, to find the strength to observe the commandments, and finally to bear the fruit of justice, peace, holiness, and service.

Discourse at the Parish of St. Maria del'Olivo, Rome, Italy, May 5, 1991

October 2

The First Commandment

Creating man, God willed to clothe him with unequaled dignity; he made him in his image and likeness, capable of doing the work for which he is responsible. In this way human work itself pertains to the work of creation, as we see already in the first chapter of Genesis. God, in fact, creating man and woman, says to them: "Be fertile and multiply, fill the earth and subdue it" (Gen. 1:28). This is, in a manner of speaking, the first commandment of God inherent in the very order of creation. Thus human work corresponds to the will of God. When we say "Thy will be done," we also apply these words to the work that fills all the days of our lives! We see that we conform to this will of the Creator when our work and the human relations it implies are imbued with the values of initiative, courage, trust, and solidarity, which are so many reflections of the divine likeness in us. But we also know that many workers find themselves in situations that are difficult or contrary to the will of the Creator.

Speech at the Arbed Steel Mill, Luxembourg, May 15, 1985

October 3

The Mission of Jesus

Jesus of Nazareth brings God's plan to fulfillment. After receiving the Holy Spirit at his baptism, Jesus makes clear his messianic calling: he goes about Galilee "preaching the gospel of God and saying: 'The time is fulfilled, and the Kingdom of God is at hand; repent and believe in the gospel'" (Mark 1:14–15; Matt. 4:17; Luke 4:43). The proclamation and establishment of God's Kingdom are the purpose of his mission: "I was sent for this purpose" (Luke 4:43). But that is not all. Jesus himself is the "good news," as he declares at the very beginning of his mission in the synagogue at Nazareth, when he applies to himself the words of Isaiah about the Anointed One sent by the Spirit of the Lord (Luke 4:14–21). Since the "good news" is Christ, there is an identity between the message and the messenger, between saying, doing, and being. His power, the secret of the effectiveness of his actions, lies in his total identification with the message he announces; he proclaims the "good news" not to justify what he says or does but by what he is.

Encyclical Redemptoris Missio (The Mission of the Redeemer),
December 7, 1990

October 4

The Future of Peace

I know that like others of your age elsewhere in Italy and the world you are very sensitive to the question of peace. It has even been echoed in this meeting. And I wish to use this occasion to confide something to you. The talk about peace, on the pope's part, with the world's powerful figures, the addressing of messages to them, the intercession in favor of our more unfortunate and tormented brothers and sisters—all of this is destined to have an influence upon the future if at the same time there grows up a new generation of persons capable of framing in a positive way the relationships between persons, groups, and nations. And here you are called to the task because, as I said to the youth of Catholic Action: "The following of Christ is the following of peace, in peace. Peace in welcoming the message of his love. Peace in welcoming his Spirit. Peace in living in his grace, in his intimacy, by means of the sacraments and especially the Eucharist." Thus in your own small way, but from this very moment, you project into the future a pledge of peace and contribute toward changing the air that we now all breathe.

Discourse to the Youth of Genoa, Italy, September 22, 1985

October 5

The Essence of God

The writings of the Old Testament emphasize *God's justice*, but also his *clemency and mercy*. They underline especially God's faithfulness to the covenant, which is an aspect of his "immutability" (e.g., Ps. 111:7–9; Isa. 65:1–2, 16–19). If they speak of God's anger, this is always the *just anger* of a God who is "slow to anger and abounding in steadfast love" (Ps. 145:8). Finally, if they always in the above-mentioned anthropomorphic concept set out in relief God's "jealousy" of his covenant with his people, they always present it as an attribute of love: "The zeal of the Lord of Hosts" (Isa. 9:7). We have already said previously that God's attributes are not distinguished from his Essence; therefore it would be more exact to speak not so much of a just, faithful God, but rather of God who is *justice, faithfulness, clemency, mercy*—just as St. John has written that "God is Love" (1 John 4:16).

Discourse at the Vatican, October 2, 1985

The Coming Kingdom

The ministry of Jesus is described in the context of his journeys within his homeland. Before Easter, the scope of his mission was focused on Israel. Nevertheless, Jesus offers a new element of extreme importance. The eschatological reality is not relegated to a remote "end of the world," but is already close and at work in our midst. The Kingdom of God is at hand (Mark 1:15); its coming is to be prayed for (Matt. 6:10); faith can glimpse it already at work in signs such as miracles (Matt. 11:4–5) and exorcisms (Matt. 12:25–28), in the choosing of the Twelve (Mark 3:13–19), and in the proclamation of the "good news" to the poor (Luke 4:18). Jesus's encounters with Gentiles make it clear that entry into the Kingdom comes through faith and conversion (Mark 1:15), and not merely by reason of ethnic background.

Encyclical Redemptoris Missio (The Mission of the Redeemer),
December 7, 1990

October 7

Our Eyes on the Face of Christ

The most important reason for proposing again the praying of the Rosary is the fact that it constitutes a valid means of fostering among the faithful *the commitment to the contemplation of the face of Christ,* to which I invited everyone at the end of the Great Jubilee of the Year 2000. The Virgin Mary is the unrivalled model of Christian contemplation. From Jesus's Conception until his Resurrection and Ascension into heaven, the Mother kept the gaze of her Immaculate heart on her divine Son: a wonderful, penetrating, sorrowful and radiant insight. It is this *Marian look* full of faith and love, that the individual Christian and the ecclesial community make their own when they recite the Rosary.

Angelus Message, October 27, 2002

---◆◆◆---

The Source of Love

The source of love is God. Love, an uncreated gift, is part of the inner mystery of God and is the very nucleus of theology. In creation and in the covenant *Love is made manifest not only as motive but also as fact,* as reality, a consequence of divine working. Precisely for this reason, the world that emerged from the hands of God the Creator is itself structured on a basis of love. To be something created is to be something "endowed" above all with existence and, together with existence, nature—which reflects different levels of being, differing degrees of perfection and good in the world, from inferior beings to more perfect ones, although St. Thomas Aquinas declares that every being is perfect according to its kind.

Sign of Contradiction

October 9

━━━━∞∞∞━━━━

From the Jeweler's Shop

Love can be a collision
In which two selves realize profoundly
They ought to belong to each other, even though they have no
        Convenient moods and sensations.
It is one of these processes in the universe which bring a
        Synthesis,
Unite what was divided, broaden and enrich what was limited
        And narrow.

The Jeweler's Shop

October 10

October 10

Amen Means "Hope"

There is one fundamental prerequisite for those who enter the City of Salvation (Zion): "firm purpose, ... trust in you, ... trust" (Isa. 26:3–4). It is faith in God, a solid faith based on him who is the "everlasting rock" (Isa. 26:4). Confidence, already expressed in the etymological root of the Hebrew word *amen*, sums up the profession of faith in the Lord, who—as King David sang—is "my strength, my rock, my fortress, my deliverer; my God, my rock in whom I take refuge; my shield, and the horn of my salvation, my stronghold" (Ps. 18:1–2; 2 Sam. 22:2–3). The gift that God offers to the faithful is *peace* (Isa. 26:3), *the messianic gift par excellence*, the synthesis of life in justice, freedom, and the joy of communion.

Discourse at the Vatican, October 2, 2002

A Young Man in Love Wonders Aloud

I remember—I also asked that woman,
"Why do you wish to sell your wedding ring here?
What do you want to break with this gesture—
Your life?
Does not one sell one's life now and again?
Does one not break one's entire life
With every gesture?
But what of it?
The thing is not to go away,
And wander for days, months, even years—
The thing is to return and in the old place
To find oneself. Life is an adventure
And at the same time it has its logic
And consistency—
That is why one must not leave thought
And imagination on their own!"
"With what is thought to remain then?" Anna asked.
"It is to remain with truth, of course."

The Jeweler's Shop

———∞∞———

The Hero Reflects About Love

This is just what compels me to think about human love. There is no other matter embedded more strongly in the surface of human life, and there is no matter more unknown and more mysterious. The divergence between what lies on the surface and the mystery of love constitutes precisely the source of the drama. It is one of the greatest dramas of human existence. The surface of love has its current—swift, flickering, changeable: a kaleidoscope of waves and situations full of attraction. This current is sometimes so stunning that it carries people away— women and men. They get carried away by the thought that they have absorbed the whole secret of love, but in fact they have not yet even touched it. They are happy for a while, thinking they have reached the limits of existence and wrested all its secrets from it, so that nothing remains. That's how it is: on the other side of that rapture nothing remains, there is nothing left behind it. But there can't be nothing, there can't! Listen to me, there can't. Man is a *continuum*, a totality, and a continuity—so it cannot be that nothing remained.

The Jeweler's Shop

October 13

⚬⚬⚬

Man's Eternity Passes Through It

Love is not an adventure. It has the taste of the whole man. It has his weight. And the weight of his whole fate. It cannot be a single moment. Man's eternity passes through it. That is why it is to be found in the dimensions of God, because only he is eternity. Man looking out into time. To forget, to forget. To be for a moment only, only now—and cut oneself off from eternity. To take in everything at one moment and to lose everything immediately after. Ah, the curse of that next moment and all the moments that follow, moments through which you will look for the way back to the moment that has passed, to have it once more and through it—everything.

The Jeweler's Shop

The Anthem of the Drama

A new love could begin only through a meeting with the Bridegroom. What Anna felt of it at first was only the suffering. In the course of time a gradual calm came. And something new that was growing, was still intangible, and above all did not "taste" of love. One day they may learn to relish the taste of that something new.... At any rate, Anna is closer to it than Stefan. The cause lies in the past. The error resides simply there. The thing is that love carries people away *like an absolute,* although it lacks absolute dimensions. But acting under an illusion, they do not try to connect that love with *the* Love that has such a dimension. They do not even feel the need, blinded as they are so much by the force of their emotion as by lack of humility. They lack humility toward what love must be in its true essence. The more aware they are of it, the smaller the danger. Otherwise the danger is great: love will not stand the pressure of reality.

The Jeweler's Shop

October 15

The Church's Preferential Option for the Poor

The Second Vatican Council underscored a specific dimension of charity that prompts us, following Christ's example, to reach out to those who are most poor: "Christ was sent by the Father 'to bring good news to the poor, to heal the contrite of heart' (Luke 4:18), 'to seek and to save what was lost' (Luke 19:10). Similarly, the Church encompasses with love all who are afflicted with human suffering and in the poor and afflicted seizes the image of its poor and suffering Founder. It does all it can to relieve their need and in them to strive to serve Christ" (*Lumen Gentium*). It should first be noted that there is a development from the Old to the New Testament in evaluating the poor and their situation. In the Old Testament we often see the common human conviction that wealth is better than poverty and is the just reward for the upright and God-fearing person: "Blessed is the man who fears the Lord, who greatly delights in his commandments. . . . Wealth and riches are in his house" (Ps. 112:1, 3). Poverty is considered a punishment for those who reject the instruction of wisdom (Prov. 13:18).

Discourse at the Vatican, October 27, 1999

October 16

─── ∞ ───

The Poor of Yahweh

In the developing reflection on the theme of poverty, the latter acquires a religious value. God speaks of "his" poor (Isa. 49:13) who are identified with the "remnant of Israel," described as a humble and lowly people by the prophet Zephaniah (3:12). It is also said of the future messiah that he will take the poor and the oppressed to heart, as Isaiah states in the famous text about the root that would sprout from the stump of Jesse: "With righteousness he shall judge the poor and decide equity for the meek of the earth" (Isa. 11:4). This is why in the New Testament the good news of deliverance is announced to the poor, as Jesus himself stressed, applying to himself the prophecy of the book of Isaiah: "The spirit of the Lord is upon me, because he has anointed me to preach good news to the poor. He has sent me to proclaim release to the captives and recovery of sight to the blind, to set at liberty those who are oppressed, to proclaim the acceptable year of the Lord" (Luke 4:18; Isa. 61:1–2). To possess the "kingdom of the poor" it is necessary to have the interior attitude of the poor (Matt. 5:3; Luke 6:20). In the parable of the great feast, the poor, the crippled, the blind, and the lame—in a word the most suffering and marginalized social categories—were invited to the banquet (Luke 14:21). St. James would later say that God has chosen those who are poor in the world to be rich in faith and heirs of the kingdom, which he has promised to those who love him (James 2:5).

Discourse at the Vatican, October 27, 1999

October 17

Mother Teresa Gave Generously

"Whoever wants to be great among you must be your servant!" (Mark 10:43). With particular emotion we remember Mother Teresa, a great servant of the poor, of the Church, and of the whole world. Her life is a testimony to the dignity and the privilege of humble service. She had chosen to be not just the least but to be *the servant of the least.* As a real mother to the poor, she bent down to those suffering various forms of poverty. Her greatness lies in her ability to give without counting the cost, to give "until it hurts." Her life was a radical living and a bold proclamation of the gospel. The cry of Jesus on the cross, "I thirst" (John 19:28), expressing the depth of God's longing for man, penetrated Mother Teresa's soul and found fertile soil in her heart. *Satiating Jesus's thirst for love and for souls* in union with Mary, the Mother of Jesus, had become the sole aim of Mother Teresa's existence, an inner force that drew her out of herself and made her "run in haste" across the globe to labor for the salvation and the sanctification of "the poorest of the poor."

Beatification Homily at the Vatican, October 19, 2003

October 18

She Saw Christ in the Poor

"As you did to one of the least of these my brethren, you did it to me" (Matt. 25:40). This Gospel passage, so crucial in understanding Mother Teresa's service to the poor, was the basis of her faith-filled conviction that *in touching the broken bodies of the poor she was touching the body of Christ.* It was through Jesus himself, hidden under the distressing disguise of the poorest of the poor, that her service was directed. Mother Teresa highlights the deepest meaning of service—an act of love done to the hungry, thirsty, strangers, naked, sick, prisoners (Matt. 25:34–36) is done to Jesus himself. Recognizing him, she ministered to him with wholehearted devotion, and in expressing the delicacy of her spousal love thus in total gift of herself to God and neighbor, Mother Teresa found her greatest fulfillment and lived *the noblest qualities of her femininity.* She wanted to be a sign of "God's love, God's presence, and God's compassion" and so remind all of the value and dignity of each of God's children, "created to love and to be loved"—this was Mother Teresa's "bringing souls to God and God to souls" and satiating Christ's thirst, especially for those most in need, those whose vision of God had been dimmed by suffering and pain.

Beatification Homily at the Vatican, October 19, 2003

October 19

The Contemplative Mother Teresa

Where did Mother Teresa find the strength to place herself completely at the service of others? She found it in prayer and in *the silent contemplation of Jesus Christ, his holy face, his sacred heart.* She herself said as much: "The fruit of silence is prayer; the fruit of prayer is truth; the fruit of faith is love; the fruit of love is service; the fruit of service is peace." *Peace,* even at the side of the dying, even in nations at war, even in the face of attacks and hostile criticism. It was prayer that filled her heart with Christ's own peace and enabled her to radiate that peace to others. A missionary of charity, a missionary of peace, *a missionary of life*—Mother Teresa was all of these. She always spoke out in defense of human life, even when her message was unwelcome. Mother Teresa's whole existence was a *hymn to life.* Her daily encounters with death, leprosy, AIDS, and every kind of human suffering made her a forceful witness to the gospel of life. Her very smile was a "yes" to life, a joyful "yes" born of profound faith and love, a "yes" purified in the crucible of suffering. She renewed that "yes" each morning, in union with Mary, at the foot of Christ's Cross. The "thirst" of the crucified Jesus became Mother Teresa's own thirst and *the inspiration of her path of holiness.*

Beatification Homily at the Vatican, October 19, 2003

October 20

Mother Teresa Suffered Too

The whole of Mother Teresa's life and labor bore witness to the joy of loving, the greatness and dignity of every human person, the value of little things done faithfully and with love, and the surpassing worth of friendship with God. But there was another heroic side of this great woman that was revealed only after her death. Hidden from all eyes, hidden even from those closest to her, was her interior life marked by an experience of a deep, painful, and abiding feeling of being separated from God, even rejected by him, along with an ever-increasing longing for his love. She called her interior experience "the darkness." The "painful night" of her soul, which began around the time she started her work for the poor and continued to the end of her life, led Mother Teresa to an ever more profound union with God. Through the darkness she mystically participated in the thirst of Jesus, in his painful and burning longing for love, and she shared in the interior desolation of the poor.

Beatification Homily at the Vatican, October 19, 2003

---⊗⊗⊗---

A Spiritual Trial

The spread of depressive states has become disturbing. They reveal human, psychological, and spiritual frailties that, at least in part, are induced by society. It is important to become aware of the effect on people of messages conveyed by the "media," which exalt consumerism, the immediate satisfaction of desires, and the race for ever greater material well-being. It is necessary to propose new ways so that each person may build his or her own personality by cultivating spiritual life, the foundation of a mature existence. The enthusiastic participation in the World Youth Days shows that the young generations are seeking Someone who can illuminate their daily journey, giving them good reasons for living and helping them to face their difficulties.

Discourse at the Vatican for the Pontifical Council for Health and Pastoral Care, November 14, 2003

───── ∞∞∞ ─────

Discovering God's Love

You have stressed that *depression is always a spiritual trial.* The role of those who care for depressed persons and who do not have a specifically therapeutic task consists above all in helping them to rediscover their self-esteem, confidence in their own abilities, interest in the future, the desire to live. It is therefore important to stretch out a hand to the sick, to make them perceive the tenderness of God, to integrate them into a community of faith and life in which they can feel accepted, understood, supported, and respected, in a world in which they can love and be loved. For them as for everyone else contemplating Christ means letting oneself be "looked at" by him, an experience that opens one to hope and convinces one to choose life (Deut. 30:19).

Discourse at the Vatican for the Pontifical Council for Health and Pastoral Care, November 14, 2003

——∞——

The Twentieth-Century Martyrs
Are Our Inspiration

Disciples of Christ are called to contemplate and imitate the many witnesses of the Christian faith who lived in the last century in the East and in the West who persevered in their loyalty to the gospel in situations of hostility and persecution, often in the supreme sacrifice of shedding their blood. These witnesses are a convincing sign of hope that is held up first of all to the churches of Europe. Indeed, they bring us a witness of the fruitfulness and vitality of the gospel also in the contemporary world. They are truly a luminous beacon for the Church and for humanity, for they have made Christ's light shine in the darkness. They strove to serve Christ and his "gospel of hope" faithfully, and by their martyrdom expressed their faith and their love to a heroic degree, putting themselves generously at the service of their brethren. Thus they showed that obedience to the law of the gospel brings forth a moral life and a social harmony that honor and promote every person's dignity and freedom. It is therefore up to us to gather this rare and most precious heritage, this unique and exceptional patrimony, as did the first generations of Christians who built monumental memorials, basilicas, and places of pilgrimage over the tombs of the martyrs to remind everyone of their supreme sacrifice.

*Message to Cardinal Paul Poupard, President of the Council for Coordinating
the Pontifical Academies, November 3, 2003*

Be Not Afraid

I state right from the outset: "Be not afraid!" This is the same exhortation that resounded at the beginning of my ministry in the See of St. Peter. *Christ addressed this invitation many times to those he met.* The angel said to Mary: "Be not afraid!" (Luke 1:30). The same was said to Joseph: "Be not afraid!" (Matt. 1:20). Christ said the same to the apostles, to Peter, in various circumstances, and especially after his Resurrection. He kept telling them: "Be not afraid!" He sensed, in fact, that they were afraid. They were not sure if who they saw was the same Christ they had known. They were afraid when he was arrested; they were even more afraid after his Resurrection. The words Christ uttered are repeated by the Church. *And with the Church, they are repeated by the Pope.* I have done so since the first homily I gave in St. Peter's Square: "Be not afraid!" These are not words said into a void. They are profoundly rooted in the Gospel. They are simply the words of Christ himself.

Crossing the Threshold of Hope

October 25

Why Are We Afraid?

Of what should we not be afraid? We should not fear *the truth about ourselves.* One day Peter became aware of this, and with particular energy he said to Jesus: "Depart from me, Lord, for I am a sinful man" (Luke 5:8). Peter was not the only one aware of this truth. Every man has learned it. Every successor to Peter has learned it. I learned it very well. Everyone of us is *indebted to* Peter for what he said on that day: "Depart from me, Lord for I am a sinful man." Christ answered him: "Do not be afraid; from now on you will be catching men" (Luke 5:10). *Do not be afraid of men!* Man is always the same. The systems he creates are always imperfect, and the more imperfect they are, the more he is sure of himself. Where does this originate? It comes from the human heart. Our hearts are anxious. Christ knows our anguish best of all: "Christ knows that which is in every man" (John 2:25).

Crossing the Threshold of Hope

———∞∞∞———

Inside and Outside

Man is called to this (the fullness of Redemption) by word of the Gospel, therefore from "outside," but at the same time he is also called from "inside." The words of Christ, who in the Sermon on the Mount appealed to the heart, induce the listener, in a way, to this interior call. If he lets them act in him, he will be able to hear within him at the same time almost the echo of that "beginning." Christ referred to that good beginning on another occasion, to remind his listeners who man is, who woman is, and who we are for each other in the work of creation. The words Christ uttered in the Sermon on the Mount are not a call hurled into emptiness. They are not addressed to the man who is completely absorbed in the lust of the flesh. This man is unable to seek another form of mutual relations in the sphere of the perennial attraction that accompanies the history of man and woman precisely from the beginning. Christ's words bear witness that the original power (therein also the grace) of the mystery of creation becomes for each of them power *that is grace* of the mystery of Redemption. That concerns the very nature, the very substratum of the humanity of the person, the deepest impulses of the heart. Does not man feel at the same time a lust, a deep need to preserve the dignity of the mutual relations that find their expression in the body thanks to his masculinity and femininity? Does he not feel the need to impregnate them with everything that is noble and beautiful? Does he not feel the need to confer on them the supreme value, which is love?

Discourse at the Vatican, October 29, 1980

———✦———

The Words "Be Not Afraid" Bear Repeating

When, on October 22, 1978, I said the words, "Be not afraid!" in St. Peter's Square, I could not fully know how far they would take me and the entire Church. Their meaning came more from the Holy Spirit, the consoler promised by the Lord Jesus to his disciples, than from the man who spoke them. Nevertheless, with the passing of the years, I have recalled these words on many occasions. The exhortation "Be not afraid!" should be interpreted as having a very broad meaning. In a certain sense *it was an exhortation addressed to all people,* an exhortation to conquer fear in the present world situation, as much in the East as in the West, as much in the North as in the South. Have no fear of that which you yourselves have created, have no fear of all that man has produced, and that every day is becoming more dangerous for him! Finally have no fear of yourselves!

Crossing the Threshold of Hope

———∞∞∞———

Freedom Is Found in the Redemption

Why should we have no fear? Because man has been redeemed by God. In pronouncing these words in St. Peter's Square, I already knew that my first encyclical and my entire papacy would be tied to the truth of the Redemption. In the Redemption we find the most profound basis for the words "Be not afraid!": "for God so loved the world that he gave his only Son" (John 3:16). The Son is always present in the history of humanity as Redeemer. The Redemption pervades all of human history, even before Christ, and prepares its eschatological future. It is the light that "shines in the darkness, and the darkness has not overcome it" (John 1:5). *The power of Christ's Cross and Resurrection is greater than any evil which man could or should fear.*

Crossing the Threshold of Hope

October 29

Love of God, Love of Neighbor

The Eucharist is the sacred banquet whose *united brotherhood spurs the believer to bring the balm of charity to those in need of it.* The liturgical assembly, gathered round the altar, authentically expresses its catholicity when the communion that binds it to God becomes concrete care for every person, especially those in difficulty who are hoping for moral and material help. In this regard, I observed in the letter *Dies Domini* that "the Sunday Eucharist, therefore, not only does not absolve the faithful from the duties of charity, but on the contrary commits them even more 'to all the works of charity, of mercy, of apostolic outreach, by means of which it is seen that the faithful of Christ are not of this world and yet are the light of the world, giving glory to the Father in the presence of men.'" All Christian tradition testifies that there is no genuine worship of God without effective love of neighbor. The Eucharist, when it is celebrated truly and sincerely, encourages acts of acceptance and reconciliation among the community's members and with regard to all humanity.

Message to Archbishop Enzio d'Antonio of Lanciao-Ortona,
Castel Gandolfo, August 6, 1999

The Importance of Social Communications

I am well aware, in this regard, of how important it is to contribute to spreading Christian values through strong and active networking in newspapers and periodicals. The courageous witness of faith that each one offers within the mass media sector constitutes a precious service for the protection and promotion of the real good of the person and of the community. The constant development of the means of social communication has a growing influence on people and public opinion, and this increases the responsibility of those who are directly involved in the sector, because it induces them to make inspired choices in the search for truth and in serving the common good. It should be stressed that in today's society there is a strong desire for good that is not always adequately acknowledged in newspapers and radio-television news bulletins, where the parameters for evaluating events are often marked by commercial rather than by social criteria. There is a tendency to favor what is "sensational" instead of what would help people understand world events better. The danger is the distortion of the truth. To prevent this it is urgent that Christians involved in the information sector work together with all the people of goodwill for greater respect of the truth. By stressing themes such as peace, honesty, life, the family, and by not giving excessive importance to negative facts, they can help establish a new humanism that opens the doors to hope.

Message to the Catholic Union of the Press, Castel Gandolfo,
September 22, 1999

October 31

The Use of the Media

A simple appeal to the individual responsibility of those who work in social communication is insufficient to ensure the control of this complex process of change. A commitment of government authorities is necessary. What is necessary in particular is an overall new awareness on the part of users, who must be put in a position where they can refuse their condition as *passive receivers* of the messages that flood their homes, involving their families. The "mass media" often risk becoming a substitute for educational bodies, indicating cultural and behavioral models that are not always positive and to which young people are especially vulnerable. It is therefore essential to provide everyone with suitable cultural instruments for dialogue with the means of social communication, so as to direct their information choices in a positive direction, with respect for man and his conscience.

Message to the Catholic Union of the Press, Castel Gandolfo,
September 22, 1999

November

November 1

My Last Thoughts

As the end of my earthly life draws close, I think back to its beginning, to my parents, my brother and my sister (whom I never knew, for she died before I was born), to the parish of Wadowice, where I was baptized, to that city of my youth, to my peers, my companions of both sexes at elementary school, at high school, at university, until the time of the Occupation, when I worked as a laborer, and later, to the parish in Niegowic, to St. Florian's Parish in Krakow, to the pastoral work of academics, to the context ... To all the contexts ... To Krakow and to Rome ... To the persons who were especially entrusted to me by the Lord. I want to say just one thing to them all: "May God reward you!" *In manus tuas, Domine, commendo spiritum meum.* Into your hands, O Lord, I commend my spirit.

My Final Testament, March 17, 2000

Revere

It is here, beneath the wondrous Sistine profusion of color
that the Cardinals assemble—
the community responsible for the legacy of the
keys of the Kingdom.
They come here, to this very place.
And once more Michelangelo wraps them in his vision.
"In Him we live and move and have our being."
Behold, the creating hand of the Almighty,
      the Ancient One
reaching toward Adam . . .
In the beginning God created . . .
He, who sees all things . . .
The colors of the Sistine will then speak the
      word of the Lord:
"To you I will give the keys of the Kingdom."
Those entrusted with the legacy of the keys
gather here, letting themselves be enfolded
By the vision left to us by Michelangelo—
So it was in August, and again in October,
in the memorable year of the two Conclaves,
and so it will be once more, when the time comes,
after my death.

The Poetry of John Paul II: Roman Triptych

November 3

Solidarity: My Seminal Thought

In 1981 during the state of emergency, I said to the representatives of the Trade Union *Solidarnosc:* "The activity of the trade unions does not have a political character; it must not be an instrument of the action of anyone, of any political party, in order to be able to concentrate, in an exclusive and fully autonomous way, on the great social good of human work and of working people." It seems that it was the politicization of the trade union—probably a historical necessity—that led to its weakening. As I wrote in the encyclical *Laborem Exercens,* the state's authority is an indirect employer whose interests do not usually correspond to the employee's needs. It seems that *Solidarnosc,* at a certain stage in history, on entering directly into the world of politics and assuming responsibility for governing the country, had no option but to give up defending the interests of workers in many economic and public sectors. May I say that today, if *Solidarnosc* truly desires to serve the nation, it should return to its roots, to the ideals that illuminated it as a trade union. Power passes from hand to hand and workers, farmers, teachers, health-care workers, and all other workers, independently of the authority in power in the country, are expecting help with defending their rights. *Solidarnosc* cannot overlook this.

Message to the Members of the Polish Solidarnosc *Union, November 11, 2003*

Adam Sapieha: My Model

Prince Cardinal Sapieha was a Polish aristocrat in the true sense of the word. He was born in Krasiczyn near Przemysl. I once made a special trip there just to see the castle in which he was born. He was ordained a priest for the diocese of Lviv. He worked at the Vatican during the pontificate of Pius X, acting as assistant secret chamberlain. He did a great deal of good for the Polish cause at that time. In 1912 he was named a bishop and was ordained by St. Pius X himself for the See of Krakow. He took possession of the see that same year just before the First World War. After the outbreak of hostilities he established the Bishop's Committee for War Victims, commonly known as the Prince Bishop's Committee in Krakow. In due course the Committee expanded its activities to include the whole country. The archbishop was extraordinarily active during the war years and for this he was greatly respected all over Poland. He became a cardinal only after the Second World War. Since the days of Cardinal Olesnicki, a number of archbishops of Krakow had become cardinals before him, including Dunajewski and Puzyna, but it was Sapieha who earned the title of "Indomitable Prince." It is true: Sapieha was a fine role model for me, *principally because he was a shepherd.* Even before the Second World War broke out, he had told the Pope that he wanted to retire from the See of Krakow, but Pius XII did not agree to this. He said to him: "War is coming; you will be needed." He died as the Cardinal of Krakow at the age of eighty-two.

Rise, Let Us Be on Our Way

November 5

───❦───

My Deepest Thought

I have lately given much thought to the liberating force of suffering. It is on suffering that Christ's system rests, beginning with the cross and ending with the smallest human torment. This is the true *messiad* (the true source or hope of belief in a Messiah).

Letter to Mieczyslaw Kotlarczyk, November 2, 1939

—∞∞∞—

My Unfolding Vocation:
The Cause of Christian Unity

I know well, as I explained in the encyclical *Ecclesia de Eucharistia,* that our being prevented by all these reasons from immediately taking part in the Sacrament of Unity, sharing the eucharistic Bread and drinking from the Common Cup at the table of the Lord, causes much suffering and disappointment. None of this should lead to resignation; indeed, on the contrary, it must spur us to continue and to persevere in praying and working for unity. Even if in all probability the path that lies ahead is still long and arduous, it will be full of joy and hope. Indeed, every day we discover and experience the action and dynamism of the Spirit of God, whom we rejoice to see at work also in the churches and ecclesial communities that are not yet in full communion with the Catholic Church. Let us recognize "the riches of Christ and virtuous works in the lives of others who are bearing witness to Christ, sometimes even to the shedding of their blood" (*Unitatis Redintegratio*). *Rather than complaining about what is not yet possible, we must be grateful for and cheered by what already exists and is possible.* Doing what we can do now will cause us to grow in unity and will fire us with enthusiasm to overcome the difficulties. A Christian can never give up hope, lose heart, or be drained of enthusiasm. The unity of one Church that already subsists in the Catholic Church and can never be lost is our guarantee that the full unity of all Christians will also one day be a reality.

Vespers Homily Commemorating the Fortieth Anniversary of the Decree on Ecumenism, St. Peter's Basilica, November 13, 2004

My Essential Ecumenical Attitude:
"In All Things Love"

How should we imagine the future of ecumenism? First of all, we must strengthen the foundations of ecumenical activity, that is, our common faith in all that is expressed in baptismal profession, in the Apostolic Creed, and in the Nicene-Constantinople Creed. These doctrinal foundations express the faith professed by the Church since the time of the apostles. Then, on the basis of this faith we must develop the concept and *spirituality of communion.* "A communion of saints" and full communion do not mean abstract uniformity, but a wealth of legitimate diversities in gifts shared and recognized by all, according to the well-known proverb: *"In necessariis unitas, in dubiis libertas, in omnibus caritas"* (in necessities unity, in doubt liberty, but in all things charity).

> *Vesper Homily Commemorating the Fortieth Anniversary of the Decree on*
> *Ecumenism, St. Peter's Basilica, November 13, 2004*

Solidarity Is the New Word for Communion

A spirituality of communion also means an ability to think of our Christian brothers and sisters in the deep unity born from Baptism "as 'those who are part of me.' This makes us able to share ... and attend to their needs, to offer them deep and genuine friendship" (*Novo Millennio Ineunte*). *A spirituality of communion* "implies also the ability to see what is positive in others, to welcome it and prize it as a gift from God: not only as a gift for the brother or sister who has received it directly, but also as a 'gift for me.' *A spirituality of communion* means, finally, to know how to 'make room' for our brothers and sisters, bearing 'each other's burdens' (Gal. 6:2) and resisting the selfish temptations which constantly beset us and provoke competition, careerism, distrust, and jealousy. Let us have no illusions: unless we follow this spiritual path, external structures of communion will serve very little purpose. They should become mechanisms without a soul, 'masks' of communion rather than its means of expression and growth" (*Novo Millennio Ineunte*). To sum up, therefore, *a spirituality of communion* means traveling together toward unity in the integral profession of faith, in the sacraments and in ecclesiastical ministry (cf. *Lumen Gentium; Unitatis Redintegratio*).

Vesper Homily Commemorating the Fortieth Anniversary of the Decree on Ecumenism, St. Peter's Basilica, November 13, 2004

---∞∞∞---

My Desire for Unity Between East and West

In the transferal of such holy relics (Sts. Gregory the Theologian and John Chrysostom, two Fathers of the Eastern Church), we find a blessed occasion to purify our wounded memories in order to strengthen our journey of reconciliation, to confirm that the faith of these Holy Doctors is the faith of the Churches of East and West. We also witness to a favorable moment to "show in word and deed today the immense riches that our Churches preserve in the coffers of their traditions" (*Orientale Lumen*). This is the "acceptable time" to join our prayer to their intercession, so that the Lord will hasten the arrival of the moment when we can live full communion together in the celebration of the Holy Eucharist, and thus to contribute more effectively so that the world believes that Jesus Christ is Lord. Beloved brother (Patriarch Bartholomew I of Constantinople), I will never tire of searching out, steadfastly and with determination, this communion between Christ's disciples; my desire in responding to God's will, is to be a servant of communion "in truth and love so that the ship—that beautiful symbol which the World Council of Churches has chosen as its emblem—will not be buffeted by the storms and will one day reach its haven" (*Ut Unum Sint*).

Address to the Ecumenical Patriarch of Constantinople, Bartholomew I, for the Transferal of the Relics of Sts. Gregory Nazianzen and John Chrysostom, St. Peter's Basilica, November 27, 2004

⸺∞⸺

Communion Within the Church Universal: An Essential Concept

Every aspect of the Church's life must be understood in relation to the profound and mysterious communion that animates and sustains the ecclesial body. The "collegial spirit," which is the soul of the *collaboration between bishops* on the regional, national, and international levels and the soul of their union with the Successor of Peter, springs from each bishop's willingness to respond to the requirements of communion. The unity of the presbyterate, the mutual esteem, support, and collaboration between priests, religious, and laity bear witness to the vitality of that communion in the local church. Sharing in communion means giving priority in thoughts and actions to the love that Christ commanded (John 13:34) and that constitutes the most authentic testimony of our fidelity to the Lord: "Truly I say to you, as you did it to one of the least of these my brethren, you did it to me" (Matt. 25:40). I wish to encourage you in your continuing efforts to promote a dynamic sense of *participation and co-responsibility at all levels of the Church.* ... Such a spirit requires an increase of personal and collective maturity on the part of all concerned. With no weakening of the principle of authority properly exercised, it requires teamwork involving self-giving and joyful collaboration in responding to the urgent challenges of evangelization. It should never be used to justify individualism or lack of discipline or of coordination in pastoral activities.

Address from the Vatican to the Bishops of Zimbabwe, July 2, 1988

The Salvific Proclamation

"I do not the good I will to do, but the evil I do not intend" (Rom. 7:19). In the reading from the Letter to the Romans (7:18–25), St. Paul, painting a picture in strong and dramatic colors, points out the human inability to do good and avoid evil. But there *is a way out:* victory over evil comes to us from God's merciful goodness, manifested to the full in Christ. And as if with an impulse of joy, the apostle explains: "All praise to God through Jesus Christ our Lord!" (Rom. 7:25). Like Paul, the Church never ceases to proclaim this great "good news," which is for everyone: Christ who died and rose has overcome evil and set us free from sin. *He is our salvation.* This salvific proclamation rings out ceaselessly in our time too and constitutes the heart of the ecclesial community's mission. Man today—as in the past—seeks satisfying answers to the questions on the meaning of his life and death. During the period of theological formation, dear young people, you prepare yourselves to be able to provide faith responses adapted to the language and mind-set of our time. May everything, therefore, be directed to this exalted mission: the proclamation of Christ and the liberating power of his gospel.

Message to the Students of the Roman Universities, October 24, 2003

The Meaning of Love

"God is love." These words are contained in the First Letter of St. John (4:16). They are the keystone of the truth about God. That truth is revealed through numerous words and many events until it reaches the full certainty of faith with the coming of Christ. These words faithfully echo Christ's statement: "God so loved the world that he gave his only son, that whoever believes in him may not die but may have eternal life" (John 3:16). The Church's faith reaches its peak in this supreme truth: God is love! In Christ's Cross and Resurrection he revealed himself definitively as love. "So we know and believe the love God has for us. God is love, and he who abides in love abides in God, and God abides in him" (1 John 4:16). The truth that God is love constitutes the apex of all that has been revealed *"by the prophets and in these days by the Son,"* as the Letter to the Hebrews states (1:1–2). This truth illumines the whole content of Revelation, and particularly the revealed reality of the creation and of the covenant. Creation manifests the omnipotence of God the Creator. But the exercise of omnipotence is definitively explained by means of love. God created because he could do so. But his omnipotence was guided by wisdom and moved by love. This is the work of creation. Redemption has a more powerful eloquence and offers a more radical demonstration. Love remains as the expression of omnipotence in the face of evil, in the face of sin. Only omnipotent love can draw forth good from evil and new life from sin and death.

Discourse at the Vatican, October 2, 1985

November 13

The Biblical Roots of My Love for Mary

This filial relationship, this self-entrusting of a child to its mother, not only has its beginning *in Christ,* but can also be said to be *definitively directed toward him.* Mary can be said to continue to say to each individual the words she spoke at Cana in Galilee: "Do whatever he tells you" (John 2:5). For he, Christ, is the one mediator between God and mankind; he is "the way, and the truth, and the life" (John 14:6); it is he whom the Father has given to the world, so that man "should not perish but have eternal life" (John 3:16). The Virgin of Nazareth became the first "witness" of this saving love of the Father, and she also wishes *to remain its humble handmaid always and everywhere.* For every Christian, for every human being, Mary is the one who first "believed" and precisely with her faith as spouse and mother she wishes to act upon all those who entrust themselves to her as her children. And it is well known that the more her children persevere and progress in this attitude, the nearer Mary leads them to the "unsearchable riches of Christ" (Eph. 3:8). And to the same degree they recognize more and more clearly the dignity of man in all its fullness and the definitive meaning of his vocation, for (as is stated in *Gaudium et Spes*) "Christ ... fully reveals man to man himself."

Encyclical Redemptoris Mater (Mother of the Redeemer),
March 25, 1987

---cRRo---

My First Role as Bishop

The bishop is to become the servant of the Word. Precisely as a teacher he sits on the *cathedra*—the "chair"—eloquently situated in the church, known for that reason as the "cathedral," from which he is to preach, proclaim, and explain the Word of God. Our times have placed new demands on bishops with regard to their teaching office, but have also offered them wonderful new resources to help them preach the Gospel. The ease of travel has enabled bishops to visit the various churches and communities in their own dioceses more frequently. They have at their disposal radio, television, the Internet, and the printed word. There are others who assist the bishop in proclaiming the Word of God: priests and deacons, catechists and teachers, professors of theology, and an ever-growing number of educated laypersons faithful to the Gospel. But nothing can take the place of the bishop seated upon the *cathedra* or standing in the pulpit of his episcopal church, personally expounding the Word of God to those gathered around him. And he, like "every scribe who has become a disciple of the Kingdom of Heaven, is like the head of a household who brings from his storeroom things old and new" (Matt. 13:52). Here I wish to mention the Archbishop Emeritus of Milan, Cardinal Carlo Maria Martini, whose catechesis in the cathedral attracted crowds of listeners to whom he revealed the treasure of God's Word. This is only one of many examples that prove how hungry the people are for the Word of God. How important that this hunger be satisfied.

Rise, Let Us Be on Our Way

———∞∞∞———

Hunger for the Word

I have always been convinced that if I am to satisfy the people's hunger for the Word of God, I must follow the example of Mary and first listen to it myself *and ponder it in my heart* (Luke 2:19). I have also come to realize that a bishop must be able to listen to the people to whom he preaches the "good news." Amid today's flood of words, images, and sounds, it is important that a bishop not be thrown off course. He must listen attentively to God and to those around him, convinced that we are all united in the one mystery of God's saving Word.

Rise, Let Us Be on Our Way

November 16

The Religious Spirit of the Adult Male

In you there are values that must remain and be further developed. In you there are also precious spiritual values that must remain and be further developed: a religious spirit rich in feeling expressing itself in confidence in God, in the meaning of prayer, and in the Christian education of children; a deep respect for the family expressed by confidence in the woman, wife and mother, by love for your own children and by fidelity in marriage; *a keen sense of solidarity, which, through living in a group, feels the need to help one another and relieve those in need.* These are values of greatest importance that you must not let disappear or be uprooted.

Discourse to the Fishermen at Fano, Italy, August 12, 1984

November 17

———— ✺ ————

Peace: My Pastoral Goal

Perhaps it should be recognized that in recent years not much has been invested in defending peace; indeed, at times preference is given to allocating huge sums for purchasing weapons. It was as if they were "throwing peace to the winds." Many hopes were dampened. The daily news bulletins remind us that wars are continuing to poison people's lives, especially in the poorest countries. For example, how can we forget the long drawn-out violence that is causing blood to flow in the Middle East and in the Holy Land in particular? How can we remain indifferent to the ever broader panorama of conflicts that are involving various parts of the earth? What can we do? Despite the difficulties, we must not lose heart. It is everyone's duty to continue to work for peace and to be peacemakers. Peace is good for all. Every person is called to be a peacemaker in truth and in love.

Message for the Peace March from Perugia to Assisi, Italy, October 11, 2003

———∞∞∞———

I Am a Priest Among Priests

We priests are the celebrants, but also the guardians of this most sacred mystery. It is our relationship to the Eucharist that most clearly challenges us to lead a "sacred" life. This must shine forth from our whole way of being, but above all from the way we celebrate. Let us sit at the school of the saints! The Year of the Eucharist invites us to rediscover those saints who were vigorous proponents of eucharistic devotion (*Mane Nobiscum Domine*). Many beatified and canonized priests have given exemplary testimony in this regard, in kindling fervor among the faithful present at their celebrations of Mass. Many of them were known for their prolonged eucharistic adoration. To place ourselves before Jesus in the Eucharist, to take advantage of our "moments of solitude," and to fill them with his presence is to enliven our consecration by our personal relationship with Christ, from whom our life derives its joy and its meaning.

Holy Thursday Letter to Priests, Gemelli Hospital, Rome, Italy,
March 13, 2005

———∞———

I Am the Bishop of Rome

The call to become a bishop is certainly a great honor. This does not mean, however, that he was chosen for having distinguished himself among many others as an outstanding person and Christian. The honor comes from his mission to stand at the heart of the Church as the first in faith, first in love, first in fidelity, and first in service. The first and most important aspect of the honor due to a bishop lies in the responsibility associated with his ministry. *"A city set on a mountain cannot be hidden"* (Matt. 5:14). The bishop is always on a mountain, always on a lampstand, visible to all. He must always be aware that whatever happens in his life takes on greater meaning in his community: *"And the eyes of all looked intensely at him"* (Luke 4:20). Just as a father shapes the faith of his children primarily by his example of prayer and religious fervor, so also a bishop inspires his faithful by his behavior. That is why the author of the First Letter of Peter begs that bishops be *"a living example to the flock"* (1 Pet. 5:3)…. A bishop is called to personal holiness in a particular way so that the holiness of the Church community entrusted to his care may increase and deepen. It is his responsibility to promote the "universal call to holiness" of which the fifth chapter of the Dogmatic Constitution *Lumen Gentium* speaks: the personal holiness of every individual gives added beauty to the face of the Church, the Bride of Christ.

Rise, Let Us Be on Our Way

———∞∞∞———

Young Adults and Young Adolescents

I want to dedicate a special part of these reflections to children and young people. Aside from my meeting with them during parish visitations, I always devoted great attention to students, particularly university students, because the city of Krakow is traditionally a lively center of academic study. There were many opportunities for us to meet: from lectures and debates to days of recollection and retreats. Of course, I also kept in close contact with the priests who were assigned to pastoral ministry in this area. As the Communists suppressed all Catholic youth associations, a way had to be found to remedy the situation. The Servant of God, Father Franciszek Blachnicki, came upon the scene and initiated the so-called Oasis Movement. I became closely involved with this movement and tried to support it in every way possible. I defended it before the Communist authorities, I supported it financially, and, obviously, I took part in its activities. During the summer vacation I would often visit the so-called oases, which were camps organized for the young people belonging to the movement. I would preach to them, speak with them, climb mountains with them, and sing with them around the fire. I frequently celebrated mass for them in the open air. This all added up to a really intensive pastoral program.

Rise, Let Us Be on Our Way

November 21

My Love for Children

On May 18, 2003, I canonized Mother Urszula Ledochowska, O.S.U., a great educator. She was born in Austria, but at the end of the nineteenth century the whole family moved to Poland. She lived in Krakow for a few years. Her sister Maria Teresa, known as Mother of Africa, has been beatified, and her brother, Wlodzimierz, was the superior general of the Jesuits. *The example of these brothers and sisters illustrates how the desire for holiness can develop in a remarkable way if it finds favorable surroundings in a good family.* So much depends on life in the home! *Saints beget and raise saints!* When I remember educators like Mother Urszula, I instinctively think of children. During my pastoral visitations in Poland, as well as those that I make here in Rome, I have always tried and still try to find time to meet young children. I have never stopped encouraging priests to devote a generous amount of time to them in the confessional. It is very important to form the consciences of children and young people.... *I have always been convinced that without prayer we can never succeed in bringing children up well.* As a bishop I encouraged families and pastoral communities to develop in young children a desire to encounter God in private prayer. In this spirit I recently wrote: *"To pray the Rosary for children* and, even more, *with children* is a spiritual aid which should not be underestimated."

Rise, Let Us Be on Our Way

As an Artist to Other Artists

With this letter, I turn to you the artists of the world to assure you of my esteem and to help consolidate a more constructive partnership between art and the Church. Mine is an invitation to rediscover the depths of the spiritual and religious dimension, which had been typical of art in its noblest forms in every age. It is with this in mind that I appeal to you, artists of the written and spoken word, of the theater and music, of the plastic arts and the most recent technologies.... A noted Polish poet, Cyprian Norwid, wrote that "beauty is to enthuse us for work, and work is to raise us up." The theme of beauty is decisive for a discourse on art. It was already present when I stressed God's delighted gaze upon creation. In perceiving that all he had created was good, God saw that it was beautiful as well. The link between good and beautiful stirs fruitful reflection. In a certain sense, beauty is the visible form of the good, just as the good is the metaphysical condition of beauty. This was well understood by the Greeks, who, by fusing the two concepts, coined a term that embraces both: *kalokagathía,* or "beauty-goodness." On this point Plato writes: "The power of the Good has taken refuge in the nature of the Beautiful."

Letter to Artists, April 4, 1999

———∞∞∞———

Devotion to the Rosary: My Spiritual Legacy

The Rosary of the Virgin Mary, which gradually took form in the second millennium under the guidance of the Spirit of God, is a prayer loved by countless saints and encouraged by the magisterium. Simple yet profound, it still remains, at the dawn of this third millennium, a prayer of great significance, destined to bring forth a harvest of holiness. It blends easily into the spiritual journey of the Christian life, which, after two thousand years, has lost none of the freshness of its beginnings and feels drawn by the Spirit of God to "set out into the deep" (*duc in altum!*) in order once more to proclaim, and even cry out, before the world that Jesus Christ is Lord and Savior, "the way, and the truth, and the life" (John 14:6), "the goal of human history and the point on which the desires of history and civilization turn" (*Gaudium et Spes*). The Rosary, though clearly Marian in character, is at heart a Christocentric prayer. In the sobriety of its elements, it has all the *depth of the gospel message in its entirety,* of which it can be said to be a compendium. It is an echo of the prayer of Mary, her perennial *Magnificat* for the work of the redemptive Incarnation, which began in her virginal womb. With the Rosary, the Christian people *sit at the school of Mary* and are led to contemplate the beauty of the face of Christ and to experience the depths of his love. Through the Rosary the faithful receive abundant grace, as though from the very hands of the Mother of the Redeemer.

Apostolic Letter Rosarium Virginis Mariae *on the Most Holy Rosary,*
October 16, 2002

November 24

My Awareness of an Abiding Secularism

The disciple of Christ is constantly challenged by a spreading "practical atheism"—an indifference to God's loving plan that obscures the religious and moral sense of the human heart. Many either think and act as if God did not exist or tend to "privatize" religious belief and practice, so that there exists a bias toward indifferentism and the elimination of any real reference to binding truths and moral values. When the basic principles that inspire and direct human behavior are fragmentary and even at times contradictory, society increasingly struggles to maintain harmony and a sense of its own destiny. In a desire to find some common ground on which to build its programs and policies, it tends to restrict the contribution of those whose moral conscience is formed by their religious beliefs.

Discourse at the Vatican to the Bishops of New Jersey and Pennsylvania,
November 11, 1993

November 25

A Marian "Be Not Afraid"

At this point we need once again to return to *Totus Tuus* (Totally Yours). In your earlier question you spoke of the Mother of God and of the numerous private revelations that have taken place, especially in the last two centuries. I responded by explaining how devotion to Mary developed in my own personal life, beginning in my hometown, then in the shrine of Kalwaria, and finally at Jasna Gora. *Jasna Gora became part of the history of my homeland in the seventeenth century, as a sort of "Be not afraid!" spoken by Christ through the lips of his Mother.* On October 22, 1978, when I inherited the ministry of Peter in Rome, more than anything else it was this experience and devotion to Mary in my native land which I carried with me. "Be not afraid!" Christ said to the apostles (Luke 24:36) and to the women (Matt. 28:10) after the Resurrection. According to the Gospels, these words were not addressed to Mary. Strong in her faith, she had no fear. *Mary's participation in the victory of Christ became clear to me above all from the experience of my people.* Cardinal Stefan Wyszynski told me that his predecessor, Cardinal August Hlond, had spoken these prophetic words as he was dying: "The victory, if it comes, will come through Mary." During my pastoral ministry in Poland, I saw for myself how those words were coming true. After my election as Pope, as I became more involved in the problems of the universal Church, I came to have a similar conviction: on this universal level if victory comes it will be brought by Mary. *Christ will conquer through her, because he wants the Church's victories now and in the future to be linked to her.*

Crossing the Threshold of Hope

————∞∞∞————

My Fundamental Thought:
"A Notion of Neighbor"

The notion of "neighbor" forces us to recognize and to appreciate what in man is independent of his membership in any community; it forces us to observe and appreciate something that is far more absolute. The notion of "neighbor" is strictly related to man as such, to the value itself of the person, regardless of any of his relations to one or another community or to the society at large. The notion takes into account man's humanness alone, the humanness which is concretized in every man, as it is in myself. It provides the broadest basis for community, that reaches deeper than estrangement; it unites human beings, all human beings who are members in different human communities. Although membership in a community or society presupposes the reality that is referred to in the notion of "neighbor," it limits and removes to a more distant plane or even overshadows the broader concept of "neighbor"; it puts to the forefront man's relation and subordination to a given community—while when speaking of a neighbor we stress, on the contrary, only the most fundamental interrelations of all men in their humanness. The notion of "neighbor" refers then to the broadest, commonly shared reality of the human being and to the broadest foundations of interhuman community. Indeed, it is the very community of men, of all men, the community formed by their very humanness that is the basis of all other communities.

The Acting Person

November 27

———— ∞ ————

Another Seminal Idea: "Participation"

We have presented in this respect participation as a dynamic enactment of the person. Enactment, which is the person's essential feature, is manifested in that performance of actions "together with others" in that cooperation and coexistence which simultaneously serves the fulfillment of the person. Participation is closely associated with both the community and the personalistic value. This is precisely why it cannot be manifested solely by membership in some community, but through this membership must reach to the *humanness of every man*. Only because of the share in humanness itself, which is at the root of the notion of "neighbor," does the dynamic feature of participation attain its personal depth as well as its universal dimension. Only then can we claim that participation serves not just the fulfillment of some individual being, but that it also serves the fulfillment of every person in the community, indeed, because of his membership in the community. We must say this participation serves the fulfillment of persons in any community in which they act and exist. The ability to share in the *humanness itself of every man is the very core of all participation and the condition of the personalistic value of all acting and existing "together with others."*

The Acting Person

359

━━━∞∞∞━━━

Love: The Necessary Component of the Human Experience

In the first place "Thou shalt love" entails the juxtaposition of my neighbor with my own ego: "thy neighbor as thyself." The significance of the system's referring to my own self, that is, everyone's self, to the neighbor, is thereby brought to the fullest light. It appears fundamental because this system underlies any other reference system existing in a human community by its scope, simplicity, and depth.

The Acting Person

———◯◯◯———

Love: The Core of the Philosophical Endeavor

The commandment "Thou shalt love" has itself a thoroughly communal character; it tells what is necessary for a community to be formed, but more than anything else it brings into prominence what is necessary for *a community to be truly human.* This is why the two reference systems—of the relationship of the neighbor and to the membership of the community—must be considered jointly and not separately or, indeed, in opposition to each other, even though their distinction is entirely justified. This also is contained in the evangelical commandment. If we were to take a different point of view, then unavoidably some mutual limitations would arise; as a member of a community man would limit himself as a neighbor and vice versa. Such limitations would be a sign of such a fundamental weakness of the person, of an absence of that dynamic feature in the person which we have defined as participation, of a serious defect in the social nature of man, etc. Does not the social nature of man have its roots in this fundamental relation and consequently in the very humanness of man?

The Acting Person

Always in the Shadow of St. Andrew

The Lord Jesus called Andrew first among all the apostles. "He first found his brother Simon, and said to him, 'We have found the Messiah' (which means Christ). He brought him to Jesus. Jesus looked at him and said, 'So you are Simon, the son of John? You shall be called Cephas' (which means Peter)" (John 1:41–42). This detail, reported in the Gospel according to St. John, had long made it necessary for me to pay a visit to the ancient See of the Patriarchs at Constantinople, which venerates St. Andrew the Apostle particularly; and for me to do so precisely on November 30, the day that the liturgical calendar of the Western and Eastern Churches links with the memory of the one whom the Lord Jesus called first. Today I wish to thank Divine Providence for this visit, which I desired so much and which—under a special inspiration of that eternal Wisdom, worshiped for so many centuries in the Church on the Bosphorus—has brought about a mutual strengthening along those ways on which Patriarch Athenogorus I and my great predecessors, Popes John XXIII and Paul VI, had started. If, then, I may be allowed to refer to the analogy derived from the gospel event, the Successor of Peter and the Roman See wishes today to express his satisfaction at having heard the call coming from the East, from that See which surrounds with special veneration Andrew, the brother of Peter, for having followed that call. Thanks to that, he found himself, again, before Christ, who confirmed the vocation of Simon Peter on the basis of the brotherly tie with Andrew.

Discourse at the Vatican, December 5, 1979

December

———∞———

〜∞〜

My Unique Vocation:
A Bridge Between East and West

A pope, son of a Slav people, is particularly moved by the call of those peoples to whom the two saintly brothers Cyril and Methodius went. They were a glorious example of apostles of unity who were able to proclaim Christ in their search for communion between East and West amid the difficulties that sometimes set the two worlds against one another. The light of the East has illumined the Universal Church, from the moment when "a rising sun" appeared above us (Luke 1:78), Jesus Christ, our Lord, whom all Christians invoke as the Redeemer of Man and the Hope of the World. Since in fact we believe that venerable and ancient tradition of the Eastern churches is an integral part of the heritage of Christ's Church, the first need for Catholics is *to be familiar with that tradition,* so as to be nourished by it and to encourage the process of unity in the best way possible for each. Our Eastern Catholic brothers and sisters are very conscious of being the living bearers of this tradition, together with our Orthodox brothers and sisters. Members of the Catholic Church of the Latin tradition must also be fully acquainted with this treasure and thus feel a passionate longing that *the full manifestation of the Church's catholicity* be restored to the Church and to the world, expressed not by a single tradition, and still less by one community in opposition to the other. . . .

Apostolic Letter Orientale Lumen, *May 2, 1995*

———⟨∞⟩———

Jesus Brings the Priceless Gift of Peace to All

The *season of Advent* begins the journey of spiritual renewal in preparation for Christmas. The voices of the prophets who proclaim the Messiah ring out in the liturgy, asking for conversion of heart and for prayer. John the Baptist, the last of these and the greatest, cries out, *"Prepare the way of the Lord!"* (Luke 3:4), because he "will come to visit his people in peace" (Isa. 9:6). Come Christ, Prince of Peace! Preparing for his birth means reawakening the hope of peace in ourselves and throughout the world. *Build peace in hearts first of all* by laying down the weapons of rancor, revenge, and every form of selfishness. The world cries out for this peace! I am thinking especially with deep sorrow of the latest episodes of violence in the Middle East and on the African continent, as well as of those that daily newspapers are recording in so many other parts of the globe. I renew my appeal to the leaders of the great religions: let us join forces in preaching nonviolence, forgiveness, and reconciliation! *"Blessed are the meek, for they shall inherit the earth"* (Matt. 5:5). In this journey of expectation and hope that is Advent, the ecclesial community is identified more closely than ever with the Most Holy Virgin. May it be she, the Virgin of expectation, who helps us to open our hearts to the One who, by his coming among us, brings the priceless gift of peace to all humanity.

Discourse at the Vatican, December 3, 2003

---∞---

World AIDS Day

This is World AIDS Day, which recalls a disease that is still spreading quickly, especially in the poorest countries. As I pray for those who are afflicted by this scourge, I encourage all in the Church who are rendering an incalculable service of acceptance, care, and spiritual guidance to these brothers and sisters of ours.

Discourse at the Vatican, November 30, 2003

The Lord Is Near

The liturgy of Advent reminds us every day that the Lord is near. This closeness of the Lord is felt by all of us: both by us priests, reciting every day the marvelous major antiphons and by all Christians who try to prepare their hearts and their consciences for his coming. I know that in this period the confessionals of churches in my country, Poland, are thronged (no less than during Lent). I think that it is certainly the same in Italy also, and wherever a deep spirit pf faith makes the need felt of opening one's soul to the Lord who is about to come. The greatest joy of this expectation of Advent is that felt by children. I remember that it was just they who hurried most willingly in the parishes of my country to the Masses celebrated at dawn. The antiphon *"Rorate ...,"* from the word with which the liturgy opens: *"Rorate Coeli,"* (*Drop down dew, O ye heavens from above;* Isa. 45:8) *still rings.* Every day they counted how many "rungs" still remained on the "heavenly ladder," by which Jesus would descend to the earth, in order to be able to meet him at midnight of Christmas in the crib of Bethlehem.

Discourse at the Vatican, December 20, 1978

The Coming of the Son of Man Is the Beginning of Life

This truth (the narrative of the end of the world), although it is recalled also in the liturgy (of the season of Advent), ... is not, however, the specific truth announced now and in the whole period of Advent. It is not the principal word of the gospel. What is then the principal word? ... It is the coming of the Son of Man. The principal word of the gospel is not "passing away," "absence," but "the coming" and "the presence." It is not "death," but "life." The gospel is the good news, because it speaks the truth about life in the context of death. The coming of the Son of Man is the beginning of this life, and it is precisely Advent that speaks to us of this beginning. Advent, which answers the question: How must men live in the world with the prospect of death? How must man, who may lose his life in a flash, how must he live in this world, in order to meet the Son of Man whose coming is the beginning of the new life, the life more powerful than death?

Discourse at the Parish of St. Leonard of Port Maurice, Achilia, Italy, November 30, 1980

⸺༄⸺

My Christmas Prayer

Emmanuel! You are in our midst. *You are with us.* [You are] coming down to the uttermost consequences [of the Covenant] made from the beginning with man, and in spite of the fact that it was violated and broken so many times ... You are with us! *Emmanuel!* In a way that really surpasses everything that man could have thought of you. You are with us as *man.* You are wonderful, truly wonderful, O God, Creator and Lord of the universe, God with the Father Almighty! The Logos! The only Son! *God of power!* You are with us as man, as a *newborn* baby of the human race, *absolutely weak,* wrapped in swaddling clothes and placed in a manger, "because there was no place for them" in any inn (Luke 2:7). Is it not precisely that because you became man in this way, without a roof to shelter you, that you became *nearest to man?* Is it not precisely because you yourself, the newborn Jesus, are without a roof that you are nearest to those brothers and sisters ... who *have lost their homes* through the terrible earthquakes and storms? And the people that really come to their aid are precisely the ones who have you in their hearts, you who were born at Bethlehem without a home.

Christmas Day Prayer at the Vatican, 1980

———— ∞∞ ————

Mary as a Virgin Mother and Daughter

This is the day [Feast of the Immaculate Conception] on which we acknowledge that Mary—chosen particularly and eternally by God in his loving plan of salvation—also experienced salvation in a particular way: she was redeemed in an exceptional way through him to whom she, as a virgin mother, was to transmit human life.... In the Letter to the Ephesians St. Paul writes: "Blessed be the God and Father of our Lord Jesus Christ, who has blessed us in Christ with every spiritual blessing in the heavenly places, even as he chose us in him before the foundation of the world, that we should be holy and blameless before him" (1:3–4). These words *refer to Mary* in a particular and exceptional way. She in fact, more than all men—and more than the angels—"was chosen in Christ before the foundation of the world," because in a unique and unrepeatable way she was chosen for Christ, she was destined to be his Mother.... And these words too—since they refer to all Christians—refer to Mary in an exceptional way. She—precisely as mother—acquired *"divine* adoption" in the highest degree: chosen to be an adopted daughter in the eternal Son of God, precisely because he was to become, in the divine economy of salvation, her real Son, born of her, and therefore the Son of Man: of her—as we often sing—*the Beloved Daughter of God the Father!*

Discourse at the Basilica of St. Mary Major, Rome, Italy,
December 8, 1981

December 8

❦

"*Tota Pulchra Es Maria*": "You Are All Fair, O Mary"

Today the Church is celebrating the Immaculate Conception of the Blessed Virgin Mary. If Christ is the day that never fades, Mary is its dawn, shining with beauty. Chosen in advance to be *the Mother of the incarnate Word,* Mary is at the same time the firstfruits of his redeeming action. The grace of Christ the Redeemer acted in her in anticipation, preserving her from original sin and from any contagion of guilt. This is why Mary is *"full of grace"* (Luke 1:28), as the angel affirms when he brings her the announcement of her divine Motherhood. The human mind cannot claim to understand so great a miracle and mystery. It is faith that reveals to us that the Immaculate Conception of the Virgin is *a pledge of salvation* for every human creature, a pilgrim on this earth. Again, it is faith which reminds us that by virtue of her unique position, Mary is our steadfast support in the arduous struggle against sin and its consequences. I invite you straightaway to join me in praying for the intercession of Mary Immaculate for the Church, for the city of Rome and for the whole world. Place your trust in the intercession of Mary, *Mater Admirabilis* (Mother Most Admirable) and Mother of the Church. May God's blessings go with you!

Angelus Message at the Vatican, December 8, 2003

December 9

It Is Through Faith That We Embrace These Things

Through faith, man welcomes the salvation that the Father offers him in Jesus Christ. The man to whom the Lord gives salvation is truly blessed; the hearts of those who are at peace with God overflow with joy: "Be glad in the Lord, and rejoice, O righteous, and shout for joy, all you upright in heart!" (Ps. 32:11). The act of faith considered in its integrity must necessarily be expressed in concrete attitudes and decisions. In this way it becomes possible to overcome the apparent antithesis between faith and action. Faith understood in the full sense does not remain an abstract element, uprooted from everyday life, but involves all of a person's dimensions, including the existential contents and experiential aspects of his life.

Discourse to the Students of Rome at St. Peter's Basilica, October 15, 1999

—∞∞—

In the Midst of Winter
There Will Always Be Flowers

In their delicate and perfumed elegance, flowers bear witness to the magnificence of the Creator. Sacred Scripture often avails itself of the language of flowers to call upon man to praise of God. I recall the words of the son of Sirach: "Listen to me, O you holy sons, and bud like a rose growing by a stream of water.... Put forth blossoms like a lily, scatter the fragrance, and sing a hymn of praise; bless the Lord for all his works" (Sir. 39:13-14). But above all, how could I fail to remind you, who live among the flowers, of the unforgettable reference that the Lord Jesus made to them in the Gospel to call us to confidence in God the Father? "Consider the lilies of the field, how they grow; they neither toil nor spin; yet I tell you, even Solomon in all his glory was not arrayed like one of these...." (Matt. 6:28-30). The wildflower, nourished only by the fruitful sap of the earth that sustains it, is pointed out by the Lord as the image and example of serene and courageous abandonment to Providence, an attitude necessary to men in all ages, subjected as they always are to the temptation of mistrust and discouragement owing to personal adversities and natural and historical perturbations.

Discourse to the Florists of Italy, November 29, 1979

∞∞∞

Reconciliation: Preparing for the Encounter with God

Our *whole life* must be a *purifying preparation for our encounter with God*: tomorrow, in eternity, but also today in the Eucharist. The Gospel in today's liturgy reminds us explicitly: "If you are bringing your offering to the altar and there remember that your brother has something against you, leave your offering there before the altar; go and be reconciled with your brother first, and then come back and present your offering" (Matt. 5:23–24). Our participation in the Eucharist, which is the source of our reconciliation with God, must be also a source of our reconciliation with man.

Dialogue with Representatives of the Lay Apostolate at the Abbey of Einsiedeln, Switzerland, June 15, 1984

The Incarnation of Christ in a World of Conflict

Our everyday life unremittingly sets before us conflicts and tensions, hate and enmity: in our heart, in the family, in the parish community, at work, among nations. The more men yearn for mutual understanding and brotherly harmony, the more unattainable these seem for them. All the more strongly then is the Church today aware that God has *entrusted to her the message of reconciliation* (2 Cor. 5:19). God, who requires of us that we be reconciled with others before we bring our gift to the altar, is at the same time ready to make us disposed to this reconciliation to Christ and his Church. For God "in Christ was reconciling the world to himself" (2 Cor. 5:19) and has given us in the Church the precious sacrament of Reconciliation. True reconciliation between divided and hostile men is possible only when they allow themselves to be reconciled also with God. *Authentic brotherly love is founded on love for God, who is the common Father of all.*

Dialogue with Representatives of the Lay Apostolate at the Abbey of Einsiedeln, Switzerland, June 15, 1984

December 13

---❦---

Love: The Heart of the Redemption

I would like to emphasize a *fundamental point,* which is that the *ultimate reality,* in its fullness, *is charity.* "He who abides in love abides in God, and God in him" (1 John 4:16). Also the final goal of every Christian vocation is love; in institutes of consecrated life the profession of the evangelical counsels becomes the main highway that leads to the highest love of God and leads to our brothers, who are called to divine sonship. Now, in the mind-set of the work of formation, charity finds expression and support and maturation in fraternal communion in order to become witness and action. The Church does not ask of your institutes that life in common that is proper to other religious institutes, because of the demands of living in the world, which are postulated by your vocation. However, She asks for a "fraternal communion, rooted and founded in charity," that makes all the members "one only special family" (Canon 602); She requires that the members of the one and same Secular Institute "preserve communion among themselves, solicitously regarding unity of spirit and true fraternity" (Canon 716, 2).

Address to the Third World Congress of Secular Institutes, Castel Gandolfo,
August 28, 1984

Love and Anti-Love

Jesus left us love as his commandment. Love was to be the main prop and stay of the spiritual identity of his followers as they faced the hatred which at various times and in various forms was to be hurled at them by the world. "If the world hates you, know that before hating you it hated me" (John 15:18). The fact that the world hates is due to the existence of the anti-Love (Satan's love of himself): "*Amor sui usque ad contemptum Dei* (the love of self even to the contempt of God)." Jesus knows that this anti-Love will catch him up and, quoting Psalm 35, speaks of those who hate for no reason. Immediately, however, he returns to the perspective of the all-conquering love that he brought into the world, the *"Amor Dei usque ad contemptum sui* (the love of God even to the contempt of the self)."

Sign of Contradiction

December 15

———— ✹ ————

A Many-Splendored Thing

Somebody once wrote that love is many-sided. How true! Love certainly has many dimensions. The love that Jesus speaks of in his farewell discourse has the dimension of the sacrifice which he himself is about to make, so it has a historical dimension that speaks to man with all the majesty of the cross. Yet at the same time love has a suprahistorical dimension that goes beyond history, the dimension of the gift refused by the *"Amor sui usque ad contemptum Dei* (the love of self even to the contempt of God)" of Satan, and very often distorted or destroyed in the hearts of mankind. This gift must therefore return, by way of Jesus, to its source, so that man may rediscover himself within the covenant of all its fullness. That is the "why" of the cross. That is why Jesus leaves the Upper Room and begins the final stage of his journey toward the cross. God, who from the beginning wishes to be a gift to mankind and who is the overflowing source of all giving, is revealed in the mystery of the Cross. *"Deus absconditus* (the hidden God)" (Isa. 45:15).

Sign of Contradiction

———— ∞∞∞ ————

The Advent Cry Is for Justice and Peace

Opus iustitia pax! The work of justice is peace! The Advent cry that invokes the Savior, the righteous one, contains within itself a reference to all of these forms, these dimensions of injustice. *The righteous one is he who indicates the path toward the overcoming of injustice; and he who liberates from injustice.* How eloquent are the words of Isaiah: "Let the earth open, that salvation may sprout forth." And at the same time the Prophet prays: *"Shower,* O heavens from above, and let the skies rain down the righteous one" (45:8). In this way he becomes witness and expression of the desire that rises up beyond the human dimensions of justice, *beyond its purely "horizontal" meaning.*

Address to University Students at St. Peter's, December 12, 1986

---◎∞◎---

Advent: The Thirst Is High and Deep

The earth awaits rain, but *the drama* of this waiting period unfolds *in man's heart.* In fact, dependent upon rain is the fertility of the earth and, along with this, the possibility of survival as well as the existence of its inhabitants.... "The poor and needy seek water and there is none, and their tongue is parched with thirst; I the Lord will answer them...." (Isa. 41:17–18). A person living in the Sahel (a region of Africa under continual drought) or in other similar regions of the world suffering from drought certainly understands this *biblical image* better than those of us gathered here today. He understands it based on his own experience. But we too must extend our faith to this experience, which manifests itself in the words of Isaiah. And thus—by means of the simile of the earth's awaiting the rain—Israel's *awaiting of Advent* becomes comprehensible to us.

Address to University Students at St. Peter's, December 12, 1986

⊶

Prayer: The Best Preparation

In his life oriented "toward the Father" and deeply united to him, Jesus Christ is the model also of our prayer, of our life of mental and vocal prayer. He not only taught us to pray, principally in the *Our Father* (Matt. 6:9), but the example of his prayer offers us an essential occasion to reveal his bond and union with the Father. One can say that in his prayer the fact that "no one knows the Son except the Father" and "no one knows the Father except the Son" (Matt. 11:27; Luke 10:22) is confirmed in a very special way.

Discourse at the Vatican, August 24, 1988

꩜

The Incarnate Jesus: The Model of Prayer

Let us recall the more important occasions in his life of prayer. Jesus spends much time in prayer (e.g., Luke 6:12; 11:1), especially during the night, seeking places suitable for this (e.g., Mark 1:35; Matt. 14:23; Luke 6:12). *By prayer he prepared himself* for baptism in the Jordan (Luke 3:21) and to appoint the twelve apostles (Luke 6:12–13). Through the prayer in Gethsemane he prepared himself to face the Passion and death on the cross (Luke 22:42). The agony on Calvary was borne completely through prayer: from "My God, why hast Thou forsaken me?" (Ps. 22:1) to "Father, forgive them; for they know not what they do" (Luke 23:34), to the final act of abandonment, "Father into thy hands I commit my spirit" (Luke 23:46). *Yes, in life and in death, Jesus was a model of prayer.*

Discourse at the Vatican, August 24, 1988

---◦◦◦---

I Have Come to Do Your Will

Concerning Christ's prayer, we read in the Letter to the Hebrews that "in the days of his flesh, Jesus *offered up prayers and supplications, with loud cries* and tears, to him who was able to save him from death, and he was heard for his godly fear. Although he was a Son, he learned obedience through what he suffered" (5:7–8). This statement signifies that Jesus Christ perfectly fulfilled the Father's will, God's eternal design concerning the world's redemption at the price of the supreme sacrifice for love. According to John's Gospel this sacrifice *was not only a glorification of the Father by the Son, but also a glorification of the Son*, in accordance with the words of the priestly prayer of the Upper Room: "Father, the hour has come; glorify thy Son that thy Son may glorify thee, since thou hast given him power over all flesh, *to give eternal life* to all whom thou hast given him" (John 17:1–2). This is what was fulfilled on the Cross. The Resurrection after three days was the confirmation ... the expression of the glory with which "the Father glorified the Son." Christ's whole life of obedience and filial devotion *was based on his prayer,* which therefore gained for him the final glorification.

Discourse at the Vatican, August 24, 1988

Jesus: The Model of a Life United to the Father

The spirit of a loving and devoted child stands out also from the episode when the disciples requested that Jesus "teach them to pray" (Luke 11:1–2). He passed on to them, and to all the generations of their followers, a prayer that commences with that verbal and conceptual synthesis that is so expressive: "Our Father." In these words is manifested Christ's spirit directed as a Son toward the Father and engaged until the very end with the "Father's affairs" (Luke 2:49). In giving us this prayer for all times, Jesus has passed on to us, in and with it, *a model of life united in a filial way to the Father.* If we are to make our own this model for our life, in particular, if we are to participate in the mystery of Redemption by imitating Christ, it is necessary that we do not cease to pray to the Father as he has taught us.

Discourse at the Vatican, August 24, 1988

December 22

─── ∞ ───

The Annunciation of Mary

"Hail [Mary] full of grace!" (Luke 1:28). The later words "The Lord is with you! Blessed are you among women" refer to the same thing. The mystery of this choice, in which God remains free and at the same time leaves the human being free, leaves us full of amazement. In one sense—a very real sense—he waits to be chosen himself. Because freedom is an essential prerequisite for loving God and giving oneself to God, the Virgin replies fully in harmony with her inner truth. Mary's inner truth was this: she had already made an unconditional choice and bestowed herself completely on the one and only divine spouse. That is why she was able to say: "How can this come about, since I know no man?" (Luke 1:34), and she said it immediately when she heard the angel announce that she would conceive and give birth to the Son. For motherhood entails "knowing a man," and this is in direct contrast with her choice. When Mary asks her question, she is not contesting the divine plan: she is simply remarking that motherhood "according to the flesh" is difficult to reconcile with the choice she *had made* "according to the spirit."

Sign of Contradiction

December 23

———— ⁂ ————

The Visitation of Mary to Her Cousin Elizabeth

In Poland Our Lady's Visitation is lived in a way very special to us Poles. For nearly twenty years now we have had the pilgrimage of the Black Madonna—or rather the faithful copy of it, which was blessed by Pius XII in 1957 at the request of the Primate, Cardinal Wyszynski, in the name of the Polish episcopate. So in 1957 the pilgrimage began, and goes on to this day, and will continue to go on: from one diocese to the next, from one parish to the next, sometimes from one church to the next in the same parish. Thanks to the initiative of both pastors and faithful, it is also customary for other paintings of the Black Madonna to be carried ... from one house to another, from one family home to another. All this is possible thanks to deep religious experience, long and thorough spiritual preparation, willingness to undertake all night vigils, and prayer that unites all parishioners, neighbors, and members of families. And when after the first chapter of St. Luke's Gospel has been read, everybody joins in singing the Magnificat, one has the impression that *Our Lady herself* has put her own words into the mouths of our people. And a deep longing too is implicit: a longing for Mary to grant us the faith with which she, the Mother of God, sang her Magnificat; a longing to share in a special way Mary's faith, the faith which can make us strong and resolute as we too maintain our stand close to Christ. "Blessed is she who believed ..." (Luke 1:45).

Sign of Contradiction

⎯⎯∞⎯⎯

In the Stable of Bethlehem

"God is born and the powers tremble—the Lord of the heavens lies naked. The star fades and the brilliance turns to shadow—the Infinite accepts limitation. Despised—reclothed in glory, the mortal—the King of eternity." That extract from a Polish Christmas carol is, in my opinion, outstandingly expressive of the mystery of God incarnate. It is a mystery embracing contrasts: light and the darkness of night, God's infiniteness and man's limitations, glory and humiliation, immortality and mortality, divinity and human poverty. People who are brought face-to-face with the *mysterium fascinosum* (the fascinating mystery) of this holy Christmas night which makes all races one become conscious that what then happened was something immensely important, something without parallel in the history of mankind. The Nativity brings us within touching distance, so to speak, of our spiritual birth in God through grace. Born through faith and grace, we have been called *children of God*; and so we are says St. John (1 John 3:1).

Sign of Contradiction

December 25

A Christmas Prayer

We thank you, eternal Father, for the Motherhood of the Virgin Mary, who under the protection of Joseph, the carpenter of Nazareth, brought your Son into the world, in utter poverty. "He came to his own home, and his own people received him not" (John 1:11). And yet, he received all of us from his very birth and embraced each one of us with the eternal love of the Father, with the love that saves man, that raises the human conscience from sin. In him we have *reconciliation and the forgiveness of sins*. We thank you heavenly Father, for the child laid in a manger: in him "the goodness and loving-kindness of God our Savior appeared" (Titus 3:4). We thank you, eternal Father, for *this love*, which comes down *like a frail infant into the history of each human being*. We thank you, because, though he was rich, yet for our sake he became poor, so that by his poverty we might become rich (2 Cor. 8:9).... *Impel* individuals and peoples to break down the wall of selfishness, of arrogance and hate, in order to open themselves to fraternal respect for all human beings, near or far, because they are people, brothers and sisters in Christ. Induce all individuals to offer the help necessary for those in need, to renew their own hearts in the grace of Christ the Redeemer.

Message at St. Peter's Basilica, December 25, 1983

———— ∞∞∞ ————

Salvation Is in Jesus Christ Alone

"Jesus Christ of Nazareth ... crucified ... whom God raised from the dead" (Acts 4:10). At the beginning of the Church, Peter's firm words echoed in Jerusalem: it was *kerygma*, the Christian announcement of salvation destined, by Christ's will, to all men and to all the peoples on earth. After twenty centuries, the Church presents herself at the threshold of the third millennium with this same announcement, which constitutes her only treasure: Jesus Christ is the Lord; in him, and in no one else, there is salvation (Acts 4:12); He is the same yesterday, today, and forever (Heb. 13:8).

Homily for the Closing Mass of the Second Special Assembly for Europe of the Synod of Bishops, St. Peter's Basilica, October 23, 1999

December 27

The Needs of Young People

The mystery of the Church is the mystery of the life of Christ, the mystery of the living Christ. And this is the mystery that we are living, together with our people. *All our pastoral efforts are aimed at assisting the faithful to share more intimately in the life of Christ. . . .* This great treasure must be presented in an especially dynamic way to *the young people of the Church.* It is they who are assailed most by the problems of the modern world: it is they who need a particular grace from Christ to endure the Christian combat with temptation and sin. In Christ the young people can find the answers to the deep questions that are the basis of all Christian choices. How greatly they need the pastoral support of their bishops, together with their priests, in order to develop and persevere in their Christian vocation. In speaking of the young people and their needs *we cannot ignore the formidable problems of narcotics* in the world today, as well as in the causes of this phenomenon and the means needed to face this crisis of humanity. The whole human community must be mobilized to confront this issue. But here the Church has a specific task of educating to human dignity, to the respect of self, to the values of the spirit, to the search for the true joy that abides in the heart and not in the passing exhilaration of the senses.

Address to the Youth of Bangkok, Thailand, May 11, 1984

My Goals and Purposes

The whole of the argument developed thus far concerning the theory of good and evil belongs to moral philosophy. I devoted some years of work to these problems at the Catholic University at Lublin. I put together my ideas on the subject firstly in the book *Love and Responsibility,* then in *The Acting Person,* and finally in the Wednesday catecheses which were published under the title *Original Unity of Man and Woman.* On the basis of further reading and research undertaken during the ethics seminar at Lublin, I came to see how important these problems were for a number of contemporary thinkers: Max Scheler and other phenomenologists, Jean-Paul Sartre, Emmanuel Levinas, and Paul Ricoeur, but also Vladimir Soloviev, not to mention Fyodor Dostoyevsky. Through these analyses of anthropological reality, *various manifestations emerge of man's desire for redemption, and confirmation is given of the need for a redeemer if man is to attain salvation.*

Memory and Identity

———✸———

A Word of Warning About Our Age

The eclipse of the sense of God and of man leads to a practical materialism that breeds individualism, utilitarianism, and hedonism. Here too we see the permanent validity of the Apostle: "Since they did not see fit to acknowledge God, God gave them up to a base mind and to improper conduct" (Rom. 1:28). The values of *being* are replaced by those of *having*. The only goal that counts is the pursuit of one's own material well-being. The "quality of life" is interpreted primarily or exclusively as economic efficiency, inordinate consumerism, physical beauty, and pleasure, to the neglect of the more profound dimensions—interpersonal, spiritual, and religious—of existence. In such a context, *suffering*, an inescapable burden of human existence but also a factor of possible personal growth, is "censored," rejected as useless, indeed opposed as an evil always and in every way to be avoided. When it cannot be avoided and the prospect of even some future well-being vanishes, then life appears to have lost all meaning and the temptation grows in man to claim the right to suppress it. Within this same culture, the body is no longer perceived as a properly personal reality, a sign and place of relations with others, with God and with the world. It is reduced to pure materiality: it is simply a complex of organs, functions, and energies to be used according to the sole criteria of pleasure and efficiency. *Sexuality* too is depersonalized and exploited from being a sign, place, and language of love.

Encyclical Evangelium Vitae, *March 25, 1995*

The Good Shepherd Lays Down
His Life for the Sheep

In the homily I preached in St. Peter's Square on October 16, 2003, on the occasion of the twenty-fifth anniversary of my pontificate, I said: "While Jesus was saying these words, the Apostles did not realize that he was referring to himself. Not even his beloved apostle John knew it. He understood on Calvary, at the foot of the Cross, when he saw Jesus silently giving up his life for 'his sheep.' When the time came for John and the other Apostles to assume this same mission they then remembered his words. They realized that they would be able to fulfill their mission only because he had assured them that he himself would be working among men." *"You did not choose me, but I chose you and appointed you to go and bear fruit that will last"* (John 15:16). Not you, but I!—*says Christ.* This is the foundation of the efficacy of a bishop's pastoral mission.

Rise, Let Us Be on Our Way

A Farewell Note

I wanted to put these thoughts in writing, so as to share with others the signs of the love of Christ, who throughout the ages has been calling the successors of the apostles so as to pour forth his grace, through earthenware vessels, into the hearts of others. The words of St. Paul to the young bishop Timothy were constantly echoing in my mind: *"He has redeemed us and called us with a holy calling, not in virtue of our works, but in virtue of his own purpose and the grace which was granted to us in Christ Jesus before the world existed"* (2 Tim. 1:9).

Rise, Let Us Be on Our Way

Epilogue

Follow the Good Shepherd

"Follow me." As a young student Karol Wojtyla was thrilled by literature, the theater, and poetry. Working in a chemical plant, surrounded and threatened by the Nazi terror, he heard the voice of the Lord: "Follow me!" In this extraordinary setting he began to read books of philosophy and theology, and then entered the clandestine seminary established by Cardinal Sapieha. After the war he was able to complete his studies in the faculty of theology of the Jagiellonian University of Krakow.

How often, in his letters to priests and in his autobiographical books, has he spoken to us about his priesthood, to which he was ordained on November 1, 1946. In these texts he interprets his priesthood with particular reference to three sayings of the Lord. First: "You did not choose me, but I chose you. And I appointed you to go and bear fruit, fruit that will last" (John 15:16). The second saying is: "The good shepherd lays down his life for the sheep" (John 10:11). And then: "As the Father has loved me, so I have loved you; abide in my love" (John 15:9). In these three sayings we see the heart and soul of our Holy Father. He really went everywhere, untiringly, in order to bear fruit, fruit that lasts.

Rise, Let Us Be on Our Way is the title of his next to last book. "Rise, let us be on our way!"—with these words he roused us from a lethargic faith, from the sleep of the disciples of both yesterday and today. "Rise, let us be on our way!" he continues to say to us even today.

The Holy Father was a priest to the last, for he offered his life to God for his flock and for the entire human family, in a daily self-oblation for the service of the Church, especially amid the sufferings of his final months. And in this way he became one with Christ, the Good Shepherd, who loves his sheep.

Finally, "abide in my love": the pope who tried to meet everyone, who had an ability to forgive and to open his heart to all, tells us once again today, with these words of the Lord, that by abiding in the love of Christ we learn, at the school of Christ, the art of true love.

Loss Is Truly Gain

"Follow me!" In July 1958 the young priest Karol Wojtyla began a new stage in his journey with the Lord and in the footsteps of the Lord. Karol had gone to the Masuri lakes for his usual vacation, along with a group of young people who loved canoeing. But he brought with him a letter inviting him to call on the Primate of Poland, Cardinal Wyszynski. He could guess the purpose of the meeting: he was to be appointed as the auxiliary bishop of Krakow.

Leaving the academic world, leaving this challenging engagement with young people, leaving the great intellectual endeavor of striving to understand and interpret the mystery of that creature which is man and of communicating to today's world the Christian interpretation of our being—all this must have seemed to him like losing his very self, losing what had become the very human identity of this young priest.

"Follow me!" Karol Wojtyla accepted the appointment, for he heard in the Church's call the voice of Christ. And then he realized how true are the Lord's words: "Those who try to make their life secure will lose it, but those who lose their life will keep it" (Luke 17:33). Our pope—and we all know this—never wanted to make his own life secure, to keep it for himself; he wanted to give of himself unreservedly, to the very last moment, for Christ and thus also for us. And thus he came to experience how everything which he had given over into the Lord's hands came back to him in a new way.

His love of words, of poetry, of literature became an essential part of his pastoral mission and gave new vitality, new urgency, new attractiveness to the preaching of the Gospel, even when it is a sign of contradiction.

"You Know That I Love You"

"Follow me!" In October 1978 Cardinal Wojtyla once again heard the voice of the Lord. Once more there took place that dialogue with Peter reported in the Gospel of this Mass: "Simon, son of John, do you love me? Feed my sheep!" To the Lord's question, "Karol, do you love me?" the archbishop of Krakow answered from the depths of his heart: "Lord you know everything; you know that I love you." The love of Christ was the dominant force in the life of our beloved Holy Father. Anyone who ever saw him pray, who ever heard him preach, knows that. Thanks to his being profoundly rooted in Christ, he was able to bear a burden that transcends merely human abilities: that of being the shepherd of Christ's flock, his universal Church.

This is not the time to speak of the specific content of this rich Pontificate. I would like only to read two passages of today's liturgy which reflect central elements of his message.

In the first reading, St. Peter says—and with St. Peter, the Pope himself—"I truly understand that God shows no partiality, but in every nation anyone who fears him and does what is right is acceptable to him. You know the message he sent to the people of Israel, preaching peace by Jesus Christ—he is Lord of all" (Acts 10:34–36). And in the second reading, St. Paul—and with St. Paul, our late Pope—exhorts us, crying out: "My brothers and sisters, whom I love and long for, my joy and my crown, stand firm in the Lord in this way, my beloved" (Phil. 4:1).

Entering Christ's Sufferings

"Follow me!" Together with the command to feed his flock, Christ proclaimed to Peter that he would die a martyr's death. With those words, which conclude and sum up the dialogue on love and on the mandate of the universal shepherd, the Lord recalls another dialogue which took place during the Last Supper. There Jesus had said: "Where I am going, you cannot come." Peter said to him, "Lord, where are you going?" Jesus replied: "Where I am going, you cannot follow me now; but you will follow me afterward" (John 13:33, 36).

Jesus from the Supper went toward the Cross, went toward his Resurrection—he entered into the Paschal Mystery; and Peter could not yet follow him. Now—after the Resurrection—comes the time, comes this "afterward." By shepherding the flock of Christ, Peter enters into the Paschal Mystery; he goes toward the Cross and the Resurrection. The Lord says this in these words: "When you were younger, you used to fasten your own belt and to go wherever you wished. But when you grow old, you will stretch out your hands, and someone else will fasten a belt around you and take you where you do not wish to go" (John 21:18).

In the first years of his Pontificate, still young and full of energy, the Holy Father went to the very ends of the earth, guided by Christ. But afterward, he increasingly entered into the communion of Christ's sufferings; increasingly he understood the truth of the words: "Someone else will fasten a belt around you." And in this very communion with the suffering Lord, tirelessly and with renewed intensity, he proclaimed the Gospel, the mystery of that love which goes to the end (John 13:1).

He interpreted for us the Paschal Mystery as a mystery of divine mercy. In his last book, he wrote: The limit imposed upon evil "is ultimately divine mercy" (*Memory and Identity*). And reflecting on the assassination attempt, he said: "In sacrificing himself for us all, Christ gave a new meaning to suffering, opening up a new dimension, a new order: the order of love.... It is this suffering which burns and consumes evil with the flame of love and draws forth even from sin a great flowering of good." Impelled by this vision, the Pope suffered and loved in communion with Christ, and that is why the message of his suffering and his silence proved so eloquent and so fruitful.

Divine mercy: the Holy Father found the purest reflection of God's mercy in the Mother of God. He, who at an early age had lost his own mother, loved his divine Mother all the more. He heard the words of the crucified Lord as addressed personally to him: "Behold your Mother." And so he did as the beloved disciple did: he took her into his own home (John 19:27)—*Totus tuus*. And from the Mother he learned to conform himself to Christ.

None of us can ever forget how on that last Easter Sunday of his life, the Holy Father, marked by suffering, came once more to the window of the Apostolic Palace and one last time gave his blessing *Urbi et Orbi*. We can be sure that our beloved Pope is standing today at the window of the Father's house, that he sees us and blesses us.

Homily of Cardinal Joseph Ratzinger, now Pope Benedict XVI,
for the Funeral Mass of Pope John Paul II,
Friday, April 8, 2005

Latin Language Documents Index

Documents of Vatican Council II

Christus Dominus—The Decree on Religious Freedom

Dignitatis Humanae—Decree on the Dignity of Humankind

Gaudium et Spes—Pastoral Constitution on the Church in the Modern World

Lumen Gentium—Dogmatic Constitution on the Church

Unitatis Redintegratio—Rediscovering Unity

Encyclicals of John Paul II

Centesimus Annus—One Hundred Years (Anniversary of *Rerum Novarum*)

Dives in Misericordia—The Revelation of Mercy

Dominum et Vivificantem—The Holy Spirit in the Life of the Church and the World

Ecclesia de Eucharistia—On the Eucharist in Its Relationship to the Church

Evangelium Vitae—On the Value and Inviolability of Human Life

Laborem Exercens—On the Meaning of Human Work (on the ninetieth anniversary of *Rerum Novarum*)

Redemptor Hominis—Redeemer of Humankind

Redemptoris Mater—The Blessed Virgin Mary in the Life of the Pilgrim Church

Redemptoris Missio—The Mission of the Redeemer

Sollicitudi Rei Socialis—The Social Concerns of the Church

Ut Unum Sint—On Commitment to Ecumenism

Veritatis Splendor—On the Splendor of Truth

Apostolic Exhortations by Pope John Paul II

Catechesi Tradendae—On Catechesis in Our Time

Vita Consecrata—On Consecrated Life and Its Mission in the Church and in the World

Ecclesia in Oceania—The Church in Oceania

Familiaris Consortio—On the Christian Family in the Modern World

Apostolic Letters of Pope John Paul II

Deis Domini—Keeping the Lord's Day Holy

Mane Nobiscum Domine—Remain with Us, Lord

Mulieris Dignitatem—On the Dignity and Vocation of Women

Novo Millennio Ineunte—The Coming New Millennium

Orientale Lumen—The Light of the East

The Rapid Development of Technology—Intended for Those Responsible for Communications

Rosarium Virginis Mariae—On the Most Holy Rosary

Salvifici Doloris—On the Christian Meaning of Human Suffering

Tertio Millennio Adveniente—On the Preparation for the Jubilee of the Year 2000

Encyclicals by Other Popes

Rerum Novarum—The Condition of Labor (Leo XIII)

Pacem in Terris—Peace on Earth (John XXIII)

Quadragesimo Anno—The Reconstruction of the Social Order (Pius XI)

Apostolic Exhortation by Pope Paul VI

Evangelii Nuntiandi—Evangelization in the Modern World

Permissions and Credits:

The Acting Person used by permission of D. Reidel Publishing Company, Inc., Lincoln Building, 160 Derby Street, Hingham, MA 02043

The Collected Plays and Writing on Theatre by Karol Wojtyla used by permission of University of California Press, 2000 Center Street, Suite 303, Berkeley, CA 94704

Crossing the Threshold of Hope used by permission of Alfred A. Knopf, Inc., 1745 Broadway, New York, NY 10019

Easter Vigil and Other Poems used by permission of Random House, Inc., 201 East 50th Street, New York, NY 10022

Gift and Mystery: A Memoir courtesy of Doubleday, a division of Bantam Doubleday Dell Publishing Group, Inc., 1540 Broadway, New York, NY 10036

Go in Peace: A Gift of Enduring Love used by permission of Loyola Press, 3441 N. Ashland Avenue, Chicago, Illinois 60657

Love and Responsibility used by permission of Ignatius Press, P.O. Box 1339, Ft. Collins, CO 80522

Memory and Identity courtesy of Rizzoli International Publications, Inc., 300 Park Avenue, New York, NY 10010

The Poetry of John Paul II: Roman Triptych used by permission of USCCB Publishing (Casa Editrice Vaticana), United States Conference of Catholic Bishops, 3661 Georgia Avenue NW, Washington, D.C. 20010

Rise, Let Us Be on Our Way courtesy of Time Warner Books Group, 1271 Avenue of the Americas, New York, NY 10020

Sign of Contradiction used by permission of The Seabury Press, 815 Second Avenue, New York, NY 10017

The Way to Christ and *Agenda for the Third Millennium* courtesy of HarperCollins Publishers, 10 East 53rd Street, New York, NY 10022

Every effort has been made to obtain permissions for pieces quoted in this work. If any required acknowledgments have been omitted, or any rights overlooked, it is unintentional. Please notify the publishers of any omission, and it will be rectified in future editions.

Grateful acknowledgment is given to L'Ossevatore Romano for quotes cited from the Pope's discourses.